CHINA'S MILLENNIALS

CHINA'S MILLENNIALS

The Want Generation

Eric Fish

ROWMAN & LITTLEFIELD
Lanham • Boulder • New York • London

Published by Rowman & Littlefield
A wholly owned subsidiary of
The Rowman & Littlefield Publishing Group, Inc.
4501 Forbes Boulevard, Suite 200, Lanham, Maryland 20706
www.rowman.com

Unit A, Whitacre Mews, 26-34 Stannary Street, London SE11 4AB,
United Kingdom

British Library Cataloguing in Publication Information Available

Library of Congress Cataloging-in-Publication Data

The hardback edition of this book was previously cataloged by the Library of Congress as follows:

Fish, Eric, 1985–
China's millennials : the want generation / Eric Fish.
pages cm
Includes bibliographical references and index.
1. Generation Y—China. 2. Youth in development—China. I. Title.
HQ799.C5F57 2015
305.20951—dc23
2015000751

ISBN 978-1-4422-7249-1 (paper : alk. paper)
ISBN 978-1-4422-4883-0 (cloth : alk. paper)
ISBN 978-1-4422-4884-7 (electronic)

∞ ™ The paper used in this publication meets the minimum requirements of
American National Standard for Information Sciences Permanence of Paper
for Printed Library Materials, ANSI/NISO Z39.48-1992.

Printed in the United States of America

CONTENTS

PREFACE

On June 4, 2014, along Beijing's Chang'an Boulevard, there was little sign that a massacre had unfolded exactly twenty-five years earlier. Shoppers toted bags from a nearby mall. Elderly women shuffled by on their morning walks. Suited businessmen filed toward their offices. All that distinguished the day from any other were the watchful public security officials stationed every few hundred feet.

At Tiananmen Square, where the protests that had prompted the massacre occurred, it was the same story. The only commemorations were those of tourists marking their trip to the capital with pictures in front of the famous Mao Zedong portrait. Those few trying to remember the events of 1989 mostly found themselves intercepted by police before they could even make it to the square. If anyone tried to post something online, it was scrubbed by censors within minutes. Thus, most of the remembering was left to foreign media.

Among the hundreds of reports in the run-up to the anniversary, many sought to compare those youth who had demonstrated in 1989 to those born after the events. In nearly all cases, the comparison reflected rather poorly on the latter. Some illustrated a state-induced "amnesia" that had taken hold. One reporter showed the iconic photo of "Tank Man," the unidentified protestor who blocked a column of tanks the day after the massacre, to a hundred college students in Beijing—to which all but fifteen pleaded ignorance.[1] Others highlighted how today's youth have simply been numbed away from politics. "They seem not to care," read one piece in the Associated Press. "They grew up in an atmosphere of nationalism and pride over two decades of strong economic growth."[2]

While accounts like these were undoubtedly true, there were facets to the story not quite captured, and it reminded me why I had first wanted to write this book. Shortly after the June 4 anniversary, I told a Chinese friend in Beijing that I was writing about youth in modern China. "Be sure to say that we post-90s people (*jiulinghou*) aren't just idiots," he suggested. "Foreigners always think we're brainwashed."

But foreigners were not the only ones selling them short. Young Chinese I was speaking to, like many youth around the world, also seemed to feel older generations at home were pigeonholing them into unflattering stereotypes. When I said I was writing about typical young people like them, they became anxious to air their grievances and struggles, as well as to defend themselves against those who would look down upon them. "You should write about the *fu'erdai*," said another Chinese friend, referring to spoiled children of the wealthy. "And how losers like me can't get a job," he added with a chuckle.

I came to China in 2007 to teach at a university. Age twenty-two at the time, I was assigned to work with students just a few years younger than myself. We were all "millennials"—loosely defined as the generation born in the 1980s and 1990s (for the purposes of this book, we will say 1984 to 1996).

I quickly discovered many threads that united the Chinese youth whom I was meeting and my American peers back home. Psychologist Jean Twenge called us "Generation Me" in her 2006 book of the same name. Through extensive surveying, she concluded that American millennials tend to be tolerant, confident, open-minded, and ambitious, but also cynical, depressed, lonely, and anxious. She drew her book title from the strong sense of entitlement and narcissism that she identified among this cohort relative to earlier generations.[3]

China's millennials get the same labels, often with survey data to back them up.[4] Like their counterparts in America and around the world, they were raised in relative comfort compared to earlier generations, leading to somewhat lofty expectations. Thanks to the one-child policy, instituted in 1979 as a way to rein in the enormous population, China's generation of "little emperor" only children have a reputation for being especially spoiled. But like their international counterparts, they are also growing into the economic and social uncertainty of a postrecession world and struggling to stay on the better end of a yawning wealth gap, arousing great anxiety about the future.

However, the Sino-American similarities start to diverge once politics is factored in. American millennials came of age as their country was triumphing in the Cold War. As the Berlin Wall fell in 1989 and the Soviet Union crumbled two years later, these youth were brought up confident as ever that their political system represented the so-called End of History. China's millennials, however, were born amid the 1989 crackdown at Tiananmen Square—one of the most transformative events in recent Chinese history. The seven weeks of protests that year and the bloody suppression that ended them were tantamount to a reset button for China's Communist Party (the CCP) and Chinese society as a whole. Amid an ideological vacuum that had helped prompt the protests, insecure leaders had to reinvent their country and justification for ruling over it. So over the following two decades, everything changed—sometimes for the better, sometimes not—and a generation gap between the Tiananmen and post-Tiananmen youth seemed to emerge, again with both positive and negative implications. The economy boomed for China's millennials, but the bigger political questions that their parents had raised at Tiananmen were put on the shelf.

During my three years as a teacher in Nanjing, I indeed saw depressing signals of political apathy and submissiveness. Jiang Fangzhou, a Chinese writer born in 1989, recognized this prevailing attitude as "an active effort to maintain the status quo," saying that young Chinese today "dare not stray from the orthodoxy for even one millimeter when they are still 10 meters away from crossing the line."[5]

Chinese youth since the uprising of 1989 have largely been kept happy by the Community Party's emphasis on opening up economic opportunities, but many signs point to a growing dissatisfaction with purely material goals and to an increasing likelihood that young Chinese will again become a vocal force for change.

After teaching, I went on to study journalism at Tsinghua University in Beijing, and later worked at a Chinese investigative newspaper with young native reporters. During my reporting at *Economic Observer* and for outlets like *Foreign Policy* and *The Atlantic*, I continued to see signs of push and pull, as the young people with whom I was speaking advanced toward or retreated from a perceived line that separated the acceptable from the taboo. This period also coincided with youth-led movements around the country that blindsided even the most adept China watchers.

These observations prompted some big questions. Could the country's youth ever spark mass Tiananmen-like demonstrations again? Could their growing list of struggles ever cause them to seriously rock the boat? As they come of age, will they steer China toward serious democratic reform, or will they carry on the Leninist tradition?

These are the million-dollar questions of contemporary China, and one would be a fool to give a definitive answer to any of them. Figuring out the present is hard enough, let alone the future. But the questions are well worth pondering. China's millennials, some 250 million in number, stand ready to exert substantial influence on the world's most populous country as it is poised to pass the United States to become the world's largest economy. How they ultimately steer that ship will have a profound impact on the rest of the world.

I do not pretend to have a finger on the political pulse of China's youth. Nobody has that detailed knowledge, not even the mandarins in Beijing. But through their personal stories, I hope to give a sense of what they are up against—socially, economically, and politically.

While writing this book, I frequently felt torn over whose stories to tell. I did not include the tattooed equivalents of Hell's Angels who cruise around Beijing on expensive Harleys. Nor did I include the group of disillusioned students who gave up on modern society to live in a Maoist hippie compound in rural Hebei. These people are rebellious in their own unique ways, and a testament to the diversity blooming among China's millennials. But the people whose stories I tell in this book are representative of common traits shared by many others with whom I have spoken. The stories depicted are those of a variety of young Chinese coming from different regional and socioeconomic backgrounds who were extremely generous with their time, spending hours and days (in some cases, over the span of several years) with me as I tried to probe their backgrounds, beliefs, and anxieties. Some of them I specifically tracked down, others I met unexpectedly along the way. I have arranged their stories into four topical areas: China's education system, the workforce, various social issues, and youth who are actively opposing the status quo.

At the request of some interviewees who felt they were crossing into taboo territory or potentially endangering themselves, I have used pseudonyms where noted or partial names in some cases. (Because some Chinese surnames are extremely common, I have also followed the practice of referring to some interviewees by their given name—which comes second in Chinese—rather than their family name.) Every story depicts unique individuals, so we must be careful not to overgeneralize from a collection of individual stories. But the collection, as I believe you will see, tells a coherent story. It speaks of youthful struggle, disillusionment, and rebellion in a system that is scrambling to keep them in line—and, increasingly, scrambling to adapt when its youth refuse to conform.

I

Getting Educated

I

BOOT CAMP

On one of my first mornings in China I awoke to the sound of hundreds of young voices belting out People's Liberation Army marching chants.

I had just arrived at a university in the ancient capital city of Nanjing, where I would spend the next three years teaching Chinese college students. As I wandered outside, I was confronted by droves of youth in matching army fatigues. Throughout the campus, the young men and women marched in lines, goose-stepped back and forth, and, in one corner, thrust bayonets into the hearts of invisible targets. As they paraded about, they glared intently straight ahead, trying to keep their shouts and their steps perfectly synchronized. At first glance, the sight seemed to validate everything I was brought up believing about China: that it is a uniform society, meticulously ordered by the state and purposefully intimidating to outsiders.

That impression quickly evaporated when I walked within eyeshot of those glares. As soon as they saw a foreigner, the stone-faced platoon broke into giggles and obnoxious "Heeeeellllloooooos." Even the drill sergeant cracked a smile.

In the years since that humid August morning in 2007, observing the college freshmen in military training—or *Junxun,* as it is officially called—has become a mild obsession of mine. The more time I have spent in China talking to young people, the more I have come to see *Junxun* as a perfect metaphor for the precarious relationship between them and their ruling party.

Since 1985, every school year has begun with this training. Upon their arrival at university, China's new college freshmen—men and women alike—undergo weeks of marching, drilling, patriotism lessons, and berating from People's Liberation Army (PLA) soldiers. Any non-conformist fashion statements are banned during the training, such as long hair and moustaches for guys, or painted fingernails and colored contact lenses for girls.[1] Participation is mandatory and a poor performance can provide a blot on students' records that will stay with them throughout their professional lives. At least, that is how it is supposed to work.

An American blogger in Shanghai echoed the reactions of many foreigners in China to the training, claiming to be "thoroughly consti-pated with disgust for the nationalism being 'brainwashed' into the in-nocent but ever-so-impressionable youth."[2] One of my more outspoken students, a nineteen-year-old English major from Sichuan, would ex-plain *Junxun* to me more succinctly: "It's to make us submissive."

Looking at history, it is hard not to come to the same conclusion. Chinese students who came of age in the 1980s appeared much less

Tsinghua University students march behind their PLA drill instructors at the con-clusion of their *Junxun* military training. (Photo: Eric Fish)

submissive. Yang Fenggang, now a Purdue sociologist, was among the first few groups of students to reenter China's universities after their decade-long closure. "People were really moving out of the Cultural Revolution mentality," Yang told me, referring to Mao Zedong's catastrophic 1966–1976 political movement to reassert power and rid the country of bourgeois capitalists. "Sometimes a single article could stir up a national debate among young people. It was an exciting time."[3]

But that excitement would come to a bloody end.

In the early 1980s, those few who emerged with college degrees could count on living comfortable lives. But by the latter part of the decade, students began graduating into an uneven job market. No longer required to accept graduates assigned to them by the state, company leaders gave the best jobs to their family members and other personal associates.[4] Meanwhile, the opening markets and growing economy presented enticing opportunities for the politically connected to leverage their power for illicit profit. Nepotism and corruption ran rampant, wealth inequality widened, and inflation spun out of control. The Communist Party's legitimacy, rooted almost entirely in socialist ideology, began to crumble.[5]

Life was still getting better for most Chinese, but many felt left behind amid the reforms as they saw unprecedented wealth accumulating around exclusive circles.[6] Those young people who had missed the chance to capitalize early in the reform period started taking a keen interest in politics. With the gates now open to the outside world, ideas of freedom and democracy trickled in from the West.

Chinese youth wondered why their rulers needed such an overarching role in their lives and such tight control over their individual freedoms—deciding what they could say, how they could love, and who could determine their future. Discussion of social and political change spilled into the open in a way that China had not seen in decades.

Student protests calling for reform began as early as the 1970s and carried on in small pockets throughout the 1980s, but after the death of a popular reformist leader in April 1989, frustrated youth were galvanized into sparking a nationwide movement that crept right up to the Communist Party's doorstep in Tiananmen Square.

Those who sparked the protests saw themselves as fervent patriots. They were carrying on a proud youth tradition stretching back to the

May 4th Movement of 1919, when students lashed out at their weak government for clinging to an outdated culture and failing to stand up to encroaching foreign powers. When the Communists came to power three decades later, they co-opted May 4, making it the national "Youth Day" holiday. They saluted the 1919 students' courage and held them up as revolutionary forebears of the Communist cause against feudalism and imperialism.

Many of the student protesters at Tiananmen were accomplished Communist Party members themselves who strongly supported reformist leaders within the government. They simply saw themselves as the descendants of May 4th—guardians of the nation's dignity and fighters against corrupted bureaucrats. Some wanted Western-style democracy, while others just wanted meaningful reform within the existing system. Almost all were united in their demands for respect and a fair chance to succeed in society.

During the protests, the song "Nothing to My Name" by twenty-seven-year-old Chinese rock star Cui Jian became the movement's anthem. Depicting a girl who ridicules her admirer for lacking material wealth, the song captured the disillusionment that many youth felt. "[It] expresses our feelings," Tiananmen student leader Wu'er Kaixi said years later. "Does our generation have anything? We don't have the goals our parents had. We don't have the fanatical idealism our older brothers and sisters once had. So what do we want? Nike shoes. Lots of free time to take our girlfriends to a bar. The freedom to discuss an issue with someone, and to get a little respect from society."[7]

After Tiananmen had been occupied for seven weeks, hardliners in the Communist Party gained control and decided they had had enough. They could have cleared the streets with nondeadly riot gear. Instead, they sent in the People's Liberation Army with machine guns and tanks, in many cases shooting almost anything that moved. Though the blood that ran down Beijing's streets was hastily scrubbed away, it left a long-lasting message for anyone who might think of stirring up rebellion again. It was a message that silenced a generation.

The massacre bought the Communist Party time, which it used to construct a new leadership model that would keep the country's hot-headed youngsters in line. Two months after the suppression in Beijing, students at Peking University—where most of the Tiananmen ringleaders had come from—were subjected to a full year of military training.[8]

Other universities were subject to intensive reindoctrination programs, and within two years, the Communist Party had overhauled its entire education curriculum for all ages.[9] It shifted from emphasizing Marxism and class struggle to pushing Chinese nationalism and how the CCP rescued the country from humiliation under violent foreign imperialists.

If the bloody crackdown of 1989 and the new education failed to dissuade any would-be instigators, then China's surveillance and intimidation apparatus has done quite well at picking up the slack. Its efficiency at identifying and silencing dissent has continually grown more sophisticated.

But the post-1989 strategy that has arguably had the most sweeping effect in preventing further uprisings is simple economics. During the 1990s President Jiang Zemin, who ascended to power amid the fallout from Tiananmen, launched dramatic market reforms that loosened the state's grip on the economy. He began dismantling thousands of inefficient state-owned enterprises and started integrating China into the world economy, while at the same time steadily retreating from the personal lives of China's citizens. The tacit bargain was simple: accept one-party rule and you can get rich.

As a result of this bargain's success, the post-Tiananmen generation has never known anything but perpetually improving opportunities. In the two decades following 1989, China saw a fourteenfold increase in per-capita income and an eightfold increase in college enrollment.[10] International travel was transformed from a luxury relegated to the elite into something that 97 million Chinese enjoyed in 2013.[11] Formerly monochromatic, once dingy cities filled with young people wearing Western brands of clothing and chatting on smartphones. They got their Nike shoes and plenty of bars to take their girlfriends to. Puritanical Big Brother even backed off and gave them sexual liberation. The material opportunities and personal freedoms that those at Tiananmen had demanded were satisfied, convincing the next generation that the more political demands were moot.

In 2008, rocker Cui Jian compared this young generation to the one that had belted out his songs in Tiananmen. "The earlier generation had a very clear direction," he said. "You know, liberation, revolution, whatever. The next generation doesn't believe in anything—just in what I can get, what I can control in my hand. I think money is most controllable."[12]

Those born into this booming era are now referred to (often pejoratively) as the "post-90s generation (*jiulinghou*)." According to one media outlet, these youths are routinely labeled "lazy, promiscuous, confused, selfish, brain damaged and overall hopeless."[13]

But just as occurred previously in the United States and Japan, China's unrestrained boom years are giving way to a painful hangover. Chinese youth are already facing a gamut of problems: dismal job prospects, out-of-control housing costs, a rapidly aging population to care for, an unprecedented gender imbalance, and environmental issues that will strain the entire nation's ability to move forward. Amid these woes, will the two-decade-old "Beijing Consensus" of authoritarian rule in exchange for prosperity continue to satisfy a generation that takes rapid economic growth for granted?

This is why the freshman *Junxun* has always intrigued me. In the span of a few weeks, it seems to force China's youth into a full-immersion experience of the Communist Party's pillars of persuasion: fear, nationalism, and prosperity. It represents a microcosm of what the government wants its youth to be: obedient, patriotic, collectivist, and thankful for the wealth that has been bestowed upon them. But I wanted to know how well it worked.

In August 2011 I met a young woman (she used her English name, Rachel) who was preparing to do her *Junxun*. Born in 1992 in coastal Zhejiang province, she was entering Renmin (People's) University, a top college in Beijing famous for its students aspiring to government careers.

A few days before her *Junxun* was set to begin, when I met with Rachel at a café on the university campus, she displayed a refreshing confidence that is rare among students emerging from the three years of virtual isolation and nonstop study that precede the *gaokao* college entrance exam. Just under five feet tall and ninety pounds, she had never done anything like military training. "I'm very nervous," she said of her upcoming *Junxun*.[14]

Rachel had traveled throughout the country with her family and hoped that her language skills would one day land her a job allowing her to branch out into the world. The daughter of a middle-class government official, she, like most Chinese her age, was an only child. "I'm so lonely," she said, laughing about her home life. "But I was very spoiled. I didn't need to worry about anything."

Rachel's upbringing was a world apart from older generations in her family. Her grandmother was nine years old when her future husband was selected for her in the late 1940s, after years of civil war and Japanese invasion. Rachel's parents were both born in the early 1960s and bore the brunt of Mao's Cultural Revolution, eating tree bark at one point to survive. It was a level of hardship Rachel has never come close to experiencing herself.

I asked Rachel to keep a diary during her twelve-day *Junxun* to get a glimpse of how the post-90s generation responds to the messages contained in this boot camp.

While many universities carry out the training on campus, Rachel and her classmates were bussed to a special military compound nestled at the foot of a mountain range twenty-five miles north of Beijing. "I found myself going back to the 1980s," Rachel said. "All the buildings are very old, made of brick. The place we lived in was very simple."

She shared a dormitory with nine other young women. The room contained five bunk beds and a deactivated air conditioner. After settling in, they were taken to a dining hall with rows of metal tables but no chairs. "When the drillmaster says you can eat, then you can eat," Rachel said. "The dishes are all very salty, so you'll eat a lot of rice."

The nearly six thousand students were given five minutes to finish their meal and were then herded together to pick up their army fatigues, which they would not wash or change for the next two weeks. "I really wanted to go back to my school," Rachel recalled.

The official training began the next morning. Students were roused at 5 a.m. to run a mile, followed by breakfast and drilling. "Today's training was about how to stand," Rachel wrote in her diary. "You should stand under the sun straight with your hands at your side for 10 minutes. Our feet, legs, and knees felt a lot of pain, but we couldn't move or we would be required to stand longer. I felt dizzy."

Later that day, a young woman in Rachel's group fainted—a common occurrence during the training. "Oh, I feel so happy that my upper eyelids are going to kiss my lower eyelids," Rachel wrote, exhausted, as she got into bed that night.

On the second day, Rachel began noticing other expectations. "No matter whether we walk, eat, take a shower, or even go to the toilet, we should do it together," she wrote in her journal. "We should walk in a line or as a group, and we can't do it before getting approval."

The training that day lasted for eight hours, most of which was spent learning to walk properly. "Don't think it's an easy thing," Rachel wrote. "Hundreds of people should walk in the same tempo like one person. The training is very boring. We have to walk hundreds of times. Even when we think it's perfect the drillmasters still aren't satisfied."

Students who made errors were required to do push-ups, run laps, endure ridicule, and sometimes sing to the rest of the group. "If you move but don't tell the master you've moved, you'll be punished," Rachel said. "If you wake up late, they'll punish you. If they think you're a little bit tired they'll punish you at any time for very little things."

The trainers ended the first few days with half an hour of criticism of the students' performance. By the fourth day, Rachel's morale was sinking. "Today was a black day," she wrote. "The drillmaster said that I'm a 'whatever person' [slang for promiscuous] just because I wore my pajamas in front of him. I cried. Never have I felt so homesick."

Michael Volkin, a US Army sergeant and author of *The Ultimate Basic Training Guidebook*, told me that many of the tactics used in *Junxun* resemble those of US Army basic training. "They're looking for people who think they're individuals and they don't want individuals," he said. "They're looking for someone who can take direction and be taught what to do."[15]

Psychologists would call this process operant conditioning. Through endless repetition, degradation, and punishment for the slightest disobedience, an individual becomes conditioned to instinctively obey. The process has long been used in militaries for training soldiers to kill or march to their deaths upon command without pausing to question the commander's wisdom.[16]

I once spoke with a twenty-five-year-old lieutenant in the People's Liberation Army who conducted freshman training twice as a drill sergeant in Nanjing. He agreed that the purpose of the drills and frequent punishments is to teach students obedience. "They're all from the countryside so they're not used to rules," he said. "It can help them have the sense of carrying out orders."[17] In fact, one of the officially stated aims of *Junxun* is to "temper [students'] willpower," in addition to "building patriotism, collectivism, and revolutionary heroism" and "developing socialist builders and successors of the future."[18]

In the middle of the training, Rachel and her classmates enjoyed a relatively relaxing day during which they played tug-of-war and watched a movie about Chinese soldiers. "The movie moved all of us because the soldier's life is much harder than ours," Rachel wrote. "But he didn't give up. So how can we want to give up when we just stand in the sun for a little while? So I've changed my mind. I'll try to be a stronger person."

Throughout the two weeks students sang patriotic songs like "Our Darling Country" and "Without the Communist Party, There Would Be No New China." Toward the end, one of the instructors told the students about life in the real military. He recounted one occasion when someone in his platoon was beaten into disfigurement for disobeying orders, and he said that sometimes soldiers live in the mountains for years at a time without a telephone. "They showed their loyalty to our country," Rachel said after the training. "Thanks to them our country will be safe."

"Ah," she said as she sat up laughing when retelling the story. "This is the aim of the training. You see? I would never say these things before, but now I'll say, 'thanks to the army, thanks to the Party.'"

The patriotic education that students receive during *Junxun* is just a small sample of what they have already encountered and will continue to experience throughout their university education. Nearly all college students are required to take political courses touting Marxism and Chinese nationalism. The lessons and historical narratives presented in these courses are not up for debate, and students have little choice but to tacitly endorse them if they want to pass their exams.

If students ever see any information about the Tiananmen uprising in textbooks, the exposure is brief and makes clear that the protestors were manipulated and that the military had no choice but to open fire on them.[19] Garnering sympathy for the PLA, which took a major hit to its image after Tiananmen, appears to be another major goal of *Junxun*.

Young people like Rachel, however, are now accessing alternative narratives. In 2009, a service was launched that arguably changed China forever. Sina Weibo, a Twitter-like microblogging platform, was used by one in every two Chinese Internet users by 2012.[20] While Weibo, like the rest of China's Internet, is heavily censored, it quickly became a platform for public cynicism that frequently indicted the official Party line. This development shook up the very command-and-control model by which the Communist Party ruled throughout its more than six decades in power. It has forced the Party to subordinate itself to the will of the people in many situations.

"This generation tends to be very patriotic," Guo Baogang, associate professor of political science at Dalton State College and author of *China's Quest for Political Legitimacy*, told me.[21] "But they may not swallow the dogmatic teaching from the Party. With the new technology I don't think the Party can use the same techniques of censorship and thought controls. They have to have a better way to deal with this group."[22]

Rachel says that she does not believe her generation will ever be bold enough to rock the political boat. "Students will never do again what happened in 1989," she said. "Even without military training, their parents would tell them they can't do this."

China's young generation today does indeed have much more to lose than the Tiananmen generation did. But while you will not often see young Chinese holding up democracy banners, their growing materialism and individualism is a different, subconscious type of resistance to the lessons put forth in *Junxun*. Chinese society is quickly evolving—perhaps faster now than the institutions that govern it—and *Junxun* cadets are no exception.

In recent years, pictures have spread online of rambunctious post-90s students posing for funny pictures in their army garb and donning non–standard-issue adornments like colorful hair scrunchies and nail extensions.[23] When a picture of two freshmen locking lips in their *Junxun* fatigues gained public notice, it was lambasted on a national news segment.

On discussion boards highlighting these instances, many lament that kids these days do not take their military training seriously and are becoming too open and Westernized.[24] Walk by any *Junxun* session and you will likely see several iPhones being whipped out during breaks.

Even the bodies of young Chinese appear to be taking a decidedly more Western turn. A health survey that has been conducted at *Junxun* six times since it began in 1985 shows that the fitness level of new students has been steadily declining over the past three decades, with an increasing number too overweight or out of shape to take part in the

Tsinghua University students undergoing *Junxun* military training photograph their PLA drill instructor during a break. (Photo: Eric Fish)

most basic physical activities. The report said that during the two-week training at Peking University one year, there were over six thousand doctor visits among the thirty-five hundred cadets.[25] Often, I have been told, unfit students who are too tired will simply sit off to the side with little protest from instructors.

These new dynamics have forced *Junxun* to evolve quietly over the years. After the disciplinary shock and awe at the beginning of the training, drill sergeants now tend to tone down their role as disciplinarians and become more like big brothers to the students.

As all the drilling and marching of *Junxun* neared its end, Rachel's attitude toward it turned distinctively more positive. "I've hurt my leg, but I still continue," she wrote during the last few days of the drills. "I've gone beyond myself. I've become stronger, more independent. I feel proud of myself."

Across the compound, however, boot camp had turned into more of a summer camp. Students played games, and one instructor even brought a case of beer to the men's dorm. The PLA lieutenant and former training instructor said that this shift is normal. "You need to give a harsh image to the students so they're scared of you," he said. "But later we get more familiar and have a better relationship, so we discipline less and less."

Several days after returning to campus, Rachel downplayed the suggestion that the training might be a form of political indoctrination. "There's a little bit maybe," she said. "We'll do what they tell us during the training, but afterwards we have our own minds. If you tell me to do something now, I won't do it. If this is the purpose, it didn't work so well."

When asked whether the training had changed him in any way, one of Rachel's classmates, Li, thought for a moment about the long days under the hot sun. "It changed my skin color," he replied dismissively.[26]

The PLA lieutenant agreed that the training probably does not have the same effect as in the past. "We're told to obey—obey the Party and the school," he said. "But post-90s students are influenced by the West more and have their own character. They tend to ask 'why?' much more than the older generation."

It is hard to say what lasting effects *Junxun* actually has on students. Many of the lessons that it tries to instill appear to fall on very cynical ears, but it does not seem to be an empty ritual either.

When I have spoken with students about *Junxun*, they have rarely expressed hostility toward it. Over the years, young people have suggested all kinds of purposes for it, including national defense, discipline, student orientation, shock therapy for spoiled children, garnering sympathy for soldiers, and instilling love for and obedience to the state. But most agree that the experience is positive, at both the individual and national levels. A 2005 survey carried out by *China Youth Daily* and the online media company Sina found that 69 percent of the respondents who had undergone the training felt that it was worthwhile.[27]

Michael Volkin, the US Army sergeant, described the benefits of this kind of training and synchronized drilling. "Everyone is going to come out with more confidence and a camaraderie they've never had before," he said. "That's the real mental reason why you do the cadence. It's [also] to follow directions, but the real reason is so you can feel as one with the people around you."

Although he cynically claimed that his skin color was the only thing changed by *Junxun*, Rachel's classmate Li did not appear completely unmoved. "I think the military training is meant to show your life now is very good," he said. "Everyone should know what the hard life is like so you'll know the life you have now is very happy."

Time and time again, the young Chinese with whom I have spoken have demurred when asked why they do not resist the principles that *Junxun* (in theory) aims to instill—the propaganda, the insistence on obedience, and the constant reminder that if you are the nail that sticks out, you will be hammered down. "It's something we all know, but it's pointless to fight it," they will sometimes say, or, more often, "You may not understand it, but it's necessary for the cohesion and harmony of the country."

But more and more voices of cynicism and dissent are emerging. As the Nanjing lieutenant noticed with his post-90s cadets, young people who feel things are not the way they should be are finding the temerity to ask, "Why?" In 2014, military training at one high school turned violent when students resisted their drill masters. The facts were disputed, but after a lighthearted quarrel between an instructor and a female cadet, the males in her class were punished with push-ups, to which they protested. Later in the day, a group of drunk military instructors allegedly sought revenge for the students' disobedience and attacked the young men, leaving several hospitalized.[28]

The episode set off a national debate about the role of *Junxun* in modern China. "Student military training has no use whatsoever," wrote one famous artist. "It's an education in how to be a slave, of a kind that should only exist in totalitarian countries like North Korea. Are we trying to cultivate a healthy, independent and freethinking populace or a bunch of obedient machines?"[29] As others saw it though, these post-90s youth were simply displaying the spoiled attitude and disobedience for which their generation had become infamous, and reaffirmed exactly why China needed student military training in the first place.

This common view among older generations in China has become a source of resentment among many post-90s, as they struggle to express that they do not have it so easy. In coming years, China will experience earthshaking demographic and economic shifts that are already becoming highly disruptive to the life that the post-90s generation has become accustomed to. Various issues that contributed to the standoff at Tiananmen are reemerging in new forms, accompanied this time by a fresh set of challenges that the world has never seen before.

The educated elite like Rachel are facing a hypercompetitive job market and learning that the path to success they were promised may no longer exist. Meanwhile, the blue-collar class is finding the gap between themselves and the privileged growing ever wider.

Gang Guo, a specialist in Chinese politics at the University of Mississippi, told me that China's political future may depend on how this young generation is treated. "Unemployment among educated youth and inequality of opportunity are a combination that could be as dangerous in China as in the Arab world," he said, referring to the 2011 Jasmine Revolution.[30]

Still, opportunities exist for those who know where to look for them. China's consumer class continues to grow and the country harbors nearly infinite economic possibilities. But even success brings its own problems, as the social order is scrambled and China's capitalist excesses clash with the socialist veneer that the Communist Party still struggles to uphold. As a result the Chinese have been left unsure of what to believe in or what moral code should be their guide.[31] "Many people in society feel kind of lost," said Yang Fenggang, the Purdue sociologist. "There are so many incidents that reflect this, like when an old man falls in the street and people don't know whether they should help."

Rachel too laments that her hometown has gotten rich but is losing its soul. She admires Western-style freedoms but is not sure if they are worth fighting for in China, or whether they would even work there. She loves her country and says she believes in it, but does not think she would stick around if an opportunity to leave presented itself. She is both optimistic about China's future and terrified of how she will fare after graduation and provide for her parents when they are old. She is confident about China's rise on the world stage, but anxious about its growing domestic troubles. These are the dilemmas that one struggles to reconcile when speaking of Chinese youth and how they will shape the country's future.

On her last night at the military compound, Rachel wrote the final entry in her journal: "I'm stronger now. Never again will I cry just because of a little pain. Growing up is a cruel thing. You must bear the pain and try to stand up again after you fall down. You should learn to smile and face all the difficulties until you finally come to the top of the mountain."

While Rachel still had a long way to climb, she had already conquered one of the greatest challenges facing Chinese youth: she had been admitted to one of China's most prestigious universities. It is a dream that nearly every Chinese family has for their child, and one that is reserved for a precious few. For every young student like Rachel that pushes to the front of the pack, dozens lag behind with an even more uncertain future.

2

THE TEST

As long as I have known Emily Fang, she has been preparing for a test.

We met through a family connection in 2009 in her hometown of Qingzhou, a city of about two hundred thousand in coastal Shandong province. She was then a scraggly fourteen-year-old with thick glasses who was always laughing at something. Born into a middle-class family with a comfortable two-story home, she had never had to worry about much more than her schooling.

Emily loved to gossip about classmates and celebrities, and she spent much of her spare time immersed in Korean soap operas. Unfortunately, she rarely had much time to spare.

The *gaokao* college entrance exam was still four years away, but it was never far from the front of Emily's mind. She was about to start her last year of middle school, at the end of which she would take a test. This test would decide whether she would gain entry to a good high school and thereby have a better chance at passing the college entrance exam three years later. That, in turn, was the only way in which she could be assured a good white-collar job. As the family's only child, she would need a good career to help her provide for her parents when they aged. The family was constantly considering these long-term issues and then pursuing the solutions to them with tunnel vision. For most of Emily's childhood, the next step involved passing a test.

China has a 1,500-year history of using exams to choose scholars and civil servants based on merit. After the disruption of higher education during the Cultural Revolution, China's *gaokao* college entrance exam resumed in 1977. Since then it has changed in many ways, but it has remained the same in its high stakes.

Each June, graduating high school seniors spend two to three days taking this written exam, which in most cases is the sole deciding factor that determines which (if any) university they will be admitted to and what they can major in. The test has traditionally been given just once a year, so a bad performance means settling for a blue-collar future or waiting another year to try again. Chinese youth spend years preparing themselves for those few days.

I was the first foreigner Emily had ever met—someone totally removed from her world and all the complications that came with it. Over the coming years, that relationship would make me a convenient outlet for her mounting pressure.

Whenever I came to Qingzhou I would chat with Emily as much as I could, but we would inevitably be cut short by her need to study. That study paid off, though. At the end of ninth grade, her test performance got her into the city's best high school. To celebrate, her family brought her on a trip to Nanjing where I was living. "I'm quite happy!" she said when she arrived. For that week she was free to eat, sleep, and play around to her heart's content. She could come up to the surface and take a deep breath.

But the respite was short. When she returned home, the three years of pre-*gaokao* hell began.

After her first semester of high school I stayed with Emily's family for a few days and could tell the heat was already on. Emily's study breaks were shorter and her playful demeanor more subdued.

One night, her parents went out and left the two of us home alone. A few minutes after they left, she started sobbing. "There's so much pressure," she said, burying her face in my shoulder. "Everyone wants so much from me. I don't know if I can pass. If I don't, they'll be so disappointed in me."

This is how it would go for the next two years. She seemed gradually busier and more exasperated each time I talked to her. In January of her senior year, I saw her one last time before she took the test. By then Emily was seventeen, still a puny ninety pounds and perpetually exhausted. Each day she went to school from 7:30 a.m. to 10:00 p.m. with a two-hour lunch. She got Saturday afternoons and Sunday mornings off—usually. If there was a topic that would not be tested on the *gao-*

kao, Emily's teachers did not waste time on it. That time was for test cramming and nothing else. Any distractions—such as makeup, social clubs, or dating—were forbidden.

Every night at 10:15, Emily's mother waited anxiously at the front door for her to return home. Upon arriving on her electric bike, Emily would lean on her horn in annoyance. Her mom bolted out the door to open the courtyard gate, but no matter how fast she came out, Emily was still irritated. She was running on fumes already and vented her frustration at the routine setback of having to wait ten seconds to get in the house.

When she got in the front door, her mom hustled her over to a warm footbath that she had prepared. Any precious second wasted was a second lost from study or sleep. But once she sat down to her footbath, she was allowed to unwind and clear her head for just a few minutes. It was the one window of time where I could talk to her. The topic, of course, was always how miserable her day was.

After we chatted for about five minutes, her mom handed her a textbook and I took my cue to head off to bed. This was just the beginning of Emily's night.

Her bedtime varied. On a rare good night, it would be a little after midnight. I once woke up to use the bathroom at 2:30 a.m. and found her passed out, her head on a book. "I'm just taking a little rest," she uttered pathetically, looking up, as if she needed to justify the catnap to me.

Mom would rouse her at 6:30 a.m. and they would bargain over whether Emily could have a few more minutes of sleep. Emily never won this negotiation. Once she was up, she would do a little morning studying, make quick work of her breakfast, and be out the door.

After subtracting the commute, Emily had an hour and a half at home for lunch. I was told by her parents ever so politely, but in no uncertain terms, that I was to be out of the house during that period. Emily did not have time to be distracted by me. She would gobble her lunch in a matter of minutes and then go straight to bed for some precious afternoon Zs—unless she still had unfinished homework, of course.

After several more hours of drilling and practice tests at school, she would come home and repeat the process. As I headed to bed each night, I would tell her, "Don't work too hard." I was the only one doling out such advice.

Some family members persuaded Emily's parents that the brain needs time to relax, so at some point they became a bit easier on her. On Saturday afternoons she would be allowed to watch soap operas and talk with me for a little while before being directed back to her study desk. Many of her classmates had their faces stuffed in books at every waking moment or had a study session with an outside tutor arranged during this time.

Teachers and parents were perfectly aware of how much stress this put on the kids. They occasionally tried organizing activities to relieve the pressure and allow some semblance of socializing. But these occasions were too little and too contrived. Shortly before my visit, they had held a class dinner to celebrate the New Year, but it was more like being let out of the dungeon to have a nice meal with the other captives. The students were happy to have it, but it was not exactly a festive atmosphere. Everyone spent the evening complaining to one another.

While Emily's Western counterparts can look back at high school with memories of parties, proms, sports, and all kinds of pointless time-killing shenanigans, Emily will have only memories of soul-crushing routine. And she is hardly alone.

Each year nine million high school seniors across China spend their days like Emily, cramming their heads with anything that might show up on the *gaokao*. Then in the weeks leading up to the exam, a sort of national hysteria takes hold. Young girls take birth control pills to prevent their periods from falling on exam day. Crowds flock to Buddhist temples to light prayer sticks. Hucksters make a killing with expensive remedies promising to enhance brain power. And a few schools even provide IV drips for students cramming around the clock.

For some kids, the pressure proves too great. Every year, several *gaokao*-related suicides are reported in Chinese media. And every year, stories of families going to bizarre lengths to free their child of distractions come to light. In 2012, it was reported that twelve days before the *gaokao* a car accident had killed one student's mother and left his father in intensive care. Traffic police and the rest of the boy's family worked together to hide the news from him until after the test.[1]

Because of all these pressures, some Chinese youth have taken to calling themselves "the Damaged Generation."[2] With the *gaokao* being the key source of that damage, there is nearly universal consensus that it is a terrible system. Unfortunately, coming up with an alternative has proven problematic.

Corruption and nepotism pervade every corner of Chinese society, and education is not immune to it. From admission to prestigious schools all the way down to where a child sits in class, preferential education opportunities can be bought or obtained through connections.[3] Starting from kindergarten, spots at top public schools in major cities—which are supposed to be allotted based on the parents' residence—are in practice often handed out to those who have powerful contacts or who fork over illegal "donations" to school administrators looking to supplement their income.[4]

The *gaokao* was intended to be the final defense against those who would leverage their wealth and connections to compensate for their child's lack of scholastic ability. For whatever inequality exists up through high school, at least the *gaokao* ensures that college admission is truly reserved for the best and brightest. At least, that is how it works in theory.

The biggest criticism of the exam tends to be that its emphasis on rote memorization of certain subjects leaves behind creative students who thrive under less conventional circumstances. When reporters catch up with top *gaokao* scorers years later, rarely have these former prodigies achieved anything more than midlevel business success. Most of China's Nobel Prize winners and prominent entrepreneurs were educated overseas.

The subject matter tested in the *gaokao* gives a pretty good idea of just what skills students learn in high school. Once, while studying for the English portion of the exam, Emily asked me when you should say "it's my pleasure" as opposed to simply "my pleasure" in English conversation. I had to admit that I did not know, and that it was a pretty pointless distinction in terms of actually being able to communicate in English. But sure enough, there was a "correct" answer to this multiple-choice question.

I flipped through the textbook and found pages full of similar hair-splitting drivel, some of which was flat-out wrong. I asked Emily what exactly they teach her in school all day. "We write many passages," she said. "And then they tell us how we should write it better [for the essay portion of the *gaokao*]."

"You know, it's not like Mo Yan," she continued, referring to the self-educated Chinese Nobel laureate in literature. "He tells very interesting stories, but we can't write anything like that. If I write what I want, I'll fail."

She was probably right. Even for the *gaokao* essays, which are supposed to give students a chance to demonstrate their creativity and writing ability, taboo answers can result in complete failure.

In one alleged story from 2010, a student used her *gaokao* essay to deliver a scathing social commentary on the breakdown of Chinese society. "I want to find my childhood back," it read. "Because back then dried milk was used as gifts rather than poison; houses were meant to shelter people, not to kill people; trenches were used to drain flooded fields, not to collect used old oil from; the hospital did not try to rob every dime out of people's pockets but actually treated the patients; education was not regarded as a means to power and fortune but something that brings positive changes to life; tall buildings were not used to jump off from but as places where people can enjoy nice scenery."[5]

Though it is hard to verify the veracity of such essays, it has been reported anecdotally that answers indicting Chinese society routinely receive crippling scores of zero, effectively barring students who are outspoken in their off-message political beliefs from seeking higher education. This, some scholars argue, is precisely the aim of high-stakes testing in China.

The *gaokao* has roots in an imperial exam system designed specifically for the purposes of social control. Nearly 1,500 years ago, the *keju* exam system was formally established under a Sui dynasty emperor concerned with keeping China unified under his rule, and it was later perfected during the prosperous Tang dynasty. The exams tested Confucian classics, which stressed obedience to authority and the importance of stability and harmony. Success on the test could lead to prestigious and lucrative positions high into the government and, contrary to previous systems that heavily favored the hereditary aristocracy, it was open to the masses. It gave hope to everyone that if they just worked hard, they could climb to a high position in the social order.[6]

While the system indeed allowed peasants to become nobles, *keju* was most effective at keeping those at the very top in power and unchallenged. The government controlled all roads to success, meaning that no matter what a man's talent was, he devoted all his time and energy toward learning the skills, knowledge, and philosophies predetermined by the country's rulers. Those who demonstrated the highest aptitude for Confucian values tested into the government bureaucracy. They became adamant defenders of the existing social order that had put them there and were forever loyal to the emperor. Meanwhile, anyone who might otherwise have been inclined to challenge the status quo could scarcely come up with the skills, time, or manpower to mount an opposition. Everyone was too busy studying for the exam.[7]

Yong Zhao, a University of Oregon education professor and author of the book *Who's Afraid of the Big Bad Dragon: Why China Has the Best (and Worst) Education System in the World,* argues that in many ways, the *gaokao* college entrance exam is just a continuation of *keju*. "College is still a gateway to most social mobility opportunities in China," Zhao told me. "So if you want to gain access to that channel, you have to go through the *gaokao* and comply with what the government authorities subscribe as the content, skills and knowledge."[8]

One of the reasons that *keju* was such an effective tool of social control was that even those who failed still believed they had had a fair chance. Little did they know that throughout the centuries the system was usually plagued by cheating and corruption.

With the *gaokao*'s similarly high stakes in modern China, more than a handful of resourceful students also try to give themselves an edge on exam day. Each year thousands are caught trying to cheat, and dozens, sometimes hundreds, of teachers, parents, and organized gangs are arrested for facilitating the cheating. In some cases, they can be imprisoned for up to three years on charges of "stealing state secrets."[9] Tactics range from rudimentary instant messaging on cell phones all the way to earpieces and miniature television screens built into classroom rulers. In 2014 in inland Henan province, 127 students were found to have hired surrogate test takers, some of whom had used special film to fool fingerprint scanners or bribed test proctors to turn a blind eye.[10]

The Education Ministry has consistently vowed to crack down on increasingly sophisticated cheating methods. Those who write the questions for the *gaokao* are kept in secluded, top-secret facilities under armed guard without access to communication devices until after the test is administered. It is not uncommon for students to go through a metal detector and fingerprint scanner, be strip-searched, and take the exam under multiple video cameras as police roam outside with radio signal detectors.[11]

But enforcement is uneven. When local proctors oversee the testing of their community's children, they are sometimes sympathetically lax. For years the small town of Zhongxiang, Hubei province, had performed suspiciously well on the *gaokao*, prompting the provincial education ministry to send in outside monitors for the 2013 exam. After test takers were blindsided by unusually strict checks and droves were busted trying to cheat, there was a near riot among two thousand parents outside a high school. Mindful of how widely cheating was still tolerated in other areas, they ironically chanted, "We want fairness. There is no fairness if you do not let us cheat."[12]

Fear of cheating is one of the main impediments to serious *gaokao* reform. Under a more rounded, Western-style evaluation system that factored in grades, essays, interviews, and extracurricular activities, there would undoubtedly be widespread cheating and bribery. A 2010 paper by Zinch China, an education consultancy to American colleges about China, estimated that roughly 90 percent of Chinese undergraduate applications to foreign universities contained falsified information of some kind, such as outsourced essays or grades altered by unscrupulous high school administrations.[13]

Starting in the early 2000s, some colleges were allowed to select a certain quota of students using measures other than the *gaokao*, or let students add points to their score based on academic, artistic, or athletic achievements. But these alternatives have also been fraught with cheaters. One school, for instance, offered extra *gaokao* points to those who could run a marathon exceptionally fast. At the Xiamen International Marathon that year, more than thirty youths were caught trying to cut ahead on the course or hiring professional runners to carry their timing chips.[14] In many other cases, school administrators were found to have simply sold spaces reserved for special talents to the highest bidder. In 2014, it was announced that these allotments would be phased out due to overwhelming abuse and corruption.[15]

Some reforms should be relatively easy to carry out, though. The aspect of the *gaokao* that most undercuts its claim of ensuring egalitarianism is how greatly it disadvantages rural students. Not only do students in cities like Beijing and Shanghai attend higher-quality schools than rural youths, but they also have *lower* standards for acceptance to the nation's top colleges.

Since China's top two universities (Tsinghua and Peking) are located in Beijing, the schools set aside a higher quota for students with a Beijing *hukou* residence permit. In 2013, eighty-four out of every ten thousand Beijing students who took the *gaokao* gained admission to one of those two universities, whereas only three of every ten thousand students from inland Henan province were accepted.[16]

In 1958, the Chinese government instituted its *hukou* residence system in order to control population distribution and the general movement of its people.[17] Though the policy has loosened over the years, it remains in place and continues to be likened to a caste system or "peasant apartheid."[18] According to the policy, citizens are classified as either rural or urban and are largely tied to their birthplace by regional restrictions on education, medical care, and other social services (which are much better in cities). It is extremely difficult for anyone from the countryside to switch to an urban *hukou*, and nearly impossible for blue-collar workers. Thus, rural migrants doing labor in cities usually must leave their children behind to attend school where their *hukou* is registered, or place them in low-quality unofficial schools for migrant children in the city.

But even if a student from Henan lived his or her whole life in Beijing with parents who worked in the city, that student would still have to return home to take a different exam from the one for which the Beijing school had prepared its students. And such students would still be excluded from the preferential Beijing quotas, simply because their parents had not been able to obtain a local *hukou*.

A number of regions, including Beijing, have announced planned reforms allowing students to sit for the *gaokao* where they live rather than where their *hukou* is. But this proposal has received stiff opposition from locals who worry that the reforms would hurt their own children's educational prospects and encourage a flood of migrants.

Even if these reforms are introduced nationwide, students from rural provinces will still be severely disadvantaged when compared to those from the coastal regions where the bulk of China's education investment has gone. Since 1995, 117 top universities have been targeted for substantial central government investment under Project 211. Students in Beijing have twenty-six of these schools locally. Coastal

Jiangsu province has eleven. But in Henan province, with a total population of 94 million, there is just one Project 211 university. [19]

In 2012, I came across a report that dozens of young people had been robbed of thousands of dollars and years of their life through an education scam. When I tracked down some of the victims, I was hardly surprised to learn that they were from Henan, and that their nightmare had begun with failing the *gaokao*.

I met three of the young men in Jinan, the provincial capital of Shandong province, where they had been lured by the scam. All were born in 1989 to farmer parents in a rural Henan town that had little besides cornfields and small concrete homes. Despite what they had been through, I was surprised to see how upbeat they were. Like many people I had met from the countryside, they immediately peppered me with their own questions about the world outside of China before I had a chance to ask them anything. On the outside, they appeared perfectly acclimated to city life, wearing the same clothes as locals and revealing only a hint of their Henan accents. But on the inside, they were still struggling to break free of their rural upbringing.

The three had similar stories. Like many poor peasants in the region, their parents had transitioned from full-time farmers to migrant workers during the 1990s when China's economic boom took off. Since then, the parents had drifted from city to city, working in construction, while the kids stayed behind with their grandparents to attend school.

Kids in this situation have come to be known as "left-behind children"—a reference not only to being physically left behind, but also to how they are often left behind peers emotionally and academically due to a lack of parental care and educational support. As of 2013, China had an estimated 61 million left-behind children. [20]

The Henan boys' parents had spent their lives doing strenuous labor in one form or another with very meager wages to show for it. But they had made the most of those wages. Ever since their kids were in diapers, they had been saving every penny that they did not need for food and shelter. For them, securing a quality education for their children was nonnegotiable. It was the only way for the family's next generation to change its fate. So the family scrimped and saved for that education while constantly reminding their children to do their part and pass their exams.

In the end, though, none of them quite made the cut. One of the boys, Chuankai, scored high enough on the *gaokao* to qualify for an obscure three-year college, but being unable to attend a four-year university was a major blow to his family. He decided to study for another year and try again.

Another of the boys, Yang Yang, was ready to throw in the towel completely. He had never really wanted to go to college anyway, and he knew a friend who was making a small fortune as a jade merchant. He figured he would be better off just starting his own small business.

But those plans changed within a few weeks. The boys all got calls from a Shandong college recruiter, who had presumably paid the high school for *gaokao* failures' contact information. He told the boys there was a way that they could still start at a four-year university in the coming semester. At the prodding of their parents, the boys all went to hear him out.

"He was a very inspiring speaker," Chuankai recalled. "He talked about how society is and how we could have prosperous jobs. The recruiting brochures said the school had all these certifications, but it meant nothing to us. We didn't know what schools needed to be legitimate."[21]

The recruiter said that after graduating, the students could even be hired to teach at the school. In spite of their parents' initial skepticism, the boys were sold. It was going to cost them, though.

The first year's tuition was 10,000 yuan ($1,600), about twice the cost of a subsidized public university. For Chuankai's parents, it was an enormous amount of money. But they decided that they could borrow from family and neighbors later if necessary. Any sacrifice was worth the chance to see their son empowered to change his fate. Chuankai and the others were off to Jinan that September.

Altogether, about sixty other students showed up at the "university," which was a building rented out from a legitimate local college. But recruiting must have been more difficult than expected, because a few months later they were moved to a smaller building across town.

It did not take long for the students to start noticing other suspicious things. They had seen the head of the school, Zhao Lianshan, several times at the old campus, but after the move they never saw him again. And the already heavy restrictions on the students started getting worse, to the point that they were allowed to leave school only once a week to run errands.

At some point during the spring semester, the school said it needed the students' tuition receipts back and would pay 300 yuan ($48) for them. Most complied, happy to get the money. "People in the country-side are very honest," Chuankai said. "So we had no sense of law."

A few started getting suspicious and demanded to see Zhao Lian-shan. But whenever they got worked up, some of the class leaders would calm them down and dissuade them from pressing the issue.

That April, though, seven months after classes had begun, the whole thing fell apart. Students were called together by a hapless middleman and told that the school was out of money. He said they should all go out and find something else to do.

Most were furious, and a few suggested calling the police. But again the student leaders talked them down, saying there was no point. Chuankai later realized that those students were probably being bribed by Zhao Lianshan all along. But since most no longer had their receipts, trying to get their money back was indeed a lost cause. In the end, one student did call the police, who told him that Zhao had already been reported for running another fake school and that there was nothing they could do at the moment.

"The only thing I learned at that school was not to trust anybody," Chuankai said. "I got hurt badly. My first contact with society was full of lies."

The school fell apart in 2010, but incredibly, Zhao Lianshan had been running a similar scam across town at the same time, one that would not be uncovered until 2012. The victims there were even less fortunate. They had been told they were getting degrees at the relative-ly well-known Shandong Institute of Light Industry. Not until they "graduated" after four years did they discover that the school where they had been studying was not affiliated with the institute or officially registered in any way. Their four years of study were essentially mean-ingless and they were out tens of thousands of yuan. Eventually Zhao was arrested, but by then he had no money left.

Situations like this one have become ubiquitous. In 2013 a private education firm published a list of fake universities known to be operat-ing in China; the list contained at least seventy in Beijing alone.[22] Many institutions like these are diploma mills where students knowingly participate in the fiction, but in some cases, like those in Jinan, students are deceived into thinking they are working toward a legitimate degree. These scams prey heavily on rural families desperate to get their kids an education. Their tight-knit communities where everyone knows each other leave them naïve and vulnerable to outside con men.

The three young men had stayed in Jinan since their school folded, and none had ever had the nerve to tell their parents what happened. "In the countryside, gossip is really bad," Chuankai said. "Neighbors all know you're studying, so if you come back [without a degree] it brings a kind of shame."

Yang Yang cut his losses and started studying e-commerce at a private three-year college the autumn after the school failed, conveniently allowing him to keep up the pretense with his family that he was getting a four-year degree.

Zheng, the third young man, continued to study for the *gaokao* while working to support himself. He was employed at a grocery store, earning 1,000 to 2,000 yuan ($160 to $320) per month, 500 yuan of which went straight to the monthly rent. Sometimes he worked as long as two months without a day off, leaving little time to make progress in his *gaokao* study.

Zheng says he would give up on the *gaokao* if he found a stable job that could ensure that he would always have enough to eat. But even that is difficult. "I feel very different from local Jinan people," he said. "I feel inferior. Many hire locals instead of us. Local people are rich and have connections, so it is easier for them to get jobs."

Chuankai remained intent on eventually passing the *gaokao* and gaining admission to Beijing's prestigious Renmin University. But he faced the same economic hurdles. His family did not have any money left to send him, so he took up selling small goods on the roadside. He made about 40 to 50 yuan ($6.40 to $8) per day, but on several occasions he had his products confiscated by *chengguan* (city management officers). Keeping ahead of his expenses left him with very little time to study.

"I feel like I'm at the bottom of society," he said. "I'm not doing well in school or life. I'm working hard, but not doing anything for my future that I can put on my résumé."

When I asked what role he thought China's education system had played in his tough luck, Chuankai said, "The *gaokao* isn't a good system, but you can't make a better system. It really needs to be equal, though. Why is it easier for Beijingers than people from other provinces?"

When Emily Fang finally took her *gaokao* in June 2013, she also scored too low to get into a good four-year university. Fortunately, her family earned enough that she could devote the following year exclusively to study—a luxury the young men from Henan did not have. After her second go at the *gaokao*, she gained admittance to an upper-tier university. Once again, the young men's poor rural background precluded them from the same opportunities available to middle-class urban families.

In late 2014, the Chinese government announced that it would be phasing in *gaokao* reforms, seeking to raise university quotas for those from poorer regions and relieve pressure by switching from a one-time exam to three exams spread across high school. Other possible changes discussed included shifting from provincially administered tests to a single national exam, as well as factoring in students' "moral character" in college admissions. Yong Zhao, the University of Oregon professor, says there are both positive and worrisome implications to these proposed *gaokao* reforms. On one hand, they look to ensure better egalitarianism and relieve some pressure, but on the other hand, the suggestions of nationalizing the test content and adding a morality requirement could be moves to assert greater central government control. "Moral character really talks about whether students comply well with teachers," Zhao told me, "because the ones who write the comments and [judge morality] will likely be teachers and others supposed to be representing the government."

With all the hardships associated with the *gaokao*, it might seem that simply skipping it and pursuing an increasingly lucrative vocational line of work would be a more desirable option. When I suggested to Chuankai that university degrees do not carry the same weight that they used to in China, and that he might be better off financially with a technical education, he demurred. "I thought about going to technical school when my college went bankrupt," he said. "But my classmates criticized me. They said, 'Your parents saved for you to go to college. How could you use their money for technical school?'"

The last time I spoke with him, he was preparing to take the *gaokao* for the fourth time. In the meantime, he was selling school supplies on a blanket outside a local university's gates, clinging to the hope that one day he would be allowed to study inside.

3

THE UNIVERSITY

One morning the university cafeteria was abuzz with gossip. Word was spreading that a student had died and speculation as to what had happened engulfed campus.

To nobody's surprise, the school administration was not saying anything and the deceased boy's roommates suddenly became inaccessible. Some departments gathered their students and cryptically warned them not to spread rumors or speak with anyone from outside the university about certain events. They did not specify what those rumors or events might be. Campus suicides were fairly routine, and similar cover-up measures unfolded every time, but this case was different. This was a mysterious death that might be linked to school policy.

In the absence of any official university acknowledgment of the boy's death, rumors ran rampant. The story with the most momentum was that the boy had suffered a brain aneurism in the middle of the night. When he tried to leave his dorm to go to the hospital, the doorman stopped him, citing a strict policy that students had to stay in their rooms during nighttime hours. Unable to bear the pain any longer, the boy crawled out his window and tried to climb down the building. On the way down, the story went, he fell to his death. Another variation said that the boy had simply fallen on his head while sneaking out to catch a train or play computer games at an Internet café. In yet another version of events, the boy had been involved in some sort of physical altercation just prior to his death.

The security cameras installed all around the building undoubtedly could have shed light on what actually happened, but no tapes were ever released. The boy's roommates returned to the dorm but would not speak about the incident or their meetings with school officials.

A few days later, the boy's parents showed up on campus in peasant's clothing. They sat on a sidewalk adjacent to the administration offices, holding a sign that demanded a full account of what had happened. Their brief meeting with a school official had yielded more questions than answers. A few sympathetic students sat with the parents and expressed remorse but said that their protest was useless. Still, the parents vainly persisted. "They've lost their only son," one student told me. "Their life is meaningless now."

In 2007, I began teaching at this university of roughly thirty thousand students in the Jiangsu provincial capital of Nanjing. It was ranked among China's top fifty colleges and was thus one of the elite schools that received substantial central government funding through Project 211.

Like state-run institutions at all levels, Chinese universities are managed in a relatively authoritarian manner compared to their Western counterparts. The Communist Party, cognizant of how crucial it is to retain tight control over young students, firmly calls the shots in higher education. From their teachers all the way up to the university Communist Party secretary (who holds more power than the dean or president), students are at the very bottom of a strict command-and-control structure. As elsewhere in Chinese society and government, this unchecked power is often abused.

This abuse would become most apparent through my students' *fudaoyuan*—an instructor appointed at Chinese universities to oversee a few hundred students and act as a sort of nanny and counselor to them. Their responsibilities include advising students academically and professionally, organizing activities, and enforcing rules. But their number one responsibility is to "establish a firm belief in Marxism" and to help students form "a correct view of the world, life, and values firmly on the road of Socialism with Chinese Characteristics under the leadership of the Chinese Communist Party."[1]

Fudaoyuan wield enormous power over those they monitor. It was they who were dispatched to warn their students when the university wanted to keep the campus death quiet. They have the power to withhold degrees or make a mark on the permanent record that stays with Chinese graduates throughout their professional lives. They are often quite popular and helpful to those whom they oversee, but my students frequently complained about theirs, whom they nicknamed "the Bitch."

The *fudaoyuan* thrived in some of her duties while shirking others. One of her responsibilities was to regularly organize social activities and field trips for students, but she chose instead to simply falsify documents at the end of each semester saying she had done so (the actual falsification work was usually outsourced to one of her students). In order to get her to do anything for them—such as giving permission to live off campus or to travel out of town—several students said they needed to give her an expensive gift wrapped in flattery.

One area where the *fudaoyuan* thrived, though, was in her Communist Party role, which was the only duty to which her superiors actually paid attention. She frequently required students to attend ideological sessions and short film screenings glorifying the People's Liberation Army and touting the Party's latest pronouncements. On one occasion, some of the *fudaoyuan*'s Party superiors from outside the university came for a visit. An obligatory banquet was held, and she chose several of the prettiest girls from the English Department to entertain and drink liquor with the cadres.

At the end of their senior year, the students were to fill out an evaluation of all their instructors, including the *fudaoyuan*. She told them ahead of time that her scores reflected on them as a department, so they should put perfect marks all the way down. As the students completed the forms, she walked around the room, conspicuously looking over shoulders. Several students, who happened to be those with whom she had quarreled in the past, arrived too late to do the evaluation because she had told them the wrong meeting time.

A student told me about this incident over dinner immediately after it happened. "Don't you think you should go to her boss and tell him all these things?" I asked.

"She has a lot of power over us," the girl replied. "If someone complains about her, she'd make their life hell and might stop them from graduating."

"Just send a note anonymously, or have a friend in another department do it for you," I suggested.

"She'd punish all of us if we did that. It'll just bring trouble for no reason. We'll graduate soon and won't have to worry about her anyway."

"Then why not tell her bosses after graduation? Don't you want to see her get fired?"

"Impossible. They'd never fire her. Her job is protected."

"Well, I think you should do something. If you tell her bosses they might at least be stricter with her so she's not so terrible to the younger students."

The girl scoffed gently, closed her eyes for a moment, and then looked at me with a resigned smile, as if I were a naïve child not yet old enough to understand the world. "There's just no point," she said.

Contrary to this pattern, there was one student whom the *fudaoyuan* did not dare cross. His name was Jackson, and he was my worst student. Despite being an English major, he could barely utter a coherent word in the language. He was so far inferior to all the other students as to make one wonder how he had managed to pass the *gaokao*.

As it turned out, he hadn't. Jackson's father was a famous professor at the university and his mother had a high position in the school hospital. By some incredible coincidence, Jackson had been admitted in spite of his dismal exam performance.

And the coincidences did not stop there. When all the students had to pass a listening comprehension test to move on to their junior year, Jackson was conspicuously absent, yet he still obtained a passing score. When it came time to write his final thesis, a teacher was dispatched to complete it for him; and he was never required to defend it like everyone else.

At the opposite extreme of the favoritism spectrum, a video that circulated online showed a graduate student in the university straddling his sixth-story window and threatening to jump. His supervisor had been holding his degree ransom, refusing to let him graduate until he did more research and completed a paper in the professor's name. The student felt that the threat of suicide was the only way to attract attention to his situation and get his rightful diploma.

When Jackson's classmates saw the video, they knew exactly what was happening and were just as quick as I to note the glaring inconsistency between Jackson's experience and that of the suicidal graduate student. But most simply dismissed it as an inescapable fact of life.

There were many such "facts of life" at the school. Another one that constantly confronted me was cheating. As a teacher I was completely intolerant of it at first, giving a failing grade to anyone I caught. But over time I came to understand the students' plight more fully. During their senior year, my students took an English certification test that is mandatory for English teaching positions. The certification is very helpful in other job searches as well.

When the scores came out, several decent students had failed while some of the worst had received the highest scores. I was quietly informed that many had bought the answer key through a bathroom stall advertisement beforehand for 3,000 yuan ($480)—a sum far out of reach for the poorer students. Realizing how these students would be competing with each other for jobs when recruiters came to campus the following month, I was furious at the advantage that the weaker ones had bought themselves.

On a social media account that most of my students followed, I expressed my disgust at what they had done. The comment caused a stir in the dorms. Apparently I had breached a taboo: everyone knew about the cheating, but no one would dare to flag it in such a public forum. Later that night, though, I got an e-mail from a student who had failed the test, thanking me for speaking up. "But many students like me can do nothing but accept the reality and blame ourselves," she wrote.

The following year, those who had failed the certification were allowed to come back and retake the test. I found out that the girl who had written to me—and just about everyone else—saved up and bought the answers the second time around. I could not blame them. The cheating was obvious, yet once again the university took no action.

In contrast to all the rules governing students' personal lives at the school, with the option of cheating so readily available, there tended to be little pressure inside the classrooms. Li Baoyuan, a professor of labor economics at Beijing Normal University, told me that this is widespread throughout higher education in China. "No matter how much attention we pay to this problem, there are still a lot of students who cheat," he said. "It's a sad thing, but more often students tell teachers that they need to pass for this or that reason, and they get passed without cheating."[2]

On several occasions after I had failed students for plagiarizing or skipping too many classes, I was gently urged by higher-ups to reconsider, or at least to offer a makeup test. Colleagues at other schools told me of receiving even heavier-handed rebukes. An American teacher at a prestigious university in Beijing recalled that when he failed a student for never coming to class and skipping the final exam, he was told to simply give her a five-minute makeup test. "The director basically gave me an 'either you do it or we will do it' type answer," this teacher said. "I was also told to pass on this information to other teachers with the explanation that it got more confusing if we failed a student."

About 54 percent of the students who enter American universities do not graduate. The attrition rate is 32 percent in the UK and 11 percent in Japan.[3] China, on the other hand, may have the world's lowest college dropout rate. In 2011, the Beijing-based MyCOS Institute estimated that only 3 percent of China's university students drop out. China's Ministry of Education immediately disputed that figure as too high, saying the true number was just 0.75 percent.[4]

China's university system is often called "narrow in, wide out" in reference to the difficulty of admission and the ease of graduation. The competitiveness of the *gaokao* explains much of China's low dropout rate. The pressure and extensive financial support coming from Chinese parents are also factors. But after the years of stress and tears that precede the *gaokao*, many students see college as a four-year hammock to lie back and relax in. This attitude is captured by a slang Chinese term that roughly sounds like the English word "university": *you ni wan si nian*, meaning to just play around for four years. It is an attitude that universities tend to accommodate.

Li Baoyuan, the labor economics professor, told me that plagiarism, cheating, and simple neglect of studies are widely tolerated throughout China's colleges. On one hand, the universities will be criticized by parents and shunned by potential students if too many fail and have to drop out. On the other hand, teachers often have little interest or incentive to crack down on subpar academic performance. He compares Chinese universities to state-owned enterprises of the 1980s, calling them inefficiently controlled bureaucracies with endemic politicking among teachers. Usually, he says, professors are more concerned with climbing the ranks and furthering their own careers than with evaluating their students properly.

Another problem may be that professors themselves are often engaged in cheating. Given that international university rankings rely heavily on output of academic papers, administrations put big pressure on professors to publish. This, in turn, has resulted in rampant plagiarism among academics. In a 2010 government survey of six thousand scientific researchers at six leading Chinese institutions, more than a third admitted to plagiarism or falsification. The previous year, Wuhan University estimated that the demand for academic papers led to a $150 million industry for fake journals and bogus research.[5] But some professors, like the one whose student threatened suicide at my university, get these services for free by exploiting students.

The exploitation sometimes even goes beyond academics. In 2009, a seventy-year-old professor at the Central Conservatory of Music —China's most prestigious music school—accepted sexual favors and 100,000 yuan from a young woman in exchange for admission to a PhD program. When he failed to deliver on his promise, she reported him to the school. For every case that goes public, countless more go unreported. A young student I knew sought help from a university administrator to get into graduate school. She thought the 2,000 yuan ($320) of cigarettes that she brought him would be enough, but his advances when they met in his office made it clear that sex would have to be part of the deal. She quickly made an excuse to leave but did not report him, fearing the potential backlash.

Yang Rui, a professor of education at Hong Kong University, has written extensively on corruption in China's higher education system. "It's so deeply rooted," he told me. "Promotions, appointment of deanship, university presidents, Party secretaries—everywhere. I'm quite worried. The political culture in China has been unprecedentedly corrupt, and this affects almost every corner of Chinese universities in different shapes and forms."[6]

Yang also said that while requests for sexual favors happen at universities all over the world, China's political culture and the traditionally poor social standing of its women makes the practice especially prevalent there. "[In Hong Kong] we have clear regulations," he said. "If professors [accept sexual favors], that's serious stuff. In China it's not. In theory it is, but in practice it isn't."

At five-year intervals, universities undergo inspections from Ministry of Education authorities as part of the accreditation process, which also influence their national ranking. It is during these inspections that serious academic or ethical problems should theoretically be unearthed. During my first semester teaching, I dealt with one of these inspections.

In the months leading up to the inspectors' arrival, drilling and jackhammers constantly interrupted classes as buildings received facelifts and vanity structures were erected. In the week immediately before the inspection, all teachers were told that they needed to prepare detailed lesson plans for each class for the remainder of the semester. Meanwhile, all students were assigned hours when they would be required to study in the library, so as to give the impression of dedicated learning.

I happened to stop by the reception center as the inspectors were arriving. Men in suits and young women in leggy *qipao* dresses were ready to give a warm welcome as the black Audis synonymous with government cadres rolled up. Throughout the week, impressive fountains that I had never seen before were turned on; elevators in the teaching building suddenly became operational; food in the cafeteria was unusually delicious and came in supersized portions; and the dark, secluded corners of campus normally frequented by couples making out were illuminated by colorful lights.

If the inspectors had ever walked inconspicuously among the students, they would have readily noticed that something was strange, as everyone was pointing in awe at all the new and pretty things. But it is unlikely that they ever got that chance. From what people in the foreign affairs office reported, it was one banquet after another, with the actual inspection work being conducted as a formal entourage that could be seen coming from a mile away.

An American friend who taught at several less prestigious colleges said that prior to his inspections, teachers would sometimes spend weeks rehearsing a single lesson with students to perform for inspectors. Faculty would also spend months adjusting grades and doctoring past student theses that inspectors might examine. And accomplished academics from higher-ranking universities were hired on paper as "visiting scholars" in order to bolster the college's credentials, even though they never actually set foot on the school campus.[7]

As soon as the inspectors left my university, everyone breathed a collective sigh of relief. The fountains and elevators were turned off and the amorous young couples got their privacy back in once-again dark corners.

Yang Rui says such inspections are par for the course. Undue influence, be it simple wining and dining or outright bribes, is very common. "Cheating is normal for this evaluation," he said.

Not a single university across the nation lost its accreditation that year. But remarkably, four schools—including mine—had an entire department shut down after numerous plagiarized dissertations were found on file. This was one of many signs that the government intended to reform Chinese universities in order to boost their world standing. Some schools were starting to use plagiarism detection software to root out cheaters. Sang Guoyuan, an associate professor at Beijing Normal University's Center for Teacher Education Research, told me that at his school, students were facing severe punishments and even expulsion when caught cheating. He says this trend is starting to take hold firmly at many of the top-tier universities.[8]

Over the years, the Chinese government has also instituted corruption crackdowns within universities. In just one province (Jiangxi), fourteen top university officials, including three university presidents, fell to corruption charges between 2008 and 2013.[9] Then in 2010, the vice head of Jilin province's education department was sentenced to life in prison for accepting $1.31 million in bribes in exchange for securing university slots for unqualified students.[10] Similarly, in late 2013 the head of admissions at Renmin University fell to corruption charges and was caught trying to flee the country.[11] While these cases are only scratching the surface of university corruption, they are raising the public's awareness of it.

The emergence of microblogging platforms has also given students greater power to expose misdeeds in their schools. In 2012, when a female student at Qingdao Qiu Shi College fell to her death after an evening of drinking with her teachers, the school tried to suppress any discussion of the incident. The story quickly exploded on the Internet and reporters discovered that several other mysterious deaths had occurred previously at the school. Though what had happened never fully came to light, the teachers involved were dismissed from their posts.[12] Then in 2014, photos of a young woman in bed with a Xiamen University history professor were posted online by a blogger claiming to be a former student who had been coerced into a sexual relationship with him. Several other alleged students then spoke up to detail similar stories, and soon after the professor was removed.[13]

As part of its effort to "comprehensively deepen reforms," the Communist Party Central Committee announced in late 2013 its intention to overhaul the country's education system by granting schools more autonomy, closing the rural–urban education gap, adding more emphasis on practical vocational education, and shaking up the university admissions system in order to accept a more diverse range of students.[14] China has also been welcoming cooperative relationships between dozens of Western universities in order to help internationalize the country's higher-education standards. Schools like New York University and the University of Nottingham have even been allowed to set up satellite campuses in China.

However, the area perhaps in greatest need of reform is still changing very little, and it may even be retrogressing. Despite the claim to be giving more autonomy to universities, the Communist Party has no intention of backing away from them. Currently the Party directly appoints top university officials, including the all-powerful Party secretary and school president. According to Professor Yang Rui, these leaders are often referred to as "parachutes" for the way they are simply dropped into universities.[15] "It's just chess," Yang said. "They move you to the next step." He explained that since leadership roles at prestigious universities can be springboards to powerful ministerial positions, higher-level Party officials frequently stack the positions with their political allies. "We often say 'Chinese Communist Party,'" as if the organization were monolithic, Yang noted. "But what is the Communist Party? These people fight against each other in different factions, and unfortunately, universities aren't immune from this. In fact, they're directly involved."

Because of this system, university leaders are far less concerned with the people below them (their teachers and students) than with pleasing the handful of Communist Party cadres above them. "In China, very few deans care about their students or teachers," Yang observed.

This heavy Communist Party influence trickles all the way down to the classroom. In addition to frequent political activities arranged by university *fudaoyuan*, Chinese college students are also subject to a slew of compulsory courses on subjects like Marxism, morality, and modern Chinese history that are meant to highlight the superiority of the Chinese system and the triumphs of the Communist Party.[16] Western philosophies are mentioned only in passing, for the purpose of highlighting their inferiority when compared to Socialism with Chinese Characteristics—a euphemism for China's brand of authoritarian capitalism. While emphasizing the advantages of one's own political system is normal throughout the world, the education in China's universities goes quite a bit further by teaching students to have the "correct opinion."

China's National Entrance Examination for Postgraduates (NEEP), which all students must take to get into graduate school, gives an idea of the subject matter contained in the undergraduate courses on Chinese ideology. One question from the 2011 test asks students to choose which of the following accurately describes China's current political system:

a. The Communist Party's great creation of combining Marxism and China's reality
b. The Communist Party's achievement of leading Chinese people through a long struggle
c. A reflection of the common interests and aspirations of all ethnic groups in China
d. The inevitable choice in the social development of modern China[17]

(All choices are correct.)

Another question from the same exam starts with this statement: "In 1989, former U.S. State Department advisor Francis Fukuyama dished out the so-called 'End of History' theory which says the Western democratic system is 'the end of human progress in social formation.' However, 20 years of history have shown us that history didn't end. What ended was the Western sense of superiority."

My students often complained about the tedium of these classes, indicating that everyone—including the teachers—knew the content was little more than dogmatic propaganda. Professors seldom tried to convince students that the subject matter was true, but simply taught them how to approach the material so that they could pass their graduate school political tests. One student recalled a teacher instructing the class that "if Lenin said it, it must be the right answer."

I received a frank explanation of the training's purpose from Professor Wang Ji, who holds a PhD in Marxism from Peking University and teaches the political subject matter at a Beijing test-prep academy. "The goal of this education is to let students achieve the same opinion," he said. "It's common that students don't necessarily agree, but we've achieved the goal when students take the test and know they need to choose according to what they learned instead of their own mind."[18]

To my surprise, many students who hated the political classes nevertheless supported their inclusion in higher education. "We are unconsciously learning to support the Party," Maggie, one of my post-80s undergraduate students, once told me. "But as huge and complicated as China is, it's hard for it to apply a two-party or multiparty system. Thus, this method the Party uses to maintain its domination is necessary to ensure the whole country's safety and stability."

Most of my younger post-90s students remained unconvinced of the political education's merits, but they tended to just laugh when I brought it up, treating it as yet another of those inescapable facts of life. "Most young people know which direction the tests try to take them," Donnie Wang, a student from Chongqing, told me. "But it does no good to be a maverick. We just want to pass so we can have a fighting chance to travel further or study abroad and know what's really going on."

Professor Wang Ji admitted that this political education does not have nearly the effect that it had even a decade earlier. "It may not be the most effective way to educate students," he said, "but it cannot be neglected, cannot be omitted."

Despite the many reforms that the government has proposed, it signaled in early 2012 its intention to intensify its ideological hold on universities. One year before Xi Jinping assumed the presidency of China, he called on universities to "increase thought control" over students and young lecturers. "University Communist Party organs must adopt firmer and stronger measures to maintain harmony and stability in universities," he said at a meeting attended by university leaders in Beijing. "Young teachers have many interactions with students and cast significant [political and moral] influence on them."[19]

Within months of assuming the presidency in the summer of 2013, Xi's sentiment would be formalized in the notorious "Document 9." This communiqué, circulated by the Communist Party's General Office to local Party committees, admonished cadres to stop universities and media from discussing seven taboo topics: constitutional democracy, universal values, civil society, neoliberalism, crony capitalism, press freedom, and historical Communist Party mistakes.[20]

The wording of the document in many ways echoed remarks by former president Jiang Zemin twenty-four years earlier. At an education conference one month after the Tiananmen Square crackdown, Jiang lamented that Western values had taken hold among many of China's youth, and he called for greater ideological control on university campuses.[21]

Both periods—from 1989 into the early 1990s, and from summer 2013 onward—were times of great paranoia for the Communist Party. On both occasions China's government responded by trying to rejuvenate an ailing economy with sweeping market adjustments, accompanied by a political clampdown to help in seeing the risky economic reforms through.

During the early 1990s, the stricter ideological controls of which Jiang spoke were indeed implemented in schools. Then, as today, few swallowed the rigid touting of Marxist socialism. However, some of the more nationalistic and troubling aspects of the indoctrination would be taken to heart, with violent repercussions years later.

4

THE PATRIOTS

To many, Rao Jin represents the ultimate Chinese success story.

His first brush with fame came at age eighteen when he shocked his village by getting into the country's most prestigious university. By twenty-one, he would become a campus sensation after cofounding "China's Facebook" and buying his very own car and chauffeur. But by twenty-three, he would be the poster child for China's "*fenqing*" (angry youth) movement and would find himself at the center of a nationalistic fervor.

In March 2008, a group of Buddhist monks gathered in the Tibetan capital of Lhasa to commemorate a failed 1959 uprising against the Chinese government. When police came to break up the gathering, it was the final straw for many locals who had long resented Communist Party rule and the presence of Han Chinese in the region. [1]

Following the police action, enraged local Tibetans began indiscriminately attacking Han Chinese and members of the minority Hui Muslim ethnic group. Government vehicles were destroyed and businesses belonging to Han and Hui owners were set ablaze. By the following day, police had suppressed the rioting with gunfire and tear gas. [2]

According to government figures, rioters killed 22 people, including an eight-month-old baby. Tibetan exile groups in India claimed that the total death toll was 140, mostly Tibetans killed by police quelling the riot. [3]

The government was quick to blame the "Dalai Lama clique" for covertly sparking the violence with the support of unspecified "Western anti-China forces." It was a familiar narrative to Chinese that some "Westerners" were about to make more believable.

During and after the riots, foreign journalists were barred from entering Lhasa, leaving much of the reporting to secondhand information from activist groups. As is often the case in such situations, several of the initial reports contained inaccuracies.[4] Several foreign media outlets mislabeled old photos of police crackdowns in Nepal and India as Chinese police violence against Tibetans. Photos showing Chinese police rescuing bystanders from rioters were also incorrectly described as protesters being arrested.[5]

The outlet that drew the greatest ire was CNN. In fact, just days after the riots the website anti-CNN.com sprang up with the aim of "identifying the lies and distortions of facts from the Western media."[6] CNN's chief transgression was a photo it published of a military vehicle in Lhasa being pelted with rocks by protesters. The photo, anti-CNN.com claimed, had been purposely cropped to hide the rock-chucking Tibetans in an attempt to downplay their aggression and demonize the Chinese military. According to the website, the Western media was twisting facts in order to defame China. Ironically, the image as it appeared on anti-CNN.com did its own cropping, deleting CNN's original caption under the photo, which read, "Tibetans throw stones at army vehicles on a street in the capital Lhasa."[7]

Patriotic young Chinese posted messages on anti-CNN.com decrying Western hypocrisy. While many users kept the focus on correcting purported media distortions, others used the platform to vent xenophobic hatred of the West and grievances dating back to the nineteenth century.

Over the following weeks, fuel would be thrown on the fire as the torch relay for the Beijing Olympics began. What was supposed to be a festive coming-out party for China quickly became an embarrassment as protesters in San Francisco, London, and Paris turned out in force to decry Chinese actions in Tibet and various other human rights violations. At one point when the torch passed through Paris, a torchbearer in a wheelchair was assaulted by French protesters attempting to extinguish the flame.[8]

While outsiders may have seen the protests as the acts of a few brazen individuals against the Chinese government, many within China saw it as a unified slap in the face of every Chinese citizen. It was a signal that "the West" could not tolerate an emerging China and would do anything to keep it down, just as it had done in the past.

By mid-April the initial wave of nationalism had become a full-blown tsunami. Soon after the Olympic torch relay incident in Paris, activists in China organized a boycott of the French superstore Carrefour and protests at outlets across the country. Thousands chanted slogans like "Oppose Tibet independence," "Go China," and "Condemn CNN."[9] When I asked students participating in the protests why they were targeting Carrefour, some cited unsubstantiated rumors that it had funded the Dalai Lama. For others, the store's French origin was sufficient justification.

Around this time a twenty-eight-year-old graduate student from Shanghai, who would later work for anti-CNN.com, created a six-minute video entitled "China, Stand Up!" Set to a chilling orchestral piece, it juxtaposed false Western media reports beside an image of Joseph Goebbels. "Finally, we're reminded of Chairman Mao's famous words: imperialism will never abandon its intention to destroy us," the video stated. "Obviously, there is a cabal, a Cold War against China!" it said while showing an image of George W. Bush and the Dalai Lama superimposed on a Nazi flag. "Stand up! We must stand up to give our voice to the world!"[10]

The video was frightening to foreigners living in China, but it was a hit among Chinese, drawing more than a million views within a week and a half and tens of thousands of approving comments. A few students e-mailed the link to me. I was not quite sure if they did so out of courtesy or spite.

As these events unfolded, many outside China assumed that they were part of a coordinated government effort to stoke nationalism and redirect attention from Tibet's ethnic conflicts. At a Foreign Affairs Ministry press conference, a foreign reporter even asked if the government was funding anti-CNN.com. "You won't ask that if you take a look at the reports by the Western media," the spokesperson replied. "It is these irresponsible and unethical reports that infuriated our people to voice voluntarily their condemnation and criticism."[11]

While a flood of state-backed editorials egged on the nationalistic sentiment, they were just fanning flames that had spontaneously erupted among China's "angry youth"—so labelled for their intense patriotism and fury at perceived slights by foreign countries.[12] The flames would not die down until an earthquake in Sichuan killed over eighty thousand people and redirected the nation's attention. But the flames continued to smolder, just waiting to reignite.

When I met Rao Jin at a Beijing café nearly five years after the Lhasa riots, it was hard to believe he had been the man behind anti-CNN.com. With his laid-back demeanor and constant grin, he appeared nothing like the vitriolic nationalists associated with his website. Rao seemed to agree. "I'm not very outgoing, so I didn't want to be famous," he laughed. "Anti-CNN was a coincidence. I'm a Libra, so I'm not really interested in politics."[13]

Rao was born in 1984 in an agrarian village of two hundred in the coastal province of Fujian. From a very young age, he was ahead of the curve. He did not want to go to kindergarten because he felt it was "too naïve" (besides which the classroom sat beside a smelly latrine), so he skipped straight to first grade.

He says his interest in media began at age fourteen when he started picking up radio signals from Taiwan that included the BBC, Voice of America, and Radio Free Asia. Sometimes he even picked up programs from the Falun Gong spiritual movement, which is banned in China as an "antigovernment cult." After having been exposed only to state-run propaganda his whole life, this was a fascinating turn of events.

"During that time I was very curious and felt quite excited," Rao said. "They're different from any Chinese media. They describe China as a hell, no light, no freedom at all, but in fact it's too political. I saw two extremes, so I learned critical thinking and balance."

Like most Chinese parents, Rao's mother and father saw a good education as the only path to success. They put gaining admission to a good university above all else and constantly locked him in his room to study. He would not disappoint them. When he took the *gaokao* college entrance exam at the end of high school, he achieved something considered miraculous in his small village: he earned admission to Tsinghua University, China's most prestigious school. The achievement made him a local celebrity. "That was a burden," he said. "I didn't want people to know me. The *gaokao* [score] was just a coincidence."

Rao had always stood head and shoulders above his classmates, but when he arrived at Tsinghua that all changed. "I found after one semester that even if I studied very hard, I wasn't a top student anymore,"

Rao said. "I was shocked and really depressed. I wanted to be different and do something that people never imagined."

After his first semester, he stopped putting so much effort into his coursework and turned to something else new to him that Tsinghua offered: Internet access. He had never gone online before college, but once he did, he would hardly ever log off again.

Rao dove into computer programming and would eventually buy his own servers to host the sites he was designing. Soon older Tsinghua alumni were tracking him down for help in building their company websites. One site that he helped to develop from his dorm room was Xiaonei, one of China's first social networks, which started out as a carbon copy of Facebook (right down to the logo). After about a year, Rao and the other cofounders cashed out by selling the company to an entrepreneur. As of 2013, under the name Renren, it remained one of China's largest social networks, with 31 million active users and a listing on the New York Stock Exchange. By his junior year at Tsinghua, these successes had enabled Rao to stand out among his peers; in fact, he had his own car and chauffeur.

However, Rao's father was mortified, thinking that this IT obsession was uncharted territory. Rao was doing well now, but who knew how long this career path could last? It would be better if he directed his intelligence toward something guaranteed to provide for a lifetime. Rao's father expected him to study hard and become a civil servant—a highly competitive occupation viewed as lucrative and stable in China.

"My father came all the way to Beijing to ask the class supervisor to persuade me to take the civil service exam," Rao said. "But the supervisor told him that I would choose my own way. My father felt very unhappy."

In a sort of compromise, Rao agreed to sell his car and buy an apartment—a much better investment in his father's eyes. Soon afterward, however, Rao would tread further into risky ground.

After the Lhasa riots began in 2008, Rao, like many of his highly educated and patriotic friends, was greatly disturbed by how some foreign media were portraying events unfolding in China. In response, he set up anti-CNN.com, choosing the provocative name intentionally in order to be noticed both in China and abroad (in 2009 he changed the name to April Media). The strategy clearly worked; tens of thousands of Chinese flocked to the site to support Rao's cause.

"There were indeed many people [coming to the site] who weren't so calm," Rao recalled. "But many overseas Chinese students and our forum members were quite calm and understood what they were doing. They just wanted to win back respect for their country."

Rao says that from the beginning he respected Western journalists and their devotion to their work, and that he wanted only to oppose the prejudice exhibited by some Western media. I asked whether he thought his website had stoked counterproductive nationalism, even if that was not his intention.

"Nationalism or patriotism, I don't know how to define it in Western culture," he replied. "In this generation we accept a lot of Western culture, like Hollywood movies. As a result many Western media didn't understand why, this time, Chinese youth reacted so nationalistically. I can understand. We just wanted justice, to be treated equally. We don't want to be discriminated against."

This insistence on respect from the rest of the world is something for which Rao's generation, which came of age after the crackdown at Tiananmen, has become known. In the early twentieth century, China's Kuomintang government had often emphasized a Chinese nationalist narrative that centered on its exceptional people as victims to pugnacious foreign aggressors. But when Mao and his Communists came to power in 1949, the national story was shifted from one of victimhood to one of socialist triumph and proletarian internationalism. In a socialist China, there was no room for "bourgeois nationalism," which Marxists view as something conjured up by rulers to keep workers of the world divided and distracted from class struggle.

After Mao was gone and China had begun to embrace capitalism, the Communist Party continued throughout the 1980s to rely on socialist ideology as its source of legitimacy. But the demonstrations of 1989 showed that this track was bunk. The Party needed a new approach . . . or perhaps more accurately, a very old approach.

Five days after the Tiananmen protests were quelled, then-paramount leader Deng Xiaoping addressed a group of generals who had been involved. "During the last ten years our biggest mistake was made in the field of education," he told them. "Primarily in ideological and political education—not just of students but of the people in general. We didn't tell them enough about the need for hard struggle, about what China was like in the old days and what kind of a country it was to become."[14]

Within two years, China would launch its "Patriotic Education campaign," shifting away from a focus on the triumphs of socialism back toward highlighting China's historical traumas. The "old days" to which Deng referred would be codified into official history as the "Century of Humiliation," which extended from the Opium War in 1839 through World War II, ending with Communist "liberation" in 1949.[15]

During the eighteenth and nineteenth centuries, China's Qing dynasty leaders still regarded their country as the center of the universe and one to which all other nations should pay tribute. Throughout history, China had indeed been among the world's most formidable powers both technologically and militarily. But Qing leaders did not realize that, while maintaining China's isolation from the rest of the world, they were missing out on the industrial revolution unfolding in Europe.

In 1839 a Qing commissioner wrote to England's Queen Victoria, requesting that she demonstrate her "politeness and submissiveness" toward China by ending the opium trade.[16] It came as a shock that, rather than complying, the British used their superior weaponry to decimate China's much larger standing army.

After that, other Western powers would carve up the country, inflicting "humiliating" treaties that required China to pay outrageous indemnities and cede territory. The ultimate humiliation came when the tiny nation of Japan defeated China in 1895 and invaded again in the 1930s, leaving behind a trail of destruction, rape, torture, and senseless murder.

Patriotic Education was introduced in 1991 and fully instituted by 1994.[17] Henceforth, Chinese schoolchildren would be bombarded with instruction on the Century of Humiliation in gory detail. China, according to the curriculum, was an exceptional, peace-loving civilization that was brought to its knees by foreign imperialists. Only when the Communist Party vanquished the Japanese army and took control of the country in 1949 did China begin to recover its former glory.

This education has fairly successfully unified the Chinese against external enemies and shifted public demands from calls for reform to an insistence on national sovereignty and stability. But it has also had the side effect of embedding a severe inferiority complex among the Chinese, along with a need for validation and respect from the West.

The 2008 Olympics were supposed to signify China's reemergence as a serious player on the world stage. But when China's youth saw the global media heaping insults rather than praise on their country, they felt that the West was once again seeking to impose its imperialistic will on China. The fact that the conflict was over Tibet especially opened old wounds.

In the end, the 2008 uproar against the West featured little more than angry rhetoric. But when that smoldering nationalism reignited four years later, things became downright violent. This time the conflict involved a series of skirmishes on the Diaoyu Islands, an uninhabited island chain claimed by both China and Japan.

In April 2012 the nationalistic mayor of Tokyo announced his intention to raise money to buy some of the islands from their private Japanese owners, place them under Tokyo's administration, and develop them. In a bid to prevent this action and reduce the risk of provoking China, Japan's national government said it would buy the islands and bar any visits or development.[18] However, Chinese did not view this alternative any more favorably; they still saw a hated foreign power once again divvying up Chinese territory.

These events alone may not have caused the Chinese to take up arms, but on August 15 the Japanese coast guard intercepted and detained a group of Hong Kong activists landing on Diaoyu.[19] By the time the Japanese government finalized its purchase of the Diaoyu Islands in September, Chinese tempers had flared and the government was ready to harness that anger to send a message.

On September 13, the state-run *Global Times* newspaper ran an editorial saying, "Japan inflicted the deepest atrocities on China in its modern history, which was full of humiliation. If China were to pick a target country to wash out the old shame, Japan is the best choice."[20]

That weekend, thousands poured into the streets in dozens of cities to protest. In Beijing, protesters descended upon the Japanese embassy, pelting it with water bottles, eggs, and rocks while hoisting Chinese flags and portraits of Mao Zedong.

Across the nation, businesses that appeared to be Japanese were targeted, even though most of them had Chinese owners. Japanese restaurants had windows smashed, retailers' shops were ransacked, and a few companies such as Panasonic and Toyota had their offices

Protestors march against Japan in front of the Japanese embassy in Beijing in September 2012 with a sign reading "Eliminate Japanese, protect our country." (Photo: Eric Fish)

torched. Japanese cars in several cities were set ablaze, overturned, or otherwise vandalized.[21]

In a particularly gruesome incident, a fifty-one-year-old Chinese man was dragged out of his Toyota in Xi'an and left paralyzed after a twenty-one-year-old migrant construction worker named Cai Yang bludgeoned him on the head with a bicycle lock. Days later, when Cai learned that he was wanted by police for his assault, he expressed surprise. He told family members that his action was "patriotic" and that "online, half the people support me and half are against me."[22]

The Japan-based *Asahi Shimbun* newspaper caught up with Cai's mother weeks later, after he had been arrested. "Ever since he was a child, he loved to watch movies and dramas about the war against Japan," she told them. "Those programs often emphasize brutal scenes of murder and pillage by Japanese troops. In Nanyang village, whenever children are asked who the villain was, they would always answer, 'The Japanese.'"[23]

Based on interviews with his family and friends, a profile in *Southern Weekend* painted a picture of Cai that was not quite as simple as a young man being brainwashed into antiforeign sentiment.[24] He had grown up in a poor and troubled rural family and dropped out of school at age thirteen. From there, he went straight into construction work and by age eighteen had migrated to Xi'an to do plastering on buildings. He toiled through unfulfilling work and rarely socialized with other workers, opting instead to immerse himself in online first-person shooter games during his off-time. He dreamed of going to university and making something of his life, but by this point, it was an impossible proposition.

On Cai's QQ microblog more than a year before his attack in Xi'an, he wrote, "In two weeks I'll be 20-years-old . . . sigh . . . will I be the same next year as I am now? Really want to find a wife to live with. Don't want to go on being a slacker. God, grant me a wife!"[25]

Cai saw himself at the bottom of society—unnoticed and irrelevant to all those around him. The *Southern Weekend* profile described a time when he had urinated on his project manager's Audi, and "felt great" about it. "He wanted to do more," the profile said. "To prove 'I

Protestors set a Honda dealership ablaze amid the 2012 anti-Japan demonstrations. (Photo: Weibo)

am important'—but lacked both the material and mental means. A clamoring protest gave him the 'opportunity' to do precisely this."

Two weeks after the bludgeoning incident and just before his arrest, Cai posted his last blog message: "Miserable post-90 generation—do we feel fortunate?"

Within two days of Cai's attack in Xi'an, the government decided that the protests had gotten out of hand. The media started urging calm and police dispersed the large gatherings. The abrupt ending gave the impression that China's leaders had skillfully manipulated the protests and then simply turned them off after achieving their desired aim.

But it would be a mistake to assume that either the 2008 or 2012 protests were the result of a brainwashed populace sheepishly falling in line behind the government, or that China's "angry youth" are all just uneducated flag wavers.

To Rao Jin, the most laughable part about his whole experience in 2008 was the idea, frequently assumed by foreign media, that he and anti-CNN.com were in league with the government. On the contrary, on several occasions Rao had been "invited for tea"—a euphemism for a soft interrogation by public security officials. "When I do media, I want to criticize the government as well," Rao said. "Otherwise I would follow my father's advice and take the civil service exam. But that's totally impossible. I like freedom."

Even among the more vitriolic or violent nationalists, there is not always as much overlap with the government agenda as outsiders might think. For example, the Mao Zedong posters prominently displayed during the anti-Japanese protests, widely assumed to be a sign of support for the Communist Party, were actually an indictment of the current government. When I asked a few protesters in front of the Japanese embassy why they were carrying the Mao Zedong posters, the consensus answer was that "Chairman Mao would never let Japan get away with this." At one of the anti-Japan protests in Shenzhen in 2012, some protesters even unfurled a banner that read "Liberty, democracy, human rights and a constitution." They were quickly arrested by plainclothes police.[26]

Off-message displays like this represent one of the Communist Party's deepest fears. On many occasions over the past century, nationalistic antiforeign protests in China have quickly shifted toward blaming corrupt domestic leaders for taking a soft line on the foreigners. From there, the protests have the potential to morph into calls for greater government accountability and even democracy. The May 4th Movement in 1919 began after Japan was awarded Chinese territory in the post–World War I Treaty of Versailles, which prompted Chinese to condemn their own leaders for standing by too idly. In 1935, protests against Japanese militarism again turned toward domestic leaders for their failure to resist invasion. Then in 1985, demonstrations against Japan that were suppressed gradually turned to condemnations of Chinese leaders for selling out their country and lacking patriotism. They eventually shifted to full-blown movements for political reform that would set the stage for the 1989 Tiananmen protests.

Jessica Chen Weiss, an assistant professor of political science at Yale and author of *Powerful Patriots: Nationalist Protest in China's Foreign Relations*, argues that over the past three decades, China's government has selectively allowed or repressed nationalist protests in order to achieve certain diplomatic aims. In 2012, Chinese leaders wanted to signal resolve when Japan refused to back down, so it tacitly allowed street demonstrations to grow. But more often, the government suppresses these movements before they become large, as it did two years earlier over another flare-up in the Diaoyu Islands dispute.[27] "When nationalist protests are raging in the streets, it's very difficult for the Chinese government to make compromises and wind those protests down without looking unpatriotic," Weiss told me. "But at the same time, the Chinese government is often quite selective in determining when those protests take place at all."[28]

One common belief holds that the Chinese government simply turns nationalist protests on and off periodically as a way to let citizens "blow off steam" and redirect anger over domestic issues toward foreign enemies. Weiss cautions that this is an oversimplistic view. "The government does play a role in allowing these demonstrations to spill forth into the streets," she says, "but often they aren't encouraging them, and even when they are encouraging them, it's more a process of stage-managing grassroots expression of anger and trying to mitigate the risk that these turn against the government."

Some have argued that these nationalistic outbursts are not so much a result of patriotism as they are a manifestation of much deeper societal dissatisfaction. A book by TV host and international affairs commentator Qiu Zhenhai recounts a conversation with a taxi driver about the possibility that China might go to war. "War is good, it reshuffles the cards," the driver told Qiu. "If I lose my life, I lose my life. I'm not like those people who own property or companies. I'm even less like the corrupt officials who have riches they can steal. I am a proletarian, with nothing to care about. These days I don't see any hope; it's better to just take a gamble."[29]

Andrew Chubb, a University of Western Australia scholar who researches Chinese nationalism and public opinion, suggested that stories like this reflect not necessarily a genuine longing to reclaim lost territory and avenge national humiliation but "a desire for something, anything, to shake Chinese society up."[30]

Chubb told me that nationalistic outbursts like those of 2008 and 2012 have various motivations, including outright racism, the novelty of protest, a sense of connection with others, and a feeling of patriotic duty. But an additional, often-overlooked motivation is a desire to vent general dissatisfaction with life. "I'm a believer in the theory that anti-foreign nationalism expresses domestic social issues of exclusion and atomization," Chubb said.[31]

This is the government's nationalism dilemma: The Communist Party is sometimes described as standing over a flame with a can of gas in one hand and a fire extinguisher in the other. It must allow enough expression of nationalism that people do not begin looking enviously at Western democracies or viewing Chinese leaders as weak and unpatriotic, but not so much that the disenfranchised redirect nationalistic fervor toward domestic issues or push the government toward an unwanted conflict.

I asked Rao Jin if he thought war could actually break out between China and Japan or a Western country. "I hope not," he replied. "But it's possible. People don't like wars, but China's population structure is quite dangerous. There are a lot of problems." As he explained, China is burdened by having too many people and too few resources. "God bless America," he laughed. "I've been there. I envy you—you have so much land and no strong neighbors, so you don't need to worry about regional political issues."

Rao pointed out that the world would be unsustainable if everyone copied the consumption practices of Americans, and in any case, China's dearth of resources precludes it. He said this situation makes it more difficult to keep the Chinese people happy, so he sympathizes with China's leaders to some degree. "I don't think [ours] is the best system, but maybe it's not the worst," he said. "If we moved 300 million Chinese to the US, the US system wouldn't work."

As the double-digit growth that China has enjoyed for the last two decades inevitably slows, it will become even harder to keep the nation's young people happy if their expectations grow faster than opportunities. The once wide-open paths to success are getting clogged as more people fight over fewer openings. Rao admits that he probably would not have been so successful had he been born just a little bit later.

"Ten or twenty years ago, if you were smart enough, you could have many opportunities for success," he said. "But now there are a lot of people as smart as you and lot of people with a better connected father than you."

II

Going to Work

5

FACTORY TOWN

On the night of May 14, 2010, a twenty-one-year-old migrant worker from Anhui province slashed his wrists and leaped to his death from the seventh story of his Shenzhen factory dorm.

Such an incident would normally fade away unnoticed. But this suicide happened at Foxconn, the Taiwanese electronics manufacturer that makes Apple's iPhones and iPads. Text messages and social media quickly spread the word throughout the 400,000-worker factory. Soon media outlets were reporting that it was the seventh suicide of the year at Foxconn. By the end of 2010 there would be fourteen, all involving workers under twenty-eight years old.

Despite having worked at the plant for six months, the man's seven roommates had hardly known him. "Working at Foxconn is pretty busy," one of them told Xinhua News Agency. "Chats are rare."[1]

The Foxconn suicides of 2010 made international headlines and hit close to home for millions around the world using Apple products (and anything made in China). They also got extensive coverage domestically, causing national introspection. They vividly depicted the conditions that young Chinese had been taught to avoid at all costs through getting an education.

After the sixth suicide, the Guangzhou-based *Southern Weekend* newspaper sent twenty-year-old intern reporter Liu Zhiyi undercover to get a job at the Shenzhen factory for twenty-eight days. "It wasn't about finding out what they died for," Liu later wrote. "But rather, to learn how they lived."[2]

A more careful investigation showed that reality was a bit more complex than the prevailing narrative. Foxconn had roughly one million employees in mainland China at the time, leaving its fourteen deaths well below the national suicide rate and even that of most developed Western countries (for instance, the US state of Montana, also with a population of about one million, saw 227 suicides that same year[3]). A Tsinghua University psychologist invited to the Shenzhen factory concluded that Foxconn's suicide rate was statistically similar to the rate among Chinese university students of the same age.[4]

Liu Zhiyi emerged from his time at Foxconn with a different though equally compelling story. "This super factory that holds some 400,000 people isn't the 'sweatshop' that most would imagine," he wrote in *Southern Weekend*. "Compared to others, the facilities here are well-equipped and superior, with employee treatment meeting standard specifications. Thousands of people flock here each day just to find a place of their own, in search of a dream that they will probably never realize."[5]

Shenzhen's strategic location at the mouth of the Pearl River and adjacent to Hong Kong allowed it to be designated China's first Special Economic Zone in 1980. Thanks to this experiment with market capitalism, the city exploded from a fishing village of thirty thousand to a metropolis of nearly ten million.[6] Following Shenzhen's lead, the entire Pearl River delta region has grown from a series of farming villages to nine major cities with 64 million people and a GDP that surpassed Taiwan's in 2006. By the end of 2012, nearly 20 percent of China's 263 million migrants were working there.[7]

The region has come to be known as "the world's workshop." China's economic miracle began here, drawing millions off the farms on which their families had lived for generations to delve into a brave new world.

For that first generation of workers in the 1980s and 1990s, factory conditions tended to resemble the Dickensian excesses of an unrestrained industrial revolution. These excesses came to a head in 1993 at Shenzhen's Zhili doll factory. In order to prevent workers from stealing goods and wandering away during working hours, the owners bolted the building's doors, barred the windows, and blocked passageways with crates. When a fire broke out, there was no escape. After the smoke cleared, eighty-seven workers—all migrant women from poor inland provinces—lay dead in heaps next to the locked exits.

During the subsequent factory investigation, a researcher discovered a box of undelivered letters containing correspondence between Zhili employees, their families, and other migrant workers in the region. The letters shed new light on the lives and worries of the era's workers. [8]

The primary concerns were not getting enough overtime and not getting wages. Paychecks generally came late if at all, and many workers appeared clueless as to how much money they were supposed to be receiving. Discussions about going to work at a different factory was common, but this could be very difficult, as bosses held months of back pay and confiscated workers' identification cards as leverage. If unable to show ID when stopped by Shenzhen police, migrants could be arbitrarily arrested and given a crippling fine.

Secondary concerns were loneliness and isolation. Few workers or their families had access to phones, leaving the sketchy postal system as the only means of communication. Workers also complained of frequent health problems and, on occasion, dangerous working conditions. "There was toxic gas in the factory," one letter read. "Yuxia [a coworker] died a horrible death." [9]

Inadequate food was yet another concern. But perhaps the most striking thing from the letters is what they did not contain. Not a single one mentioned a worker complaining to a boss or to authorities. Except for instances of clear and present danger, working conditions went unmentioned as well. The workers appeared to have very modest aspirations, primarily for a regular income. Only when they could not get paid consistently did they tend to think about leaving the factory.

Workers at that time were scarcely in a position to complain. They were highly replaceable, easily silenced, and not prone to complain anyway. Having toiled endlessly in the fields for a subsistence existence, they knew things could be worse. Their meager earnings and repressive working conditions still presented better prospects than what they had had back home.

Today, the Pearl River delta has its second generation of workers, many of them the children of migrants. Some things have changed. Some have not.

When Liu Zhiyi showed up at Foxconn's behemoth Longhua, Shen-zhen, plant in 2010, he was directed to wait in line with thousands of other prospective workers. Even in the year following the suicide incidents, Foxconn reported that eight thousand jobseekers showed up each day to compete for the four thousand daily openings.[10]

The lines were chaotic and noisy, prompting a manager to yell that the quietest would be employed first. Liu waited more than six hours and was eventually hired. After a health check the next morning, he was assigned to move goods in the storage department. His dorm room had ten beds and more space than he had expected. "The quality wasn't bad—no worse than my [Tsinghua] university dormitory," Liu later told me. "It also provided hot water twenty-four hours a day, so it's actually better than the university."[11]

He would never really get to know his roommates. Most worked twelve-hour days and shifts continued around the clock. Even if they happened to be in the room at the same time, workers did little other than sleep there. Many lived together for months without learning each other's names.

Liu felt fortunate with the job assigned to him. It was not too busy, so he had time to explore the factory and mingle with others. But for ordinary workers, the job would have been a disappointment. One of the greatest criticisms of Foxconn, and of Chinese factories in general, is the ungodly work hours, often seventy to eighty per week—but most of the workers want this. Since they have traveled so far to make money, to them days spent not working are days wasted.

Employees signed a "voluntary overtime affidavit" to waive the thir-ty-six-hour legal limit on monthly overtime (which still left Foxconn in violation of the rarely enforced overtime law). "This isn't a bad thing, though," Liu wrote. "Many workers think only factories that offer more overtime are good factories. For the workers desperate for making money, overtime is like a pain that can breathe. Without it, the days without money make them suffocate."[12]

Workers would actually leverage their relationships with superiors in order to get more overtime hours. Holidays were especially contentious periods, since they brought triple the normal hourly pay. "May 1st [China's Labor Day] festival is a concern for some, because it's hard to toil through the days when you spend money without making any," Liu

Southern Weekend reporter Liu Zhiyi. (Photo: Liu Zhiyi)

wrote. "That day, workers would rather not celebrate any festival, and wish for more overtime pay."[13]

The factory's conditions did not appear likely to drive workers to suicide, but they did have a psychological impact, which Liu found not so much repressive as tedious and unfulfilling. "I felt I had entered a system," Liu said. "It can provide what I need for my body. They have a gym, a swimming pool, an exercise room—all of that. The only thing they don't provide is time."

Eighty-five percent of Foxconn's workers were under age thirty, and departments tended to be heavily skewed toward one gender or the other.[14] Liu recalled that while working in the storage department he could go an entire day without seeing a woman. In their limited time off, men would go to bars or skating rinks around the factory to meet girls. "If you have a girlfriend, then your life can be colorful," Liu said. "If work is the disease, then finding a girlfriend is the pill that can cure it." Other common activities for men included going to Internet cafés to view pornography or visiting one of the area's many brothels.

Fights broke out easily over girls and other minor issues. "The workers have a very limited life," Liu said. "It's only work, and the work is of no interest. They have some emotions they want to release."

The squabbles were not just between individuals. Workers came from all over the country, leading to culture gaps and prejudice between those from different regions. So people gravitated toward those from the same background and stuck closely together. Sometimes these groups even came to resemble gangs. Mix days of tedium with the heightened testosterone of young girl-hungry males in roving packs, and the results could get ugly.

In 2012 a fight broke out at Foxconn's 79,000-worker Taiyuan plant in northern China, reportedly between groups from Shandong and Henan following a drunken quarrel between two young men. Accounts varied, but things apparently spiraled out of control when factory guards overzealously started beating up brawlers, prompting some two thousand workers to get involved in a rampage through the factory. Paramilitary police were called in to quell the violence, forty people were injured, and the plant was shut down for a day.[15]

Female factory employees are less likely to get into brawls, but they face their own problems. In a 2013 survey of female workers in Guangzhou, 70 percent reported having experienced sexual harassment from coworkers, about one in five had quit a factory job in order to escape the problem, and 9 percent said they had been asked for sex outright by a colleague or superior.[16]

In the end, Liu Zhiyi felt that Foxconn was distinctive only because of its size. After his reports appeared in *Southern Weekend*, workers from around the Pearl River delta sent him e-mails like "If you come to Dongguan, you'll think Foxconn is heaven." Indeed, unlike many companies, Foxconn never shortchanged employees or paid their wages late. It offered a stable environment and provided for all its employees' physical needs. But like most factories, it did not provide one key thing that this generation had come to crave: a sense of direction.

"I wouldn't say the people were happy or miserable," Liu said. "In their ordinary life they just felt puzzled. I think the most astonishing thing for me is how puzzled they were about the future."

Whenever Liu asked workers what their goal in life was, they would say almost the same thing: to make money and get rich. But their explanations of how they would get from where they were to where they wanted to be were evasive. "They often dream, but also repeatedly tear apart their dreams, like a miserable painter who keeps tearing up his drafts," Liu wrote in his article. "They manufacture the world's top electronic products, yet gather their own fortune at the slowest possible pace."[17]

In autumn 2013 I met a worker named Liu Peng at his dormitory in a small electronics factory within Shenzhen's Longhua industrial district. The rooms were concrete shells, each with eight bunk beds. Some had broken windows and all had crisscrossing clotheslines, creating a jungle of hanging T-shirts and underwear. Liu Peng emerged from his room wearing a flannel shirt, jeans, Adidas sneakers, and a big grin on his face.

We went to lunch at the Chairman Mao Restaurant, where he was anxious to talk about factory life as he puffed on his cigarettes, though he had as many questions for me as I did for him. "How much do American workers make? Do Americans also hate Japan? Did you vote for Obama?"[18]

Liu Peng had come from Hubei province six years earlier when he was eighteen, having never harbored any illusions of going to college. His parents were poor rice farmers and he was a weak student. He shunned a high school that would have put him on the *gaokao* track in favor of attending a technical institution teaching machine electronics.

When he graduated, the decision to go to Shenzhen was not a hard one. In the 1980s and 1990s, leaving for migrant work was seen as brave and dangerous, but by now nearly all the young people in his hometown were doing it. They were going primarily for the higher salaries, but also for lifestyle reasons. Liu wanted to branch out to a place where he could become more knowledgeable and sophisticated. "In fact, I still don't know what I want to learn," he said. "I'm too young. I just want to work in a big city for survival and learn something through my work."

In six years, he had worked in four factories—a common situation for workers in the region. His first job was producing hot plates at a plant with a few dozen workers. He sat on the assembly line for a year, but quit because the boss frequently delayed payments.

His second factory was Foxconn, where he worked for two years. "Foxconn life is pretty good," he said. "Work is simple, but you just do the same thing every day. After work, you sleep, then wake up and work again. It's a point-to-point life." Ultimately he left for a smaller factory. "Work in Foxconn was stable and you get a good salary, but I wanted to learn more," he said. "In a small factory you can learn different jobs and there are more opportunities. You can work up to salesman."

In all his jobs Liu usually worked twelve-hour days, six days per week. In his free time he would read books about Chinese history and sometimes drink beer and sing karaoke with friends.

At his fourth and current factory, which had about thirty workers, he had finally gotten his chance to move up the ladder. That was the reason for his grin: he had just been promoted to a sales position, which meant a nicer dorm room and a higher salary. After numerous horizontal steps in Shenzhen, he felt this was his first real step up.

Contrary to the prevailing trend among the first generation of migrant workers, Liu had no intention of ever moving back to his rural hometown. His ultimate goal was to save enough money to start his own factory in Shenzhen. But when he spoke of his dream, it seemed abstract if not impossible. He seemed well aware of the financial and political hurdles that would stand in his way. "China is a *guanxi* (relationship-based) country," he explained. "If you want to do a project but another factory has a relationship with the government, they'll succeed, even if your product is good and theirs isn't."

Moreover, his income, although rising, would be hard pressed to keep up with the responsibility to care for his parents and the cost of housing. "I'd spend my whole life saving to buy a house," he said.

These are two of the most common concerns for young Chinese. Liu Peng's parents, being poor farmers, cannot count on living off a pension when they age. Any medical problems that arise could be a financial catastrophe for Liu Peng and his younger brother, also a migrant worker. Even if their parents stay healthy, the two children will be expected to provide almost entirely for them when they retire. Having a sibling lightens the burden, but most do not have this luxury, given the family planning restrictions that were especially strict (though unevenly enforced) in the 1980s and early 1990s.

Housing is an even more overwhelming concern, as, when I spoke with Liu Peng, runaway speculation had left China with some of the highest real-estate costs in the world. Buying even a small family-sized apartment outside the Shenzhen city center would cost him twenty-seven years' worth of his factory wages at 2013 prices.

Given these two factors, climbing the ladder to the point of financial security would be extremely difficult, and reaching the point where he could open his own factory would take little short of a miracle—a fact he seemed to recognize. "Many post-70s people who came to Shenzhen are bosses now," he said. "But now there's so much competition—every day a new factory."

Later I would meet another worker in Longhua named Huan Cheng, a twenty-three-year-old son of Sichuan brick sellers who had become migrant workers themselves in the early 1990s. Like Liu Peng, Huan had come to the city at age eighteen after skipping the *gaokao* altogether. But he had slightly more modest dreams, hoping only to save enough money to start a small business back home and "improve himself" in the process.[19] Contrary to popular belief, money is not the only reason why young Chinese travel so far from home to work on assembly lines. According to one study, 60 percent of young rural migrants reported personal development as a "very important" reason for migrating.[20]

Unlike most of the workers I met in Longhua, Huan did not work on weekends. He cherished his free time, which he used to play basketball, practice tai chi, and read books. His favorite book was Dale Carnegie's

1936 self-help bestseller *How to Win Friends and Influence People*, a popular title among workers in the area.

Huan even had time for dating. He said the best day he had ever had since coming to Shenzhen was when his first girlfriend accepted him. But the romance, like most things in Shenzhen, was fleeting. She was from another province and her family would not allow her to marry Huan. He would later date another girl he met in a factory, but they gradually lost touch when she left for another job.

Everyone was always on the move in Shenzhen, and long-term relationships, whether romantic or platonic, were hard to maintain. Though technology had made communication cheap and instant, loneliness and isolation persisted.

Huan himself had already been through four factories in his five years. At the first one, which produced labels for drink bottles, the machines were too hot and Huan believed that the chemicals in the air were hurting him. "The salary was paid on time," Huan said, "but the boss cared only about profit, not about improving the workers' environment even with simple things like an air conditioner."

Giving up a reliable income without having lined up a new job is something that Huan's parents never would have considered two decades earlier when they came to Guangdong. But the market has changed dramatically, giving workers much more leverage. "It's not hard to find a job now," Huan said. "The key is finding a *good* job."

Two factors were driving this market change: Shenzhen's rapid development and the dwindling labor pool. In my time in China, I had been through many gritty industrial wastelands; Longhua was not one of them. The streets looked like those of any other developed Chinese city, with shopping malls, Western fast-food restaurants, and large electronics markets with neon lights dotting the building fronts. If not for the occasional groups of young women locking arms in matching factory uniforms, one might not even guess that it was an industrial hub.

As Shenzhen developed, factories started competing with the service industry for the workers flocking to neighboring restaurants, shops, hotels, karaoke bars, and massage parlors. By 2012, the situation was even more competitive, as China's labor pool started to shrink for the first time ever. The population of working-age people between fifteen and fifty-nine fell by 3.45 million that year, and this trend is expected to continue until at least 2030 as the Mao-era baby boomers retire and the smaller one-child generation takes over the workforce.[21]

At his first factory in 2008, Huan Cheng was paid 800 yuan ($127) per month. When I spoke with him in 2013, he was making around 3,000 yuan ($480). This 275 percent wage increase in five years was common among workers in Longhua. Liu Peng's wages had risen 380 percent over six years. But these raises have not always come easily. Workers have often had to fight to improve their circumstances—something they have been increasingly willing to do.[22]

Though wages have risen dramatically, so have costs. Workers complain that as soon as a factory starts paying its workers more, surrounding food and clothing shops immediately raise their prices. In 2010 and 2011 China's inflation rate spun out of control, peaking at 6.5 percent. To make matters worse, factories started cutting corners because of reduced orders amid European and North American economic woes.

Not coincidentally, these two years were also a banner period for labor unrest in China. One of the most high-profile incidents began at a Honda plant in Foshan, a manufacturing city of five million people across the river from Shenzhen. In summer 2010, a twenty-three-year-old worker fed up with price increases outpacing his wages pressed the emergency stop button on his assembly line and yelled, "Let's go on strike." He and the other workers, with whom he had conspired in advance, joined him, demanding that their pay be nearly doubled.

The Chinese media widely reported the story, and workers at another Honda factory a hundred miles away joined the strike, also demanding the right to elect their own union leaders. Forming independent unions remained illegal in China, and the officially approved organizations were usually more loyal to bosses than workers. After a two-week standoff involving negotiations with the Foshan government, the dispute was settled when Honda agreed to increase wages by 24 to 32 percent—although the protest leader and his main accomplice were fired for "sabotage."[23]

The Honda strike was unusual in that it attracted extensive media coverage in China (likely because it targeted a Japanese company), but similar strikes were occurring across the country at the same time. While economic factors played a major role, the shifting mindset of young laborers and the new tools at their disposal were also significant contributing factors. The country had seen worse periods of belt-tightening and runaway inflation, but workers had rarely reacted so boldly en masse.

Better education and various new means of spreading information are making workers more aware of their rights and more empowered to communicate with each other. Liu Peng recalled that while he was at Foxconn during the suicide controversy of 2010, word of each new death spread quickly among the workers through text messages and social media. Workers also went online and were amazed to discover that their factory was getting so much international media attention. In fact, one study attributed an abnormal spike in Foxconn suicides in May 2010 to the Werther effect, according to which publicity inspires copy-cats.[24]

Two years later, workers at another Foxconn plant in Wuhan would even leverage the attention from the suicide controversy to improve their working conditions. After a new assembly line was hastily set up under dangerous conditions without proper training, 150 employees stood on the factory roof threatening to jump. "It was not about the money but because we felt we had no options," one worker told *The Telegraph*.[25]

Professor Anita Chan of the China Research Center at the University of Technology in Sydney, Australia, believes that incidents like these do reflect growing awareness of rights by workers. "But it's still very low," she told me. "I have yet to see Chinese migrant workers really coming out in an organized way."[26]

Chan pointed out that the government has been consistently raising the minimum wage due to concern for social stability. It also often steps in to broker solutions when labor unrest gets out of control. "[The intervention] is good enough to ward off big upheavals," she said. "Of course they are worried, but I think the biggest protests don't come from workers."

In spite of great improvements, many problems remain in China's factories. Stories constantly emerge of bosses cheating employees, exposing them to dangerous working conditions, employing underage workers, abusing subordinates physically or sexually, and firing (with impunity) those seeking redress. In difficult economic times, workers may show up one day only to find that their boss has fled with months of their back pay. The more distant a factory is from the scrutiny of major cities and honest labor law enforcement, the worse these issues become.

Still, few factory workers today would deny that they are better off now than a few years earlier. Almost none of them yearn for the world their parents lived in.

As I ate with Liu Peng at the Chairman Mao Restaurant, I asked if he thought he had a fair chance to succeed in modern China. "No, no!" he said in English, laughing. "There's no fairness in the world." Nevertheless, he expects that things will be fairer after China goes through a period of growing pains. "I'm satisfied with the direction of my life," he said. "And mostly satisfied with the direction China is going. The government is very corrupt, but every country has this problem. It's moving step by step."

In early 2013, some analysts said that China (or at least the Pearl River delta) had begun to enter the all-important "Lewis turning point." This is a critical time for developing countries, when worker wages begin to rise faster than the rate of inflation because the surplus labor pool has been exhausted. Until that point, employers can still attract new workers from rural areas without raising wages.[27]

In Shenzhen and the rest of the Pearl River delta, this turning point means that factories are being forced to offer higher wages, better working conditions, and a better overall quality of life. These rising costs have sent companies like Foxconn farther inland in search of cheaper untapped labor. The arrival of these large manufacturers in central regions is allowing migrant workers to live closer to home and find well-paying alternatives to farm work or the harsh factories that previously dominated these areas. In 2011 the populations of several Pearl River delta cities including Shenzhen, Guangzhou, and Dongguan declined for the first time in three decades.[28]

The International Monetary Fund predicts that between 2020 and 2025, China as a whole will reach the Lewis turning point and rural wages will approach parity with those of urban areas. This transition presents a mixed blessing for China and the government that tries to manage this massive nation. On one hand, much of the working class will continue to see its quality of life improve, while its growing disposable income creates a new consumer base. On the other hand, rural migrants will come to more fully resemble their urban neighbors and

will begin making similar demands for rights that have traditionally
been denied to them.

In 2013, the case of Shenzhen worker Wu Guijun appeared to be a
sign of growing government intolerance of labor movements. Wu was
elected as an intermediary between his fellow workers and the bosses of
his furniture factory after the company decided to relocate without
paying employees the legally mandated compensation. Ultimately, dis-
content spiraled into a two-hundred-person demonstration outside a
district government office, for which—despite coworkers' testimony to
the contrary—Wu was blamed. He was threatened with three years in
prison for "gathering a crowd and disrupting public order"—a catchall
charge frequently used to suppress dissidents. Under pressure from
Wu's supporters, judicial authorities ultimately dropped the charges
after Wu had already spent one year in detention.

China Labor Bulletin, a Hong Kong–based worker rights group,
documented nearly 1,200 strikes in China between summer 2011 and
the end of 2013. And in contrast to the conciliatory approach that authorities had tended to take in prior years, the group saw a "noticeable
increase" in police interventions in the second half of 2013. Forty percent of the protests were reportedly in manufacturing industries hit
especially hard by the global economic downturn.[29] The following year,
the group noted a 180 percent increase in worker protests between
2012 and 2014.[30]

This could be a preview of things to come as China's economic
growth continues to slow and rising wages push manufacturers inland
and overseas. In the process, factories will close and bosses will likely
continue trying to shortchange increasingly bold workers, heightening
the level of labor unrest. If its economy is to keep steaming ahead,
China must transition from its heavy reliance on cheap labor to a more
innovation-driven economy.

To have any hope of achieving this goal, China's young educated
class will have to create new industries and make its increasingly expensive workers more efficient through technological development. It does
not bode well that, rather than creating new industries that add value to
China's economy, many of these educated young people are instead
finding themselves on assembly lines along with their uneducated
peers.

6

THE ANTS

Outside Workers Auditorium in central Beijing, group after group of dejected recent college graduates shuffled out from the job fair inside.

It was August 2013, more than two months after this cohort had finished school, and their already dismal prospects had just become even grimmer. Most had been hitting these fairs since spring. Some had graduated the previous year but were still jobless.

Two young men from neighboring Hebei province who had studied in Beijing said they were nearing the end of their rope. "We've been looking for six months, but there aren't any good jobs," one of them said. "My family is starting to get really worried."

Across the country, there were nearly seven million new college graduates—at the time, the most ever in Chinese history—but 15 percent fewer open jobs than the previous year. When school ended, only one-third of these graduates had secured a position.[1] Chinese media dubbed it the toughest job-hunting season ever.

By August, applicants were nibbling for scraps. Nobody walking out reported having seen any booths that interested them. Most participating employers were real-estate companies offering low-level sales positions of dubious potential to anyone willing to work on commission.

It was the worst year to date for Chinese college grads (until the record was broken again the following year), but the market had been bleak for a long time. For years, China's universities had been pumping out students with few skills that interested recruiters.

A few weeks after the job fair, I met a twenty-five-year-old man named Liu Geng who had confronted the same situation four years earlier. I met him in the sprawling Tiantongyuan low-income housing complex in North Beijing while he was eating at a cheap noodle restaurant. The community's tightly packed high-rises held nearly a million residents. Liu had smoothly combed hair, small glasses, and spoke very slowly and deliberately. He dreamed of one day becoming a novelist.

He had graduated with excellent marks from a second-tier university in his home province of Hubei, with a degree in Chinese. Like most young college graduates, he figured that would be enough to get him a decent white-collar job. But when he started sending résumés in his college town of Wuhan, he quickly learned that little was available. "I was really surprised it was so hard to get a job," he said. "In university, you get no concept of what society is really like."[2]

Liu went to Beijing where his older sister was working, thinking that there must be better prospects in the nation's capital. He hit the job fair circuit, looked online, and sent résumés to hundreds of companies. "I had no specific goal," he said. "I just applied for any job."

Despite all that effort, he found only the usual scraps, settling for a string of sales jobs at real-estate and insurance companies. "Those businesses recruit almost anyone," he recalled, shaking his head. "They have incentives to get as many recruits as possible. I handed out fliers to sell homes, but nobody trusts those people. I worked on commission and basically got no income."

Liu spent more money than he could earn, borrowing heavily from his sister and parents. Eventually he gave up on Beijing and returned to Hubei to move boxes in a medicine factory. "That kind of job . . . ," he sighed wistfully. "It takes you only a few days to realize that you're worthless, basically just a machine."

Over the next three years, he hopped across the country chasing leads for respectable white-collar jobs but always fell into something far below his hopes. He put in time at factories in Guangzhou and a grocery store in Tianjin, rarely staying at any job for more than a few months.

Though his hometown was usually hundreds of miles away, it was hard to keep secrets from his old neighbors. His rural village of about a thousand thrived on gossip, and everyone knew of Liu's plight. "Some people used me as an example showing it's useless to study," he said.

"They would say, 'Look, he went to college, but so what? He can't even get a job.'"

Liu's success on the *gaokao* had been a major source of pride for his family, especially since so many others in the village had failed. But now, families of those who had bypassed college for the labor force were quietly reveling in Liu's failure, subtly raising the topic with his parents. For Liu, his family's loss of face was the worst part of all.

Millions across China were feeling the same pressure. By 2012, Chinese under twenty-five with a college degree had a 16 percent unemployment rate, twice that in the United States. For those with only a high school education, the unemployment rate was 8 percent, and for persons with just an elementary education it was 4 percent.[3] The perverse implication was that, in China, to improve your job prospects you needed to have *less* education.

This paradox can be traced back to a hasty decision in 1999, when China was still reeling from the Asian financial crisis. Workers in the late 1990s were already being laid off by the millions each year as thousands of state-owned enterprises were dismantled.[4] When the crisis broke out in 1997, it abruptly slashed China's exports from an annual growth rate of 17.3 percent in 1996 to a mere 0.5 percent in 1998.[5] China's leaders looked on nervously as similar pressure from the crisis prompted student protests in Indonesia, which eventually forced President Suharto out of power.[6] There was speculation that China could become "another Indonesia."[7]

To keep the economy afloat, China needed to boost domestic consumption, and economists realized that education was one of the few sectors where demand was still far greater than supply.[8] Increasing college enrollment would stimulate spending associated with education, keep more young people out of the job market for the time being, and hopefully create a more skilled workforce down the line. Serious discussion about radically increasing college recruitment began in March of 1999, and in order to be implemented in time for the following school year, it would have to be finalized before the *gaokao* entrance exam three months later.

Against strong objections by the Ministry of Education, the all-powerful Politburo Standing Committee pushed the plan ahead without commissioning any feasibility studies.[9] A high-level Education Ministry official warned that China's economy may not be able to provide enough jobs for these students once they graduated, and consequently, the social status they ended up with could be far below their expectations.[10] Nevertheless, the plan went forward.

In the aftermath, schools undertook massive expansions. They converted vocational schools into full universities, built new classrooms and campuses, and tried to pack them with students and professors. China enrolled 42 percent more students in 1999 than it had the previous year.[11] The country went from one million college freshmen in 1998, to two million in 2000.[12] Within the following decade this number surpassed seven million.

"It's just crazy," Yong Zhao, the University of Oregon education professor, told me. "They weren't ready for any of this. A lot of professors in China aren't ready to teach, and the facilities aren't ready."[13]

This massive increase in students, combined with institutions unprepared to educate them, led to a rapid devaluation of college degrees. Even though he was surprised by the dismal job market upon graduation, Liu Geng had sensed earlier that his education was not preparing him for much. "What you learn has nothing to do with society," he said. "But I just wanted to meet my parents' expectations, pass the *gaokao*, and graduate university. I didn't really believe in the education."

There is a famous saying in China that "getting an education is above all; everything else is inferior." For years after the beginning of reforms in the late 1970s, the saying was unquestionably true. When the *gaokao* was reinstated and universities reopened in 1977, as many as 5.7 million sat for the exam.[14] The 273,000 (4.8 percent of the candidates) who made the cut were the first to enjoy the spoils from the new economic policies unfolding then. Many went on to make staggering fortunes, and through the 1990s a college degree in China continued to guarantee great opportunities.

By 2010, in contrast, about three-quarters of those who took the *gaokao* were admitted to some type of college.[15] Only those who qualified for the very top-tier universities could count on their degree guaranteeing anything; over a quarter would still be jobless a year after graduation.[16] But that did not stop parents from instilling in their children the expectation that passing the *gaokao* would open big doors, just as it had for their own generation.

In 2009, Chinese professor Lian Si published the groundbreaking book *Ant Tribe*, which described college graduates living in cheap, squalid homes on the outskirts of major cities. Scuttling downtown each day to toil in unfulfilling work, they had little upward mobility. "They share every similarity with ants," Lian wrote. "They live in colonies in cramped areas. They are intelligent and hardworking, yet anonymous and underpaid." [17]

Lian estimated that there were over a million of these "ants" throughout China, three hundred thousand of them concentrated in Beijing and Shanghai. They come mainly from poorer rural families, and they persist in the major cities for fear of the shame that returning home would bring. They slave at low-paying jobs or dubious unpaid internships on the conviction that things will turn around and someone will finally recognize their talent.

Soon after Lian's book was released, reporters descended on the area on which it had focused, the Tangjialing community on the out-skirts of Beijing's Haidian district. Once a small village of three thou-sand, it experienced rapid growth beginning in 2003. Offering some of the city's lowest rental prices, it eventually became home to some fifty thousand "ants." [18] Muddy, unpaved roads were surrounded by dilapi-dated buildings packed to the brim with people. Dozens sometimes crammed into a single room, fashioning hammocks or other improvised beds into tightly cramped spaces. Those who worked downtown had to endure a two-hour commute in each direction.

Amid the media coverage of this community of squalor, the Haidian district government announced that it would completely overhaul the area and demolish most existing structures, as it was doing with other "ant colonies" around town. There were plenty of legitimate reasons for doing so. Buildings violated scores of safety and health codes. There was also money to be made in the area amid soaring real-estate prices. But some analysts speculated that these were not the only reasons for the slated demolition. Yu Jianrong, an outspoken sociologist and mem-ber of the Chinese Academy of Social Sciences, said that the concentra-tion of well-educated but disillusioned youth posed a risk. "As we learn from history, grassroots intellectuals are the most likely to cause social turbulence," Yu told *China Daily*. [19]

At the same time these "ant tribe" colonies were growing in major cities, so were the "rat tribes"—people living in dank apartment complex basements and former bomb shelters. Liu Geng, my twenty-five-year-old acquaintance, had spent time as both an "ant" and a "rat"; at one point he lived in a windowless, underground Tianjin flat for several months.

When I first moved to Beijing, I myself stayed in one of these rooms for a few days while searching for an apartment. As soon as I walked down the stairs, it was clear that the basement was never meant for human habitation. I had to crouch to walk through its narrow concrete passages and dodge leaky pipes spiraling out in every direction. My room had thin plywood walls and was barely big enough for a small bed and nightstand. Unlike most of the rooms in the basement, it actually had a small window at eye level, enabling me to view the ankles and shoes shuffling by on the sidewalk outside. Using the bathroom required a walk to a neighboring building and a fee of three yuan ($0.47).

The basement's approximately two dozen residents were a strange mix of twenty-something university graduates and uneducated migrant workers in their thirties and forties. By 2012, the average entry-level wage for university graduates in China had fallen below that of migrant laborers.[20] These people with very different backgrounds and expectations were living in equality, quite literally, at the very bottom of society.

By the end of 2012 the Tangjialing community had been almost entirely leveled and the Beijing government began a campaign to clear out people living in illegal basement abodes. As most expected, though, the "ants" and "rats" just branched out to new areas even farther from the city center as real-estate prices bolted upward.

Lian Si, the *Ant Tribe* author, explained that in spite of disheartening conditions, few of these graduates were willing to leave the big cities. Working in Beijing or Shanghai brings a certain prestige and allows young people to be immersed in the poshest cultural and social networks. Leaving represents a major failure and a tumble down the social ladder.[21]

Lian also pointed out that many job seekers actually find the metropolises of Beijing and Shanghai fairer than provincial cities or smaller towns, where opportunities depend on local relationships, and *guanxi* rules the employment market. Because the populations of the top-tier cities consist predominantly of migrants, local networks are less entrenched.[22]

In any case, rampant nepotism and corruption in the job market are hard to avoid anywhere in China. In a 2013 poll, 80.4 percent of those surveyed believed that young people who achieve career success in China do so because of their family connections. Only 10 percent thought that hard work, creativity, and academic achievements beat having a well-connected father.[23]

Among the most sought-after workplaces for college graduates are banks. Almost entirely state owned, they offer stability, prestige, connections, and numerous financial opportunities. In 2013 the *Economic Observer* newspaper caught up with a Guangzhou bank employee who oversaw interns. She recalled that she had been one of the last persons hired under open recruitment back in 2007. The interns working under her years later included several children of influential government cadres. "I wouldn't dare make them work overtime," she told the paper. "If they did something wrong, I didn't dare say anything about it."[24]

Around the same time, a man who also allegedly worked with interns at a state-owned bank posted an essay online illustrating how crucial family background had become in attaining employment. He described the internships as little more than a ruse for free labor, since almost all the permanent positions would be divvied out to those with connections. Naturally, those from rich and official family backgrounds went on to do well, whereas the interns from rural or blue-collar upbringings never came close to landing a job at the bank. The writer's conclusion was that young people should accept their limits and not be so naïve as to think they can overcome their class background. Whether or not the account was true, it struck a chord and was reposted on Weibo some twenty-two thousand times.[25]

Those who lack good family connections often compensate by purchasing a path to employment. Recent graduates frequently report that securing a good job requires a hefty bribe—sometimes amounting to several years' worth of the position's salary.[26] But these bribes can have disastrous results. In May 2013 it was discovered that a criminal ring in Shanxi province had scammed more than five hundred college students out of 50,000 to 350,000 yuan ($8,000 to $56,000) each by promising to secure them jobs at banks and other state-owned companies. The ruse was so successful because this was a routine way to go about getting a cushy job. The scam also apparently involved real government officials, whom the students assumed could deliver on their end of the corrupt deal.[27]

Whether it is connections, bribes, or genuine ability that decides a job, rural youth once again get left far behind their urban counterparts. A 2013 survey found that 12 percent of urban college graduates were unemployed, whereas unemployment for rural graduates was over 30 percent.[28] Because of the uneven playing field, *fu'erdai* (second-generation rich) and the even more despised *guan'erdai* (second-generation officials) have come to be some of the most reviled people in China. These are the privileged children of the extremely wealthy and the politically powerful, respectively; though there is considerable overlap between the two groups.

The reckless excesses that these young people enjoy with impunity have become a major sour point among Chinese youth. In 2010 a twenty-two-year-old Hebei man named Li Qingming struck two college students (one of whom died) in his Volkswagen Magotan while driving drunk with his girlfriend. He fled the scene but was later stopped, whereupon he defiantly exclaimed, "Go ahead, sue me if you dare. My father is Li Gang!"

Li Gang was deputy director of the local public security bureau. In the past, such brazen, well-connected youth could keep such incidents secret and literally get away with murder. But by 2010 the Sina Weibo microblogging platform had emerged. Despite government efforts to suppress the story, word spread rapidly and "My father is Li Gang" became an Internet meme that remains synonymous with out-of-control official privilege. Li Qingming was later sentenced to six years in prison and ordered to pay over $80,000 in compensation.[29]

Two years later, when Bo Xilai, a Politburo member and one of China's twenty-five most powerful leaders, was arrested on corruption charges, many analysts speculated that his then twenty-four-year-old son Bo Guagua had played a role in his downfall.[30] Pictures of the half-dressed youth cozying up with girls at high-end parties had circulated on the Internet in China, depicting him as a wealthy playboy. One *Wall Street Journal* report even made a disputed claim that he had been spotted driving a Ferrari through Beijing.[31] At a time when public disgust with privileged *guan'erdai* was already undermining government trust, Bo's downfall served as a warning to other leaders that they had better keep their kids in line and out of the public eye.

While Liu Geng was working as a cashier at the grocery store in Tianjin, customers would yell at him frequently. "Sometimes people opened food, ate it, then tried to return it," he said. "They'll start a fight over 1 yuan [$0.16] or even 1 mao [<$0.01]." His boss also criticized him constantly for being too slow and making mistakes. Between working twelve-hour days and living in a dank underground cell, Liu could not take it anymore. He quit his job and went back to Hubei to live with his parents. "That was my lowest point," he said. "I just stayed at home and watched a hundred movies over the next month."

Liu's parents were wealthy enough that he could lounge at home with their support after his job hunt failed. This privilege is something largely unique to his generation, and something for which youth like him are often chastised. A 2014 survey by Peking University found that a full one-third of recent college graduates in China continued to rely on their parents for money.[32] A common complaint among recruiters at job fairs in China is that young people today feel entitled to laid-back, well-paying, fulfilling careers. The jobs are there, they say, but kids these days are just too spoiled and unwilling to pay their hardship dues. In 2013 Foxconn founder and chairman Terry Gou even lamented that young people are less and less willing to work at factories.[33]

After three years of job hunting and an introspective month at home, Liu Geng finally came to terms with the fact that his college diploma was worth little more than the paper it was printed on. At his mother's urging, he surfed the Internet to find which skilled trades were in the highest demand. His parents gave him 10,000 yuan ($1,600) and he settled on a four-month computer programming course back in Beijing. He excelled in the program and, shortly thereafter, landed a job in the city designing video games for mobile phones. "I called my parents and they were really happy," he said. "It made me really proud."

He quickly became an integral part of the company and got a raise to 12,000 yuan ($1,917) per month, putting him firmly in China's middle class. But he still did not feel secure. His parents were nearing retirement age and he was worried about their future. "I want to work hard and build a house for them," he said. "Their house is in bad condition. I don't want them to live there." Then there was the question of marriage and buying his own house, still very difficult in Beijing even on his decent salary.

Though he could afford to rent a nicer apartment, to save money Liu moved to the Tiantongyuan community, where he paid 1,000 yuan ($160) in rent each month. Since several "ant colonies" around the city had been torn down, this low-income complex's population had nearly doubled. From the outside its buildings looked nice and modern, but inside, the improvised beds and overcrowded rooms of young migrants bore the marks of Tangjialing.

Liu worked sixty hours per week at his company and commuted an hour each way, leaving little spare time. He felt stable, but the stress never really subsided. He constantly worried about earning enough money and saved as much as he possibly could.

Like Liu, even many young professionals who manage to secure office jobs continue to live in stress. A 2012 Regus survey of eighty countries found that Chinese office workers had the most anxiety in the world, with 75 percent reporting that their stress had gone up in the past year.[34]

Several causes have been blamed, including an unreliable social safety net and the fear of being unprepared for a family crisis. The spiraling costs of what are commonly called the "three mountains"—real estate, education, and healthcare—have imbued a perpetual need to earn more.

There is also the importance of face. One of Liu Geng's greatest motivators was his family's status in the village. In a 2013 survey of twenty countries, 71 percent of the Chinese respondents agreed with the statement "I measure my success by the things I own"—a higher proportion than in any other country—and 68 percent agreed that "I feel under a lot of pressure to be successful and make money."[35]

In early 2013, a twenty-four-year-old employee of the Ogilvy public relations firm died of a heart attack after allegedly working overtime for a full month. His last Weibo post before dying showed the disheveled but smiling man saluting the camera as he left work, making him an especially sympathetic figure.[36] Ogilvy denied that he had actually worked a month of overtime, but the story sparked debate about how much Chinese are sacrificing in order to stay ahead in the rat race. Every few months, similar stories come to light of white-collar employees literally working themselves to death. More than 80 percent of company employees say they frequently work overtime, and Chinese receive among the world's fewest vacation days.[37]

Still, all this hard work usually fails to bring the status that young Chinese crave. The highly visible success stories reported over the past three decades have left many today feeling that they have missed the boat. With nepotism and corruption thriving, there is an impression that the best resources have already been distributed and will continue to accumulate among the already wealthy. China's Gini coefficient, an international measure of wealth distribution where zero means perfect equality and 1 signifies total concentration of wealth, surpassed the "danger level" of 0.40 in 2000. The government did not release the figure for the following twelve years until 2012, when it claimed the Gini to be 0.47 and falling after having peaked in 2008. However, independent researchers estimated that in 2010 the true number was 0.61, which would make China one of the most unequal societies in the world.[38]

This inequality is painfully felt among educated young people as they watch jobs, promotions, and social status drifting toward those who won the birth lottery. It is becoming an ever greater source of inadequacy and resentment.

In 2013, an essay entitled "Why Generation Y Yuppies Are Unhappy" went viral in the United States.[39] It mapped the root of widespread professional dissatisfaction among American youth, but it could just as aptly be applied to China.

The essay started with a simple premise: "When the reality of someone's life is better than they had expected, they're happy. When reality turns out to be worse than the expectations, they're unhappy." It explained that the "Greatest Generation" of Americans, those who lived through the Depression and World War II, had become obsessed with economic security and raised their children with modest expectations. When those kids, the Baby Boomers, grew up through the 1970s to 1990s, the American economy took off. They had more prosperous lives than they had expected, and thus they were happy. But they then raised their Generation Y children with a very optimistic outlook and much more ambitious dreams.

After the US economy began to suffer in the 2000s, Generation Y was left with unfulfilled ambitions and severe disappointment, manifested with particular intensity in the 2011 Occupy Wall Street movement as disgruntled American youth protested a broken and corrupt system that enabled skewed wealth distribution.

The same dynamic was ringing true in China, but to an even greater extreme. The generation of Liu Geng's parents rode the wave of double-digit economic growth for three decades. Many toiled in dangerous factories or spent long days doing backbreaking farm work, but they were happy to have it. They made money and had food in their stomachs—and that was better than the experience of their own parents, China's "Greatest Generation," who had suffered through endless wars, famine, and a long string of insane political campaigns that made mere survival a daily struggle. When the political chaos finally settled and the economy took off in the 1980s and 1990s, China's baby boomers were perpetually optimistic and passed that optimism on to their kids. Now that China's millennials are struggling, feelings of disillusionment are taking hold.

When the Occupy Wall Street movement began in the United States, Chinese state media initially reported it with glee. Highlighting political dissatisfaction and capitalist exploitation in Western countries is a self-legitimizing staple of the Communist Party. However, the media quickly changed its tune when young Chinese began expressing sympathy with the Occupy movement tweeting messages like "Occupy Beijing" and "Occupy Shanghai." As one Chinese social commentator put it: "China faces more serious problems of financial oligarchism, corruption and inequality than America. But 'Occupy Chang'an Jie' [the street that runs past Tiananmen Square] is no more than a fairy tale. In China, a jobless, homeless protester would not reach Beijing before disappearing mysteriously."[40] Indeed, searches for "Occupy" terms were blocked on Weibo and Chinese journalists were reportedly told to stop covering the movement.[41]

A few months after the job fair in Beijing, I called the two young college grads from Hebei whom I had met there. They had both given up on the capital and returned to their hometown to search for jobs. Each one had reluctantly begun working in a factory while looking.

Unemployed and discouraged college graduates like these have not yet presented any obvious threat to the government or to social stability. Only a few years have passed since the job crunch began. As the persevering ant tribes of Beijing demonstrate, there is an optimism that things will turn around eventually. One study in 2014 found that 85 percent of Chinese post-90s youth were confident about their country's economic prospects, and 76 percent were optimistic about the country's political future.[42] And like Liu Geng, many still have parents on whom they can fall back when the going gets tough.

The key question is whether these educated youth will remain quiet in future years if the job market does not pick up as their parents begin to age and become more financially dependent on them. Zhou Tianmin, a member of China's top political advisory body, told the *Global Times*, "They were told education could change their lives, but now that they can't find a job after college, they might feel angry at society."[43]

China's Communist Party has assiduously studied where previous political institutions went wrong and there is ample reason for concern. One cautionary tale is that of Hong Xiuquan. A poor peasant in the mid-nineteenth century, he excelled academically from a young age and was determined to enter the exclusive government bureaucracy. But he was thwarted. He consistently failed the civil service exam while wealthier applicants bribed their way to passing scores. Sickened with failure, he began to see visions and ultimately decided that he was Jesus Christ's younger brother, destined to set the kingdom straight.

Hong had little trouble whipping up followers; many were similarly disillusioned after failing the exam and plenty more were fed up with inequality and Qing dynasty corruption. Hong gradually amassed an army by preaching utopian communalism and bastardized Christianity. By the time his Taiping Rebellion was suppressed in 1864, some 20 million Chinese lay dead.

Frustrated students and graduates from the May 4th Movement in 1919 through the Tiananmen uprising in 1989 have similarly proven a dangerous and disruptive force when they felt that their government had failed them. And there is evidence of a comparable gathering storm today. The year after Lian Si published *Ant Tribe*, he conducted another survey of the nation's "ants." He found that 57 percent of troubled college graduates blamed their difficulties on social circumstances rather than any faults of their own. Lian said this is a worrying statistic, because it indicates a loss of trust in the government and could lead young people to band together against the society that had failed them.[44]

But for all the frustration that young people express toward the government, they are nevertheless lining up in record numbers to become part of it.

7

THE GOLDEN RICE BOWL

If you were a corrupt Chinese official in the late 1990s, there was perhaps no swankier place than the "Red Chamber" in Xiamen, Fujian province.

Beloved businessman Lai Changxing ran a not-so-secret smuggling ring that brought everything from foreign cigarettes to petroleum into China's black market. But keeping the wheels turning in the illicit empire required a lot of grease.

The Red Chamber was Lai's seven-story sin palace. Its dance floors, jacuzzis, steam room, and extravagant bedrooms hosted hundreds of law enforcement officers and cadres reaching high into the Fujian provincial government (and perhaps even higher). Working girls from across the country were on hand to entertain the powerful guests, and a famous singer was allegedly coaxed into disrobing for millions of yuan.

Eventually, the operation got out of hand and national authorities cracked down on it. Dozens of officials were arrested and Lai fled to Canada (only to be extradited; he received a life sentence in 2011). Hoping to use the sordid affair as a cautionary tale, the government opened the Red Chamber to the public as an anticorruption museum. But the opulence of this "Graceland of Graft" apparently sent the wrong message. Giddy tourists swarmed in, along with wealthy industrialists keen to take notes on the building's features. The museum was shut down soon after it opened.[1]

During a 2002 interview in Canada, Lai Changxing said, "The whole system in China is corrupt. To get ahead, you have to become part of that system."[2]

Today many young Chinese appear to be coming to the same conclusion. The obvious doors that officialdom opens and the bleak prospects elsewhere have sent graduates flocking to apply for government jobs.

For more than 1,400 years, China has used imperial exams off and on to determine admittance to the government bureaucracy. The civil service exam was reinstated at the national level in 1994, and today it is usually the first step that an aspiring cadre must pass on the way up the political ladder. The Communist Party touts this merit-based exam, saying that only the brightest and most deserving gain government posts.

Most who take the exam have no intention of becoming politically active, though. Civil service jobs have long been part of what is known as China's "Iron Rice Bowl," referring to stable state jobs with housing benefits, generous pensions, and immunity from layoffs. More recently, some have taken to calling these jobs the "Golden Rice Bowl" in a nod to the wide range of perks, legal and otherwise, that they can provide. Passing the exam is regarded as a golden ticket to sidestepping the many uncertainties in China's economy.

In 2013, a record 1.52 million people registered for the test—more than twenty times the number a decade earlier. They competed for just 19,500 available posts, a ratio of 77 applicants per job.[3] Some openings had as many 9,000 applicants, with some of the more popular posts concentrated in sectors with substantial power such as security, personnel, and customs.[4]

In 2008 I met a young undergraduate law student named Mae (a pseudonym). She was soft-spoken, but incredibly sharp. From primary school through college, she had always been among the top students in her class. She rarely spoke up when in a group, but when she did, she left an impression.

Her father had been a civil servant and prodded her to try the exam. She had been focusing on getting into graduate school but obliged him by diving into civil service exam prep books just two weeks before the test. To the envy of her classmates who had spent months and years studying for it, she passed.

Mae had never seriously considered civil service; she had dreamed of becoming a lawyer or judge. But what she learned during her college years cast a dark shadow over that plan. "It's ridiculous to talk about law in China," she said. "What determines the winner of a case isn't the law."

Her civil service test results sealed the decision. Her score meant that she would be assigned to the coveted customs bureau in Beijing— an opportunity too good to pass up.

"Historically, customs has had its glory days in China," Mae said. "But it has a very negative reputation now. People say it's extremely corrupt with a lot of illegal income, but the people who say these words actually want to be part of it."

Mae started at the bureau at age twenty-two and was housed in a large dorm room with three coworkers. She had generous perks like free cafeteria meals and pool and gym memberships. Moreover, in stark contrast to most white-collar workers in the city, she had a stable work schedule of 9:00 to 4:30 each day. But the salary was a modest 4,500 yuan ($720) per month. "People think I make a lot," she said. "When I tell them how much I actually make, they don't believe me, or they wink and say, 'yeah, but you have other benefits.'"

Her work assignment made her essentially a paper pusher, but one with great power over multi-million-dollar companies. Importers would come to her window and she would determine the classification and tariff amount on the goods presented, or she could deem the claim suspicious and send it for inspection. If she gave a company a bad mark, it could make importing harder for them for years. But she could also make their lives very easy. "Even at the bureau's very lowest level, everyone has the power to be corrupt," she said.

At first Mae worked hard and was nice to everyone, but she quickly learned what a mistake that was. "If you're really nice, people won't take you seriously and will regard you as a weak target," she said, referring both to importers and coworkers. "Now I just have a bad attitude so I don't get caught in their trap."

Mae had little threat of ever getting fired if she underperformed. In order for a civil servant to be terminated, they must be deemed "incompetent" on their annual assessment for two consecutive years. In 2010, less than 1 percent of civil servants in China received this censure, and only about 0.05 percent are actually dismissed each year (as of 2009).[5]

In theory, Mae and the other three who held the same position had a daily quota of claims to process. In practice, everyone purposely worked far less efficiently than what they were capable of. They feared creating high expectations and leaving the impression that they were trying to outshine colleagues. They rarely exceeded half the daily target, and their superiors never complained. "I'm an example of how a hardworking, positive person can become the opposite," Mae scoffed.

But Mae drew the line at accepting expensive gifts; that was a slippery slope she had no desire to go down. She had never been offered outright cash, but importers often brought presents. She felt it was their way of testing the waters. If they became too pushy, she would just hand the case off to a superior.

Her refusal to take part in corruption, Mae opined, would probably keep her from advancing very far in the department. At her low rank, she could stay honest without stepping on anybody's toes, but if she rose to a higher position her unwillingness to participate in standard practice could put a target on her back. "Most people work for the government just for money," she said. "Otherwise, what's the point?"

A 2013 study by Tian Guoliang of the Central Party School, the CCP's preeminent cadre training center, found that among corrupt officials who were sacked, the average period between their first crime and their exposure was less than a year during the 1980s. That time period expanded to over four years in the 1990s and was nearly nine years when he conducted the study. Tian also found that 63 percent of the sacked officials had been promoted while engaging in corruption—a trend that had been getting worse over time.[6]

According to Ren Jianming, a governance professor from Beijing University of Aeronautics and Astronautics who studies graft, corruption can spread like a virus through a department. A corrupt official will promote other corrupt officials in order to keep him or herself safe, whereas anyone clean will be distrusted and disdained.[7] As time goes on, entire bureaus become irreversibly tainted and honest cadres either become corrupted or languish in isolation at the bottom. This may be one reason why, as one government source (citing an internal Communist Party survey) told Reuters in 2014, more than 30 percent of Party, government, and military officials are involved in some form of corruption.[8]

People did periodically get busted in Mae's bureau. She recalled hearing of a predecessor who became a bit too bold, buying a car after his first year of work and a house after the second. By the third year he was in jail. Such instances were rare, however, and when people did get caught it was usually the result of an internal power struggle. "If two of us take bribes, for example, but I want to replace you or we have conflict, I'll report you or set you up," she explained. "It's almost never a matter of authorities just finding out on their own."

It was hard to guess who was corrupt and how much they were profiting. The parking lot had several luxury cars, but many cadres came from rich families. Furthermore, it was becoming more difficult to define what constituted a bribe, let alone detect it. Cadres getting married might invite importers that they worked with to the ceremony, receiving as a wedding gift a customary *hongbao* (red envelope) stuffed with thousands of yuan. Or they might be invited out for an expensive night of feasting and karaoke with hostesses who might offer to go home with them. A former "hostess" at Lai Changxing's Red Chamber later recalled entertaining, during the 1990s, a big-nosed Beijing customs official who would come on retreats to one of the building's luxury suites.[9]

This kind of schmoozing was also common internally at the customs bureau, and it could be a critical part of getting promoted. "Once at a banquet a girl ignored protocol, sat right beside the leader, and drank a lot," Mae recalled. "He was impressed, and soon after he moved her from airport customs to a better job in the main office. Drinking is a great asset."

Mae had no interest in playing these games. As cynical as she had become, she was perfectly content to punch in at her stable position and leave it at that. "I feel I'm an upstanding person," she said. "If I get promoted, my official salary won't change much and I'm not willing to abuse my power for money, so I don't really want to move up."

Promotions actually depended in part on merit-based testing, which Mae viewed as progress from past practices. And occasionally people up the power chain actually needed a good worker, so they would promote based on ability. But according to Mae, there were three much more reliable ways to climb the ladder: joining the corrupt circles of superiors, having a family member with a high government position, or "being a beautiful girl." When I naïvely asked whether it was enough to simply be beautiful, Mae rolled her eyes and scoffed, "What do you think?"

In 2014, even the Communist Party Organization Department came to a similar conclusion. An internal survey involving thousands of cadres revealed a "deeply flawed" promotion system, with nepotism and position selling running rampant due to leaders monopolizing the process for their own purposes. [10]

I told Mae the story of Frank Serpico, the 1960s-era American police officer who shunned corruption in his department and ultimately tried to clean things up, earning him disdain (and possibly a murder attempt) from the dirty cops. "I'm not as upstanding as Serpico," she replied. "Everyone has their own way to get by in this country. I won't do it, but if you want to take bribes, it doesn't concern me. I won't stop you."

Over the years I talked with many young people who had come to believe that there were few clean paths to success. The best bet, they believed, was to learn the tacit rules and exploit them. After all, if you did not become a beneficiary of the system, you were sure to become a victim of it. When Education Ministry officials came to inspect the university where I taught, I asked one student—who was planning to take the civil service exam—whether he thought they took bribes. "Probably," he replied with a half-smile. "That's why we all want that job."

Many who do not go into civil service still seek benefits by pursuing Communist Party membership. The CCP has over 80 million members throughout the country, but gaining admission is tough. Eight out of ten students want to join, according to a Ministry of Education survey, but in 2010 only 14 percent of the 21 million applicants were accepted. [11]

From a very young age, Chinese pupils are taught the value of Party membership through the Young Pioneers. Participation in this group, overseen by the Communist Youth League, is required for most children age six to fourteen. They wear red scarves, representing the blood shed by the Revolution's martyrs, and they pledge: "I love the Communist Party of China, the motherland, and the people; I will study well and keep myself fit, preparing to contribute my efforts to the cause of Communism." [12]

When they turn fourteen, they can join the Communist Youth League, which most high school students do for at least a few years. This is where grooming of potential Party members begins in earnest. It is also where young people preview the perks that Party membership offers and the politicking needed in order to rise. Members who stand out (or make the right connections) can be appointed to higher positions with actual power in the organization, which can help them get a job or full Party membership later.

Those who want to pursue the political track might seek a position in their college's student government. These "student unions," as they are called in China, are a bit different from their Western counterparts in that they are overseen by the university's Communist Youth League faculty. Their duties include organizing school activities, maintaining connections with other universities, and preparing reports for Party officials.

The best candidates for selection as student government members are excellent students who are also politically reliable. Compared to their Western counterparts, the student body president holds more power over the student government. The person who fills this position is chosen directly by Communist Youth League faculty from a pool of candidates recommended by the union. Selection as president is highly prestigious and puts a student on the fast track to Party membership and great opportunities in government or state-owned enterprises after graduation. According to media interviews with student government officers, male student presidents also tend to become very popular with girls after securing this position. Even rank-and-file student union members are known to get preferential treatment at their universities, which can cause them to become alienated from other students.[13]

When it comes time to apply for full CCP membership, top students are again singled out for invitations to apply. Others can ask Party acquaintances for nomination. This begins a lengthy process that can involve one to two years of ideology classes, background checks, interviews, and self-criticism sessions with peers. Applicants must also keep a journal in which they record their activities, thoughts on society, and motivations for joining the Party.

In 2001, a CCP-friendly pop singer released a music video entitled "Application to Join the Party" depicting a model candidate. "As young as eighteen I'd already written my Party application," the song begins.

A group of college students become Communist Party members at their swearing-in ceremony. (Photo: xiaogushi.com)

"I've read the Party Constitution countless times, but always felt I wasn't worthy of its standards." The lyrics describe how the young man drew inspiration from the countless martyrs who shed their blood for the Party's cause, seeking neither fame nor fortune. "What is a Party member?" the vocalist asks while looking longingly at a Mao Zedong statue. "They're a servant of the people; the backbone of the common man; the red candle that burns itself to bring light to others."[14]

The video elicits laughter from young Chinese, but I have been told that it represents exactly the sort of flowery language Party applicants must use in their journals if they hope to be accepted. Others have said that a better approach is to write the journal as a love letter, simply substituting "the Communist Party" for your lover's name.

It would be an exaggeration to say that no young Chinese applicants still believe in the Party's ideological underpinnings. I have met some youth who sincerely believe that socialist egalitarianism can be achieved if only a few kinks in the government apparatus could be worked out. One fiercely loyal student wrote in a class essay that his life's goal was "to die for the Party."

But most peers tend to mock such people as hopelessly naïve. Even back in 2001, a university survey among those who had already joined the Party found that only 4 percent did so because of a genuine belief in Communism.[15] Perhaps the surest sign of the low number of true idealists entering China's political system is the existence of civil service positions that struggle to find applicants. While posts with significant power attract thousands, jobs that might have a more deeply meaningful impact are virtually shunned. Posts in disaster relief that require frequent trips to dangerous areas get little interest; positions in poor, remote regions with few opportunities to make connections or get attractive promotions often fail to attract a single applicant.[16]

For most people, Party membership is a purely pragmatic decision. Employers know the highly selective CCP application process, so being accepted is a major résumé booster. And for those who hope to climb the ladder as a civil servant or in a state-owned company, Party membership is compulsory.[17]

In 2013, Professor Zhang Xi'en from the School of Politics and Public Administration at Shandong University lamented that too many people were using Party membership as a path to personal gain. "They swarm into the Party, rapidly expanding its scale, and bringing tremendous danger to it," he said, suggesting that it downsize from over 80 million members to around 50 million.[18] Later that year, the Party did in fact add more requirements for young students and lengthened the application process. The following year, the number of new applications dropped for the first time in ten years.[19]

However, the Party's eagerness to snap up the most capable and ambitious students—regardless of their motivations—will likely never abate. While it does want the best and the brightest to fill its ranks, sweeping up these elite students is also a way of co-opting capability and ambition that could become a threat if directed against the prevailing system.

Meanwhile, the Communist Party has also tried to polish its image to escape being viewed as a corruption-ridden old boys' club. In 2011 *The Founding of a Party*, a high-budget film depicting the Communist Party's birth featuring dozens of the country's hottest stars, was released. But even the scintillating star power and vigorous promotional efforts by the state apparatus failed to draw much popular interest. After early box-office returns disappointed, schools, government bureaus, and state-owned companies were ordered to buy tickets in bulk and give employees and students half a day off to see the film.[20] Some online commentators derided the hypocritical glorification of the Communist Party's early struggle against corruption and one-party dictatorship.[21]

In a more practical effort to restore the government's reputation, President Xi Jinping in late 2012 vowed to go after both the "flies" and the "tigers" (low- and high-level officials) in an anticorruption crackdown. He also instituted a raft of government austerity measures meant to quell extravagant spending and graft. The measures included toning down official banquets, limiting the use of expensive government cars for private use, and barring cadres from having ostentatious weddings or holding membership in high-end nightclubs. While the campaign did in fact snag several "tigers" and was lauded by the public, it did little to address the root cause of corruption—namely, that the police, courts, and media are controlled by the same people. Party sources also told Reuters in early 2014 that one of the motivations for Xi's campaign was to purge opponents and replace them with his own people.[22]

Still, the anticorruption drive appeared to have real effects that were further-reaching than the countless campaigns that had preceded it over the years. A year after it began, the liberal *Beijing News* conducted a survey of one hundred government cadres. As fear that Xi's campaign might finally be for real spread across Chinese officialdom, 92 percent said their "outside work income" had fallen and 79 percent said they had stopped taking gifts. One anonymously quoted cadre said that the restrictions had made life simpler. Whereas he was previously obligated to entertain and drink four nights a week, he could now spend time at home and let his liver recover.[23] Industries heavily associated with corruption, like luxury items, *baijiu* liquor, and high-end restaurants, saw sales tank.[24]

Xi's austerity campaign was also clearly felt within Mae's customs bureau. It canceled its annual New Year's party, which in years past had featured expensive alcohol and hired dancers. Official banquets also switched from serving Maotai (a Chinese liquor costing thousands of yuan per bottle) to imported wine. However, public perceptions did not change immediately. A few months into the campaign, workers at the customs bureau were amused to discover, as they poured into the parking lot at the end of a work day, that someone had written "Can I be your mistress?" in dust on the Mercedes belonging to Mae's boss.

Mae said that working in the government had left her with an even greater distrust of higher-level officials, but it had also given her an appreciation of how much they have to juggle: "Now I feel it's hard to solve a problem since it concerns all kinds of interest groups. In my work, sometimes I see a small issue, but in order to solve it we have to change many things. That's nothing compared to the task of solving a complex nationwide problem."

Though she had long ago abandoned her dreams of a law career, Mae still had a fondness for the field and thought that the rule of law was what China needed most. She invoked the writings of the philosopher Mencius (third century BC), who believed that poor moral character is the result of bad societal influence. "Chinese society and Chinese people's nature in general are worse today than before," Mae said. "In the past there were morals. People cared about what others thought and didn't dare do evil things. That's not how it is now. There's no lawful system, so people have abandoned the old morals and do whatever they want."

During my years in China I met numerous young people like Mae, quite smart but coldly realistic about their options. On several occasions, high-performing students asked me whether joining the Communist Party would hurt their chances at getting an American green card later (it does). For the best and brightest, the two most promising paths seemed to be either to extract what they could from China's broken system or to get out of it altogether.

Like Mae, many who are thrilled when they pass the civil service exam quickly learn that this success does not mean they have won the game. They have only earned the right to play. If they are not deft enough to understand the unspoken rules, they will not advance far.

"The more idealistic you are, the more painful it is," Mae said. "Some people don't want to change society because they benefit from it. I don't like society and want to change it, but I can't, so what's the point of thinking about it?"

Mae knew that she was too smart for her job, but she had been lulled into complacency. She was content to milk what she could from a system she could not change. Her biggest fear was that someday the milk might dry up. "I used to worry about losing my job because of the regime changing," she said. "But the chances of that are small. Maybe the CCP won't collapse, but maybe China will become really good and no longer need this ridiculous job."

8

THE ENTREPRENEURS

Soon after Xi Jinping ascended to China's presidency in 2013, he continued a longstanding tradition by marking Youth Day on May 4 with outstanding students. At the country's leading spacecraft development facility, he hosted a group of aspiring young innovators ranging from space technology engineers to agricultural researchers. Uniformly well-groomed, they crowded around Xi for a picture, flashing big smiles.

On the surface, the meeting was little more than a routine photo opportunity, but there was an important subtext. China was exhausting its ability to grow on the back of cheap labor and exports as it had done for thirty years. Wages were rising and the yuan was appreciating, slowly stripping the country of its "workshop of the world" appeal. Analysts warned that China could soon fall into the "middle-income trap."[1] This occurs when a country maximizes the level of economic growth attainable through the low-hanging fruit of cheap exports and catch-up growth in existing industries, but still lacks the technological prowess to compete at the higher end of the value chain and create new products. If the Chinese economic miracle was to keep steaming ahead, it would have to become more innovative.

Xi invoked what had become the cornerstone slogan of his presidency at this meeting, calling the younger generation the hope for realizing the "Chinese dream."[2]

What was this Chinese dream? In many ways it seemed to echo the American dream, envisioning a nation where all would have equal opportunity to work hard and fulfill their ambitions. But Xi's Chinese dream had a slight difference.

He first used the phrase in 2012, weeks after becoming general secretary of the Communist Party. Flanked by the new Politburo Standing Committee, he stood in the National Museum's "Road toward Renewal" exhibition adjacent to Tiananmen Square, which detailed foreign atrocities committed during the "Century of Humiliation" and explained how the Communist Party finally rejuvenated China's drive toward world prominence. The Chinese dream described by Xi included a tinge of nationalism and would be a source of emotional legitimacy for the CCP. One analyst called it "a collectivist counterpoint to the American dream."[3]

At the May 4 gathering, Xi encouraged students to "emancipate the mind, advance with the times, forge ahead, and innovate." But then he added a caveat: "Only by integrating individual dreams to the national cause can one finally make great achievement."

An official Party journal would later elaborate on the slogan by saying, "Only the path of Socialism with Chinese Characteristics, found through untold hardships experienced extensively by the Chinese Communist Party, is the correct path in the human world to realize the Chinese dream. Socialism with Chinese Characteristics lets our dreams take flight."[4]

Shi Kaiwen apparently did not quite fit this conception of the Chinese dream. This young piano prodigy seemed a perfect role model for the innovative entrepreneurship that China needed. By age twenty-three he had already started three different companies. His current venture was an online radio service called Jing.FM, which applied acoustic analysis to algorithms and thereby allowed users to listen to music that matched their mood. Over $1 million in investment had found its way to the company by 2013, as it grew to thirty employees. It was creating buzz in tech circles and landed Shi on a Forbes list of disruptive Chinese entrepreneurs under thirty shaking up the tech market.[5]

Shi's success intrigued a state-owned Beijing television station that was doing a series on young people living out the Chinese dream. But when the film crew showed up, they found a self-described hippie with shoulder-length hair and a goatee. In a clear contrast to the clean-cut kids in Xi Jinping's photo opportunity, Shi was scruffy and rarely wore anything nicer than a T-shirt and jeans, even when speaking to investors.

The interviewer probed Shi about his upbringing and what had prompted him to take the entrepreneurial plunge; he replied that his musical talent and innovativeness were a direct result of his parents' divorce. When asked about his study habits, Shi said that he often skipped classes in school and argued with his teachers. "No, no, no, this is inappropriate," the interviewer huffed, before shifting gears.

Before leaving, the producer told Shi in so many words that his story did not quite match the theme of the series. The segment never aired.

"The hope of this nation is free thinkers, not just good students," Shi later told me when recounting the interview. "The Chinese dream should be about many people pursuing their own dreams."[6]

Before China's civil war in the 1940s, Shi's family had ties to the ruling Kuomintang Party. When the Communists took power, this status consigned his grandparents to laborious work assignments in the far reaches of China's northern frontier. His parents likewise suffered throughout their childhood, which coincided with the Cultural Revolution. They were both just eighteen when pushed into marriage in 1981. Shi was born in 1988, but his parents divorced several years later when dissolving marriages became less socially taboo.

His father's business had pulled Shi from city to city, never leaving him in one place long enough to complete a full school year. Then, amid the divorce, Shi and his sister were handed off to a series of different family members. During this time he used piano as his escape, just as he had done since age four. "Music saved my soul," he said. "It made me optimistic. Otherwise I might have gotten caught up in drugs or crime."

Shi's rough upbringing had a silver lining. He did not face the same pressure to study and pass tests that most of his peers did—his parents simply did not care. Instead he poured his energy into his own creative pursuits. "Maybe people from broken families have more independent thinking and are more artistic," he suggested. "They're more willing to think and communicate with others, which is very important for a start-up company."

In high school writing classes, Shi would come up with odd poems and stories that did not exactly fit the desired answer on assignments.

Some instructors gave him a zero, but one teacher encouraged Shi's unconventional musings. "There's a big contrast between teachers who encourage creativity and those who don't," Shi said. "Many teachers don't like students who are too creative."

He remained devoted to piano and, at age sixteen, was admitted to China's top music college, the Central Conservatory of Music in Beijing. But even the education at that prestigious school failed to inspire him. "Some subjects are nonsense," he said. "That's why I skipped classes—they don't make sense and some teachers aren't even as good as the students. The most useful stuff I got at university I got from self-study."

One skill he taught himself was computer coding, which he used to start a music website at age eighteen after scrounging up investment from family members. He later sold that company and started a second project, a social music-sharing service, which lasted two years until a change in copyright law scared away his biggest investor. "That was my worst day," Shi recalled. "I suddenly realized I had no money and everybody left. I felt my life would be a failure."

He stayed in bed for days and then took on a few jobs at other music companies, but the itch to create something of his own persisted. By the following year, Beijing's startup ecosystem had grown and Shi had the idea for Jing.FM. "My biggest motivation was to influence people," he said. "To give them a different kind of thought, a different kind of mind."

When we spoke in autumn 2013, he had grown the site to about two million users and was receiving significant interest from investors. Shi wanted to capitalize on the endless opportunities available in China's Internet, which at the time had nearly 700 million users and growing. But there were still a lot of worries.

Some were cultural. Although he had lived his life entirely in China, Shi felt that his level of objectivity—his ability to stand back and view things from a detached perspective—made him an aberration in his own country. He added that his style of expression was unusual: "I'm very straightforward, but Chinese usually use indirect ways to express themselves."

At a more practical level, he worried about the legal landscape for his business. "We don't have a well-developed law system, so many competitors are kind of illegal," he said. "If they try to copy your ideas, the law may not protect you."

His larger fears, however, were political. Shi worried about trying to grow a business in an environment that could quickly become unstable. He had lived in an era of peace and stability, but he knew from his family's previous generations how unpredictable Chinese politics could be. Most of all, he worried that he would be forced to change his vision. "If you do any cultural stuff or music, then you're going to be watched by Big Brother," he said. "Just like if you make films, you have to get censored. My biggest concern is whether I can keep going and still be myself."

These are common concerns among Chinese entrepreneurs, and they dissuade many from pursuing private entrepreneurship in the first place. Though the private sector has come to dominate China's economy (accounting for roughly 80 percent of industrial output by 2014),[7] state-owned enterprises remain very powerful. For private startups, entering territory where these behemoths graze is an intimidating prospect. Small-time entrepreneurs like Shi Kaiwen worry that once they put a good idea out there, a state-owned competitor will snatch it up and use its considerably greater resources to develop that idea. If the rival breaks the law by doing so, there is little faith that government arbitrators will act impartially in a conflict between their state-owned brethren and an obscure startup.

One cautionary tale came in 2013 when mobile apps allowing people to electronically hail taxis started becoming popular in several major cities. Their efficiency was a hit with passengers and drivers alike, but local government interests saw a threat. There was talk of the apps destabilizing the industry, and some wondered why big (mostly state-owned) taxi companies would even be necessary if drivers could so easily be managed electronically. Some cities, like Beijing, instituted regulations favoring latecomer state-owned taxi apps, thereby putting several private startups out of business. The Shenzhen transportation authority responded by banning the apps altogether.[8]

Unpredictability is bad for business, but politics may be hindering Chinese innovation and entrepreneurship in an even more fundamental way. Political scientist Francis Fukuyama has described the critical role of social trust in a developing country's economic transition. According to his theory, trust gives people a high degree of "spontaneous sociability," allowing them to form strong relationships outside the family, build large companies, and collaborate to stay at the forefront of industrial innovation. If a nation lacks this basic level of trust, then innovation stagnates and economic growth plateaus.[9]

A 2012 study by the Institute of Sociology within the Chinese Academy of Social Sciences found that the general trust level in China had fallen more than three percentage points in just two years. Less than half of the people surveyed for the study agreed that "most people can be trusted." Only about 30 percent said that they trust strangers.[10]

A decade earlier, a paper entitled "How Political Institutions Create and Destroy Social Capital" aptly articulated the most common root of this mistrust. "A deteriorating, biased, corrupt administrative system in general goes hand in hand with low levels of social capital, particularly when measured as generalized trust," its authors concluded.[11]

Professor Steven White, who teaches aspiring young businesspeople at Tsinghua University's Department of Innovation, Entrepreneurship and Strategy, said that China's administrative weaknesses are just one of many factors hindering the innovative drive of young Chinese. He explained that his students consistently approach class activities, such as simulated negotiations, with an "eat or be eaten" mentality. They refuse to give up any information for fear of making themselves vulnerable, and they show little or no guilt about having to cheat to get ahead. White's real-world observations have shown the same tendencies; he noted that cheaters have a sense of shame only if they get caught. "There are also elements of cohesion and loyalty, but that's the exception here," White said. "The rule seems to be you get ahead, and using others is part of getting ahead. It's very antithetical. Innovation emerges from trust-based collaboration."[12]

White tells his students a simple story to illustrate the widespread fear of thinking outside the box and challenging authority. In the story, a shopkeeper tells his two assistants to complete a task in a way that they both know will not work. One assistant adjusts the instructions and succeeds, while the other follows orders precisely and fails. The shopkeeper berates the one who failed and commends the one who succeeded, but later quietly fires the latter for not directly obeying orders.

"You can see that kind of obedience to authority [in China]; even when you shouldn't," White said. "It really goes through their heads.

You never come up with your own ideas, and if your boss asks you to, it's a trap. I can't really say what I think the best idea is unless I know that's exactly what my boss wants."

This pattern of thinking in China likely stretches back far before Communism. With an enormous population and limited resources, the country has always been a scarcity society. Competition over resources has frequently been a life-or-death struggle, making misplaced trust or unnecessary risk potentially catastrophic. Couple this social culture with a political environment hostile to risk taking and innovative endeavors, and you have a difficult combination to overcome.

A 2013 survey of engineering students at top universities in the United States and China sought to compare attitudes toward startups among young would-be innovators in the two countries. It found that most students in both nations were interested in starting their own company. However, only 3 percent of the Chinese respondents actually planned to do so, compared to 22 percent in the United States. On the flip side, 52 percent of the Chinese wanted to work in government, compared to just 5 percent of Americans. [13]

The uninviting atmosphere for innovation has led to what even Chinese state media have dubbed the world's worst "brain drain." According to government figures, of the 2.64 million Chinese who left the country to study abroad between 1978 and 2012, only 41 percent returned. [14]

Factors contributing to the brain drain are numerous, ranging from environmental issues to educational opportunities. There also tend to be better facilities and support circles for research in the West. China is trying to improve its standing in these areas, but there is one big area where it seems to be moving backward: the Internet.

One does not have to stay in China long before getting frustrated with its Internet. The "Great Firewall" censorship system blocks popular foreign sites like Facebook, Twitter, and YouTube, key resources that people in many different fields use to communicate with one another around the world. Even less sensitive collaboration sites like GitHub, SourceForge, and LinkedIn have also been periodically blocked, as have several major foreign news sites. And even if one has no need for these resources, Internet processing is slower because of the Great Firewall. This hindrance to efficiency and international collaboration

gives China a gaping disadvantage in the information technology industry, where most of the hope for future innovation lies.

Students at prestigious Peking University, whom the government is
particularly concerned with keeping in line, face even tighter restrictions. Their campus Internet subscription limits them exclusively to
domestic sites unless they are willing to shell out twelve times the
normal fee in order to use foreign sites that the rest of China already
has access to. Most students opt to save their money.[15]

At neighboring Tsinghua University, Steven White worries about
what China's broken political atmosphere is doing to his best students.
"There are two groups, broadly," he says. "One says that the system is
bad, but there's not much hope to change it, so sooner or later they're
going to try finding ways to get away from it. The other group seems to
say 'that's the game.' You figure out how to play and make loads of
money."

"For me, the worrying part is that there's a non-randomness to who's
leaving," White continued. "Those coming out of a place like Tsinghua
or Peking University have the potential to be influential in society. But
if those who see the need for change are doing as much as possible to
leave the system or distance themselves from it rather than become
actors of positive change, you're left with a lot of people trying to work
the system the way it is, which reinforces it. Extrapolate that out, and
it's not very positive."

Vivek Wadhwa, vice president of research and innovation at Silicon
Valley's Singularity University, agrees that this kind of political environment is incompatible with innovation. At a debate hosted by *The Economist* in 2012, he said that innovators have to challenge authority, break
the rules, and take risks. "You can't do that in China," he continued. "If
you do, you're going to be put away unless you happen to be part of the
Communist government, in which case you have subsidies and the entire system is rigged in your favor. But also you're relying upon stolen
technology. That ain't innovation."[16]

Wadhwa added that China is investing massively in attempts to be
innovative, but the results have been akin to "throwing a thousand
monkeys" at a problem and getting a small innovation by mistake. He
said the only people who believe China is going to become a world
leader in innovation are book authors and venture capitalists who can
bank on government subsidies.

Steve Bell is one venture capitalist who begs to differ. The shaved-headed New Yorker started coming to China in 2002 to sell software. Over the next several years he became so impressed with the country's young entrepreneurs that he decided to put all his eggs in their basket, forming Trilogy Venture Capital with the aim of funding young Chinese startups. "They're very cost-effective," Bell told me while eating in a trendy Beijing café. "I can invest in ten young Chinese startup teams for the cost of one in the US."[17]

His strategy involves traveling to meet students through startup salons and at talks by successful entrepreneurs. But his activity that yields the biggest results is ChinaStars, a three-day competition where teams of students must create and present a new product. The winners get thousands of yuan in investment and continued guidance from Bell in order to develop it. When we spoke in early 2014, he had held nearly a hundred of these events, which had yielded some fifty active investments. About a dozen of them had already paid off, including a dating app and a video game. Bell is convinced that within a decade or so, a student-founded game changer like Facebook or Google will emerge from China.

"The thing going for tech students in China is nobody believes in them except very few of us," Bell said. "In the US, at Stanford, MIT, or any top school, there are five hundred good investors competing with me. The amount of competition [for me] as an early-stage investor in startups focusing on Chinese students is basically none at all."

Over the past decade, Bell has seen Beijing's startup community blossom while benefiting from a rapidly growing middle class. Millions across the country continue to urbanize, stepping off the farms and into cities that offer a brand-new world of purchasing opportunities. Consumption from urban Chinese households is projected to grow from 10 trillion yuan ($1.56 trillion) in 2012 to nearly 27 trillion yuan ($4.3 trillion) by 2022.[18]

The generation spending all this new money is also the one primed to create new products to spend it on. Steve Bell concedes that enormous educational, cultural, and political barriers currently constrain the country's ability to innovate, but he sees them as speed bumps rather than road blocks. With a little time, he believes, they will be overcome just as they were in Japan, Korea, and Taiwan. "I think the Western media paints a very one-sided, sometimes ignorant picture of China," he said. "The only people who say that China doesn't innovate are the people who haven't been here, because there's a ton of innovation happening in every area."

Bell prefers investing in young people because they are not constrained by families, jobs, or a knowledge of what has not worked previously. In China, there is still usually a reluctance to deviate from the prescribed path of getting a degree and then a job, but he is starting to see more young people recognize that shifting toward their own pursuits is not as foolish as they were taught. "Ask a group of Chinese students what the biggest most important startups in the last thirty years are and they yell out Microsoft, Facebook, and Apple," he said. "The first things that come to their mouths every time were all started by dropouts."

One of the entrepreneurs to receive Bell's money was twenty-two-year-old Jerry Yue. The Xi'an native had always been a bit ahead of the curve, getting admitted to a top college at age fifteen. A year before that, he had started developing software that allowed teachers, students, and parents to communicate about classwork on an online platform. By age sixteen he began attracting investment in his idea and poured himself into it, neglecting his studies in the process. His grades sank and he did what was once unthinkable for a Chinese student: he dropped out.

Yue subsequently went to a lesser university and sold the company he was developing, but then he dropped out again. He said one major reason was that he could not focus on his classwork when he had the constant urge to create something new of his own. "We already have a huge ball of jobs in existing industries," he said. "The only thing that pushes us forward is to make something outside that ball."

Yue may appear a shining example of Chinese entrepreneurship, but there is one hitch in the story: the colleges he attended were Stanford and the University of Illinois. His parents, both academic researchers, had lived and worked in the United States, so they knew the value of a Western education. They sent Yue to the United States for high school and encouraged him to stay there for college. "I've been through both education systems," Yue said. "They are very, very different. In China there's no way to interact; it's just like a factory. The only way you can interact with the teacher is to answer questions, and there's only one answer."

Returning overseas students like Yue, colloquially known as *haigui* (sea turtles), represent China's hope for stemming its brain drain. The country's potentially gigantic market, with fewer skilled competitors than the West, has drawn many native innovators with Western ideas and skills back to their homeland. Those ideas, in turn, are being passed on to locally educated Chinese. Since returning home, Yue has taken a personal interest in cultivating entrepreneurial youth who were educated entirely in China. He has continued to develop software companies and recruited young, indigenous standouts to help him.

On a cold Beijing morning in early 2014, I attended a meeting that Yue hosted at a Beijing television station with eleven post-90s entrepreneurs. The young students, most of whom had taken a year-long break from their studies to work with Yue, had all designed software. One student's product, an electronic magnet that tracked food in a user's refrigerator, neatly complemented another student's grocery-ordering app.

The purpose of the meeting was to design an upcoming reality TV show starring a famous real-estate magnate. Viewers would interact with the host and the show through a mobile app as they viewed descriptions of the students' products.

Yue, with his spiked hair and a small goatee, led the meeting wearing sweatpants, sandals, and a T-shirt while casually eating his breakfast. The students shouted out ideas and took copious notes on how they might engineer the show's software. "There are very few independent thinkers in China, so [these students] are very different," Yue told me afterward.

He said he selects the students because their values differ markedly from those of most young Chinese, in many cases because their parents have supported their unconventional pursuits. Most of them come from second-tier universities, since those from the very best schools tend to show little interest in entrepreneurial thinking. "The culture here has decided that all the talented people in China want to go to a huge corporation," Yue said. "Our parents have been through a lot of unstable times. They've starved, so they teach us that the most important thing is stability—having a stable job."

Do Jerry Yue and Shi Kaiwen represent an emerging trend of young entrepreneurial risk takers in China, or are they simply among a small group of outliers who will not meaningfully impact the economy? The answer is uncertain. While hugely optimistic, Steve Bell conceded that his investment strategy depends on the "law of large numbers" and on his ability to pluck a few standouts from an enormous pool. "There's a whole cultural bias against innovation and creativity throughout society in China; the fear of failure is very different," Bell said. "There's not a startup culture yet, but there will be."

Jerry Yue agreed, citing the rapidly improving resources for Chinese startups. He told the story of a sixteen-year-old engineering student who quickly created a self-heating coffee mug with a 3D printer. "I was smart but we just didn't have these tools back in my day," the twenty-two-year-old said without a trace of irony. "It's really neat how people can innovate nowadays."

Even if China's current crop of young entrepreneurs is just a small pool of outliers, the pool is likely to get much bigger. The further young people and their parents are removed from the social taboos and rigid thinking of Mao's era, the more they are branching out into individualistic pursuits and unconventional ways of thinking. The government is encouraging strategic innovation with residency benefits, cheap office space, subsidies, and cash grants. And while there has been little movement in easing political constraints, plenty of young thinkers seem to be working around them just fine.

Shi Kaiwen, like many Chinese entrepreneurs, points to Steve Jobs as his greatest inspiration. The Apple founder was put up for adoption as a baby and was later viewed as a goof-off by teachers due to his disinterest in formal schooling. A college dropout by age eighteen, he taught himself the skills that would later help him to found one of the world's most recognizable companies. "It's not only about his success," Shi said. "He was a weird person according to society. He had personality problems. Most Chinese startups find him very inspiring. If you're not recognized by society now, don't give up."

Jobs's story is well known and admired in China. After his death in 2011, tributes were posted throughout the country and the first 250,000 prints of his translated biography sold out in less than a day.[19] At the time, Chinese pondered what it would take to produce a Steve Jobs of their own. "Of course you're restricted by society, but at least your mind shouldn't be restricted," Shi concluded.

Shi added that he will not be constrained by Xi Jinping's narrow vision of "the Chinese dream," but will live out his dream on his own terms. "There is innovative and inspiring thinking here; and we do have hippies in China," he laughed. "We want the outside world to know that we're trying to change the direction of this country."

III

Coping

9

THE LEFTOVERS

Every weekend in Shanghai, hundreds of people descend upon People's Square to trade in the city's biggest market: the marriage market, that is.

Umbrellas propped up on their sides in neat lines contain pieces of paper listing the vital statistics of marriage candidates: age, height, education level, job, salary, and workplace. An interested suitor can simply call the number listed at the bottom.

But the eligible bachelors and bachelorettes themselves are rarely present at the market. In fact, there is a good chance that they are opposed to the whole thing. The market is almost exclusively attended by parents, desperate to set up their children.

"She's just not trying," one mother complains about her daughter's lack of determination in searching for a husband. "She has a good education and is very beautiful," says another, seeking to persuade the mom of a young man that her daughter would be a good match.

The candidates advertised at the market are overwhelmingly female, reflecting the panic that urban Chinese parents feel when a daughter reaches her late twenties without a man. In their eyes, as soon as she crosses the threshold into her thirties, she will be undesirable and thus doomed to die childless and alone, a "leftover woman" (*shengnü*).

Kathy, a twenty-eight-year-old Shenyang native, hears this refrain constantly—from her friends, family, the media, and pretty much everyone else in society. "I don't mind," she laughed. "I sometimes tease myself and other girlfriends, saying that we're leftovers."[1]

Parents at People's Park in Shanghai put their children's vital stats atop umbrellas, hoping to find them a marriage partner. (Photo: Eric Fish)

When we met at an upscale Beijing Thai restaurant, she spoke confidently in colloquial English. With her smooth short hair, milky skin, and wide smile she resembled Courtney Cox. A researcher for a prestigious foreign media bureau in Beijing, she is the product of China's top journalism college and holds a master's degree from England.

With this background, one might consider Kathy a catch. But that is not necessarily how she has been perceived on the dating scene. She broke up with her first boyfriend, a Chinese man she met in England, after failing to reach a compromise on where they would live. He wanted her to follow him as he racked up degrees around Europe, which would have effectively delayed her foray into journalism for several years. She could not accept it.

Her second relationship, with a businessman six years her senior, ended similarly when he expected her to move to his hometown near Shanghai, thus cutting off her blossoming career in Beijing. "I think that's not respectful," Kathy said. "He just decided that's what he wants and lectured me about how a man thinks of women."

Kathy recalled the man declaring that he would still be regarded as charming well into his late thirties, and that since he was rich, he could basically have any woman he wanted. "Why should I marry someone over twenty-eight? They're leftovers," he asked rhetorically.

"He told me I should settle down," Kathy recalled bitterly. "'Don't just play around wasting time. It's time for you to have a family.' He actually said that."

Undoubtedly many women like Kathy become frustrated when men expect them to take a backseat to the man's career aspirations. This may be one reason why 55 percent of university-educated Chinese men choose to marry a less educated spouse (compared to 32 percent of university-educated women).[2]

After she broke up with her second boyfriend, Kathy's family started getting worried. They were attending a steady stream of weddings and baby showers for her childhood friends. Much to their social chagrin, they had to deflect questions about their daughter reaching the ripe old age of twenty-seven with no spouse and no prospects.

Some of the marriages, however, occurred largely because aging women caved to social pressure. Kathy recalled one twenty-eight-year-old girlfriend who was unhappily single. As the peer pressure and family prodding became unbearable, she decided that she would marry by age twenty-nine and have a baby by thirty—no matter what. "Everything was just arranged very, very neatly," Kathy said. "She set up a very busy schedule, meeting three guys each week."

This woman had just three requirements for her husband: he needed to have a stable job and income, be well-educated, and care about her more than himself (this last requirement was flexible). After rapid-fire setups and tireless browsing on dating sites, she found a man who earned all three check marks. Within six months they were married. On their wedding night, the man asked if she actually loved him. "I'm not really sure," she replied, to which he said, "I'll show you I'm worthy of marrying you."

Kathy laughed as she related the story. "It's like they're dating *after* getting married," she said.

This urgent sense of desperation to marry is hardly unique to China, which has a tradition of early marriages that goes back to antiquity. But part of the stigma attached to educated, unmarried Chinese women can likely be traced to a 2007 campaign launched by none other than the government's official feminist organization, the All-China Women's Federation. That group popularized the term "leftover women" and even divided them into categories based on age and chances of marriage: those age twenty-five to twenty-seven still have a fighting chance, but things get tough thereafter and downright dismal at thirty.

The campaign manifested itself in state media articles belittling leftover women. One Women's Federation piece from 2011 warned "average-looking" or "ugly" girls who might try to increase their competitiveness through higher education that "as women age, they are worth less and less, so by the time they get their MA or PhD, they are already old, like yellowed pearls." A separate Xinhua column proclaimed that most leftover women do not deserve sympathy because they squander their youth "going to nightclubs in search of a one-night stand, or they become the mistress of a high official or rich man."[3]

Leta Hong Fincher, who was the first to bring wide attention to these articles, argues in her book *Leftover Women* that the campaign has been remarkably effective in convincing women that their clock is ticking and that they should rush into marriage regardless of the excessive personal and financial compromises it entails.[4]

Anyone acquainted with educated, urban Chinese women would likely recognize the effect. After I finished teaching in Nanjing, I kept in touch with three graduating female students who were also moving to the capital. Their attitudes toward marriage evolved almost exactly as the leftover woman campaign hinted. Between ages twenty-two and twenty-five, they aggressively went on blind dates with one man after another. At that point, they had high standards. For one girl, Sara, the man needed a Beijing *hukou*, a salary of 15,000 yuan per month, and a height of at least 1.8 meters (5'11") before she would agree to meet him.

But by the time age twenty-five rolled around without a mate, a sort of hysteria took hold. The families became unrelenting in their pressure. Sara, who was living with her parents, quietly snuck into the house when she got home so she could avoid her mother at all costs. She had been given strict instructions to find a husband within one year, and each day brought renewed interrogations about her dating tactics.

After the girls turned twenty-six, two of them underwent plastic surgery—one to erase facial blemishes and one for trendy Western-looking double eyelids. Before they reached twenty-seven, their standards fell precipitously. Sara dropped the *hukou* requirement and lowered the salary expectation, settling on a man of satisfactory height with whom she got along well enough. At the time of writing, the other two were still desperately hounding everyone they knew to introduce single male friends to them.

Kathy, meanwhile, was still resilient and able to deflect her family's pressure. "If I'm looking for a job or trying to get a high score on an exam, I know what I should do," she said. "But that's not how it should work in a relationship. If you rush it, that will end very badly."

She had trouble convincing the men she encountered to hold the same progressive attitude. The third man with whom she got involved, nine years her senior, decided at the end of their first date that they should get married. The wisdom of his thirty-six years, he explained, made him certain that she was the one. And besides, he was getting tired of going out on dates.

A man whom Kathy met at a speed dating event informed her on their first formal date that his mom was bugging him to get married so he could deliver her a grandchild as soon as possible. "I thought 'wow, you really moved to the next step,'" Kathy laughed about the date. "It's not about you and me at all. It's about a child."

Kathy, patient about making commitments and resistant to pressure from family, may be in the minority among her peers, but she is hardly alone in China. Chinese women, focusing more heavily on education and careers as the economy has developed, have followed the global trend of marrying later. Between 2000 and 2010, the average age of first marriage for Chinese women rose from 23.4 years to nearly 25.[5] In cosmopolitan Shanghai, women are now waiting until over 30 on average, defying the leftover label en masse (much to the dismay of the parents at People's Square).[6]

One might expect a government that came to power promising liberation and equality for women to embrace this trend. Instead it has reverted back to patriarchal policies and put forward the patronizing leftover woman campaign.

Part of the reason lies with Mr. Yang in a village outside Huanghua, Shandong. When I passed through this small farming community on a bike trip, it was brimming with activity. It was October, the harvest season, and the surrounding fields were full of corn ripe for the picking. Farmers uprooted it, husked it, ground it, and raked the kernels onto the road to dry.

Yang's home had a sign advertising rooms for just 10 yuan ($1.59) per night—a deal too good to pass up. When I approached, Yang was outside with several male cousins, feeding cobs of corn into a husking machine and loading them onto a small pickup truck.

In any Chinese city, one of the easiest ways to understand what local governments are worried about is to look at the propaganda. In this village (and almost every one that I rode through in Shandong) the message was crystal clear.

"Give fewer and better births, be happy the whole life," read one message in blue paint on the side of a shop. "Delivering girls is just as good as delivering boys. Girls are descendants too," said another outside a pharmacy. On the wall surrounding Yang's farm, the local government had spray-painted in big bold characters: "Today's girls are the builders of tomorrow." Around the corner, a placard got straight to the point: "Ban nonmedical sex determinations and sex-selective abortions."

These signs and hundreds like them were conspiring to hammer home a simple message: obey the birth limits and do not abort girls. But the people, it seems, have not been receptive to that message.

Due to a lethal combination of the one-child policy, accessible ultrasounds, cheap abortions, and a traditional patriarchal culture that prefers sons over daughters, China has the world's largest gender imbalance, with 117 boys born for every 100 girls. The problem supposedly peaked in 2008 with a national birth ratio of 120 to 100, which has been declining slightly since then, according to government figures.[7] But even if that decline continues, a generation of damage has already been done. A surplus of roughly one million Chinese men enters the marriage market each year. The number of Chinese men age twenty to forty-nine who are destined to live a life of bachelorhood is projected to surpass 20 million in 2015 and grow beyond 40 million by 2040.[8]

"Having boys is the same as having girls. Delivering less leads to fortune and happy music." One child/anti-sex-selective abortion propaganda in a rural Anhui province village. (Photo: Eric Fish)

Yang was twenty-six years old and muscular, with a middle-school education and sun-glazed skin. He had worked around Shandong as a migrant construction worker, helping to put up massive residential complexes that dotted urban areas. But lately the jobs had dried up, pushing him back onto the farm to wait out the dry spell. His family had diversified beyond agriculture, putting up the small inn and a restaurant for those passing through town. But the income was still a far cry from even the modest construction pay.

I ordered dinner and started chatting with Yang, asking questions that he clearly found a bit silly. After discussing his background and work on the farm, I jumped a bit brusquely into a question about his love life. "I've never had a girlfriend," he laughed.[9] Nor had most of his cousins or peers, for that matter.

Looking around town, it was not hard to see why. Most of the women who lived there were in their forties or older, and already taken. The few younger women with whom I spoke to were mostly home for a short visit or to lend a hand in the harvest, and they were taken as well.

China's gender imbalance has led to a particularly harsh reality in rural areas. The low supply of females means that a woman can be very selective in choosing a spouse, usually marrying a man who can improve her socioeconomic status and leave a sizable bride price (reverse dowry) for her family. Therefore, women in the poorest villages marry up into more comfortable areas. Unfortunately, for the men like Yang who are left behind in the most secluded and poor villages, there simply are not any women left.[10]

Whether Yang earned several hundred yuan each month on the farm or a few thousand by doing migrant work, his chances of attracting a mate appeared bleak. Saving up for a bride price, which can run into the tens of thousands or even hundreds of thousands of yuan, would be hard enough. Yang hardly had a prayer of ever affording one of the urban homes that he had helped to build. In all likelihood, he would be among the one in five Chinese men consigned to the status of "bare branch" (guanggun)—unable to continue his family line.

Men a bit higher up the socioeconomic food chain do not have it easy either. This became apparent in the Jiangsu port city of Lianyungang, which has an urban population of seven hundred thousand and the distinction of being China's most gender imbalanced city, with 163 boys for every 100 girls under age five.[11]

I visited a high-end nightclub there where the cheapest drink was a $7 Budweiser. It was an interesting mix of well-off professionals, carefree fu'erdai (second-generation rich), and about a dozen tall young women milling about in leggy evening gowns. I would later learn that these ladies were not looking for exactly what I first assumed; rather, the club had hired them to mingle and schmooze patrons into buying more drinks—though if it was anything like most similar clubs, everything has its price.

As soon as I entered, I was enthusiastically greeted by Zhou Kai, the club's chubby twenty-two-year-old assistant manager. He led me to his table and offered me a beer. After the standard probing about my nationality and length of stay in China, he asked bluntly, "How many girlfriends do you have?"

"Just one," I laughed. But he would return to this question several times throughout our conversation, apparently unwilling to believe that a Western (and presumably wealthy) man would settle for just one woman. I asked in turn how many he had, to which he just shook his head and waved me off with his lit cigarette.

"You have all these beautiful girls hanging around," I pushed. "Surely you've dated one."

"No, no, no," he replied. "They don't want me."

He took another puff of his cigarette and pointed to a balding, middle-aged man sitting in the corner with a hostess. "He probably makes more than 50,000 yuan per month," Zhou said. "I make 3,000. They'll be his second or third girlfriend before they'll be my first."

"I guess we're both just *diaosi*," I said in a pathetic attempt at solidarity. He smirked and clinked his beer to mine. "How many girlfriends do you really have?"

Diaosi has become a popular term in China. Crudely translating to "penis hair," it migrated from its origin in online forums in 2010 as a self-deprecating label for unattractive men from humble backgrounds with no house or car. Contrary to their tall, rich, and handsome (*gaofushuai*) counterparts, they yearn for a beautiful lover but lack the confidence to pursue one. Unable to make a name for themselves in China's hypermaterialistic society, they escape into fruitless hobbies like video games. (*Diaosi* has subsequently evolved into a more encompassing term for self-identified societal losers of both genders who feel stuck in dead-end lives.)

Diaosi is a funny word with a very serious underlying problem. For the foreseeable future, one of every five Chinese men will be denied the fundamental human desire for a lover and offspring. Experts are expecting very little good to come from this situation.

In her book *Unnatural Selection: Choosing Boys over Girls, and the Consequences of a World Full of Men*, *Science* magazine writer Mara Hvistendahl put it bluntly: "Historically, societies in which men substantially outnumber women are not nice places to live. Often they are unstable. Sometimes they are violent."[12]

Studies have shown a compelling correlation between testosterone levels and aggression, and young, single men have the highest testosterone levels. A 1998 study carried out by Syracuse University researchers explained that single men spend more time in the company of other males. This association tends to expose them to more confrontations with other men, which in turn boosts their testosterone further.[13] Unmarried men between twenty-four and thirty-five years old are thus three times more likely to kill another male than married men in the same age bracket. They are also more likely to steal, rob, rape, engage in substance abuse, and take risks involved in acquiring the resources needed to attract women.[14]

China is already starting to feel the same effects. One study found that from 1988 to 2004, every 1 percent increase in China's gender imbalance resulted in a 3.7 percent increase in violent and property crime.[15]

Even without these studies, history provides ample evidence of the same tendency. From ancient Athens to the American Wild West, places with severe male surpluses have been lawless and violent. China's own history gives a glimpse of the upheaval that restless "bare branches" can spark.

In the nineteenth century, the country experienced relentless cycles of drought, floods, and famine. Due to the dwindling resources and the rigid patriarchal culture, many families began selectively neglecting or outright murdering their young daughters, thereby creating gender imbalances as high as 129 men for every 100 women in some areas. When the surplus bare branches grew up, they were easily recruited into militias or gangs of roving bandits that would coalesce into larger rebellions. Occupying foreigners, as well as corrupt Qing dynasty mandarins with their harems of concubines, made appealing targets for the pent-up angst of these men. This pattern manifested itself in the Nien Rebellion, the Black Flag Army, the Boxers, the Eight Trigrams Uprising, and the deadliest of them all—the Taiping Rebellion with its 20 million casualties.[16]

In this context, one can understand a little better why the Chinese government is urging women to put marriage ahead of education or professional goals. An edgy Communist Party wants to deploy every available woman to mitigate what could turn into widespread instability.

The danger could even spill over China's borders. Scholars Valerie Hudson and Andrea den Boar warn in their book *Bare Branches: The Security Implications of Asia's Surplus Male Population* that governments presiding over large male surpluses tend to co-opt bare branches through nationalistic pandering, which results in "a swaggering, belligerent, provocative" foreign policy.[17] Remember Cai Yang, whom we saw bludgeoning a Toyota driver during the 2012 anti-Japan protests? He was a bare branch.

In 2012, amid a Beijing crackdown on foreigners who lacked proper visas, one famous CCTV anchor played on a resentment of foreigners dating Chinese women. "The Public Security Bureau wants to clean out the foreign trash: To arrest foreign thugs and protect innocent girls," the anchor, Yang Rui, wrote on his Weibo account. "Foreign spies seek out Chinese girls to mask their espionage and pretend to be tourists while compiling maps and GPS data for Japan, Korea and the West."[18]

Plenty of Chinese derided the comments as ignorant and harkening back to the 1900 Boxer Rebellion, wherein the indiscriminate massacre of foreigners in northern China prompted a retaliatory invasion by eight nations. But Yang also had plenty of supporters. With the growing number of expatriates living in China coupled with the widening gender imbalance, the topic of foreign men dating Chinese women is polarizing.

The relatively small (but very visible) number of foreign men sweeping up Chinese women only adds to the sense of crisis for Chinese men in the marriage market. Their desperation has led them to ferociously pursue capital and assets in order to make themselves more attractive to potential wives. In China, financial considerations still weigh very heavily in marital matchups. In rural areas, a man's family often has to pay eight to twenty times their annual household income for costs associated with his marriage, including the wedding, bride price, and new house.[19] Men who do not own a house are less likely to ever marry.[20]

In most countries this may not be an insurmountable challenge, but for Chinese men it can seem all but impossible. In 2014, the average Chinese home cost twenty-six years' worth of the average income, compared to eight years of income in Japan and just two in the United States. In Beijing, the average home cost was an incredible thirty-three times the average salary.[21] The financial markets were largely responsible for this imbalance. China's stock market is widely seen as a rigged roller coaster (less than 9 percent of Chinese own shares[22]), and the government has for years pushed bank interest rates artificially low—usually lower than the inflation rate—in a move to fuel economic growth through cheap capital. Real estate has thus remained the only consistently reliable investment. Rampant speculation, driven by wealthy investors buying dozens or even hundreds of homes at a time, has left China with some of the highest housing costs in the world.

For young status-conscious Chinese, home ownership is a symbol of arrival to the middle class. For single men, it is often viewed as the baseline for adequacy in the marriage market. So saving up for a down payment can become an all-out effort for a man and his family. A 2009 study for the US-based National Bureau of Economic Research estimated that, during the years immediately preceding the study, the gender imbalance had accounted for 18 percent of the rise in urban savings rates and a whopping 68 percent in rural areas.[23]

Even if a woman decides to throw material concerns to the wind and marry based on love alone, that does not necessarily mean her family will sign off on the arrangement. One of my female friends from east China decided to marry her high school sweetheart after dating him for five years, even though his family was far less affluent than hers. From the moment they announced their engagement, there was conflict between the two sides. In a serious break with local tradition, her parents insisted on walking out first at the wedding (since they had paid for it), which caused a major loss of face for the man's parents. Then there was bitterness over the fact that the man's family could pay only a small token bride price to her family and could not contribute a fair share of the down payment for the couple's home. The family tensions eventually became overwhelming and within several months of the wedding the couple divorced.

Given the skyrocketing housing prices, purchases are increasingly requiring a joint effort by the husband, wife, and both families. Unfortunately for the woman, she will usually get the short end of the stick if the marriage ends in divorce. In 2011, China's highest court reinterpreted the country's marriage law, deciding that home ownership is determined by whose name is on the deed. Thanks to prevailing social norms, in 70 percent of cases only the man's name is on the deed, even if the woman contributed money.[24] Conveniently for a government that wants to see as many men married as possible, this situation makes it much harder for a woman to leave her husband or exert equal power in the relationship.[25]

An outside observer might conclude that home ownership in China is more trouble than it is worth. But few within the country see it that way. Men need a home in order to be attractive in the marriage market.

Status-hungry youth need to keep up with the neighbors. And nearly everyone craves the stability and financial security that a home supposedly offers. On top of these factors, real-estate companies, dating websites, and government propaganda use advertisements, op-eds, and misleading surveys to promote the idea that young people should buy a home and scramble to find a spouse.[26] Few with the means to join the exclusive club of Chinese homeowners will forfeit the opportunity.

This harrowing housing situation has introduced some new terms into the Chinese lexicon. One is *kenlao* (chewing on the old), which describes young people who depend on their families to support their lifestyle. With the importance of home ownership, parents are usually more than willing to chip in (especially if their child is a man at risk of becoming a bare branch). But with this support comes extra pressure to earn more money and find a spouse.

Even more widely used is *fangnu* (house slave), used for people who work tirelessly in order to stay ahead of their mortgage. On average, Chinese families now have 66 percent of their assets tied up in their homes, compared to 41 percent in the United States. In Beijing, the figure is an astounding 84 percent.[27] The accompanying mortgage obligation means constantly striving for that promotion while scrimping and saving for the other two financial "mountains" of healthcare and education, along with any other necessary expenditures and status-building toys.

All this pressure may help to explain why struggling Chinese youth are not more politically active. When they complete their education they promptly embark on their next daunting challenge, with the faint promise of a spouse and home beckoning them at the other end of the tunnel. Moving up the pay scale and the social ladder while finding that special someone command far more attention than deeper political questions.[28]

Back on his farm in Shandong, Mr. Yang was preoccupied with many things, but politics was not one of them. He was not even aware that Xi Jinping was about to assume control of the Communist Party and become China's most powerful man. I asked Yang what he planned to do in the future. "I'll just go wherever the jobs are," he replied.

But it is always possible that China's hopelessly single men will present a more volatile wild card in the future. As the authors of *Bare Branches* wrote, "The mere presence of dry, bare branches cannot cause a fire, but when the sparks begin to fly, those branches can act as kindling, turning sparks into flames."

Back in Beijing, Kathy seemed content for the moment with being single, but remained a bit apprehensive about the future. "I think sooner or later I'll get married," she said. "I don't buy what my boyfriend told me about marriage, but I think he's right that if you get to a certain age, it's hard to have a child. I think I'll start to worry when I'm thirty-two."

Whether or not Kathy ever found a man was not of great economic consequence. She was fortunate to have a comfortable urban upbringing, a successful career, and a high degree of financial independence. But for those young women brought up under poorer conditions in rural areas, life can be quite bitter.

10

EATING BITTERNESS

As Yang Sijia lay down in the coffin, her mind was fluttering with the anger, guilt, and despair that had consumed her previous few days and, in fact, most of her life. Between the twenty pounds she had lost in the past two weeks, the abortion, and the suicide attempts, everything had come together in an unholy storm. But when the coffin's lid slid shut, it left her in a dark isolation that put everything in perspective. During those few minutes she vowed that she would turn things around.

Sijia was born in 1990 in a rural Shaanxi province town near the provincial capital of Xi'an. In 2011, while studying at a film college in Xi'an, she was introduced to a director making an independent film about a rural "ghost marriage" custom.

The region has a longstanding superstition that those who die before marrying will spend eternity in loneliness unless they are posthumously married and buried with a partner. The practice has led to a thriving black market for corpses, with pretty young females bringing in top dollar thanks to the prevalence of "bare branch" men.

One of the themes of the film, called *The Cremator*, was the Chinese concept of "eating bitterness," where one silently pushes ahead in the face of extreme hardship. It is a concept with which rural Chinese women are all too familiar.

Early in the film a young woman in a small Shaanxi town is dredged from a river, presumably after committing suicide, and taken to the local morgue. When presented with the unclaimed body, the morticians start arranging to sell it for a ghost marriage. However, Old Lao, the morgue's terminally ill cremator, wanted the girl to be his own eternal bride.

Sijia's character, a young girl named Xiuqiao, shows up from a poorer region looking for her missing sister, who had come to the area to do migrant work. But Old Lao turns her away, saying that no young women have turned up.

Lao later finds the girl prostituting herself to fund her ongoing search. He tries persuading her to give up and go home but eventually admits that a young woman was indeed brought in. He leads her to the morgue, opens the cold chamber, and prods her to have a look at the corpse's face. She reluctantly obliges and then slumps to the ground in despair, but she does not shed a single tear.

The film alludes to many issues that disproportionately plague rural Chinese women: suicide, alienation during migrant work, financial desperation leading to prostitution, and complications stemming from the gender imbalance.

When I saw the film at a small screening with its director in Beijing, I was intrigued by the character of Xiuqiao. In a country where censorship has left most films sticking to tried-and-true themes and trite overacting, Xiuqiao's anguish seemed real. Though the viewer can tell that she is shattered inside, she keeps stoically biting her lip.

The director said that he used only nonprofessional local actors in order to authentically depict rural Shaanxi life. If Yang Sijia's quiet agony was convincing, it was because her real life had entailed even more bitterness than that of her character.

I met her at her small Beijing flat eighteen months after filming was complete. Bundled in a sheepskin coat, her eyes would often wander, and at times they began to swell as we spoke. But she never lost her poise as she recounted how her personal story gave authenticity to the character of Xiuqiao.

Sijia's mud-brick childhood home sat in an agricultural Shaanxi community of a few thousand people. During her first years, in the early 1990s, sleepy villages like hers were just beginning to wake up and send people off to the cities to make more money than they had ever seen before. Soon after Sijia was born, her father went to Guangdong to paint walls. When he returned after a few years with the money he had saved, he was considered rich in the village. But it would be short-lived.

Her father quickly got entwined with the wrong crowd and became addicted to gambling. Before long, his riches turned into debt and the family moved to urban Xi'an to do more migrant work. The couple sold things on the street and later set up a stand selling videos while Sijia attended a local primary school. Today, only an hour's drive on a new highway separates her hometown from Xi'an, but in the late 1990s the two might as well have been in different countries.

Sijia's Xi'an classmates did not accept her. Her rural background and strange-sounding dialect made her an outsider. Even the school regarded her as second class. With her rural *hukou* she was considered only a "temporary" student. As soon as she left class each day, she immersed herself in movies at her parents' video stand. Her favorites were Jackie Chan Kung Fu flicks.

After five years she went back home to live with her grandparents and attend middle school. By that point she had spent the formative years of her life in Xi'an. Her accent and manner had changed enough to alienate her from her new rural classmates. "I felt like a foreigner in my own hometown," she recalled. [1]

After less than a year at the new school, Sijia was diagnosed with a serious heart condition. The family exhausted all the money they had saved and began borrowing from friends and extended family members to pay for her treatment. Then, as now, superstitions were rampant in the countryside. Sijia's grandparents hired a local "wise man" to cure the affliction before it killed her. He told the family that God must want Sijia to work for him, so they should find a girl of the same age and height who had died recently to offer in her place.

Sijia's grandparents asked around, scoured cemeteries, and eventually found a candidate. Sijia and her family accompanied the wise man to a famous Buddhist mountain, where they all said a prayer together for God to take the other girl instead. Soon afterward, Sijia recovered.

When she went back to school, rumors that she had been in the hospital with an infectious disease kept her isolated. In retrospect, she feels that being an outcast during this time was a blessing. She buried herself in her studies and became a star student. For once, she felt good. Perhaps she could be happy after all.

"But then, during the summer between middle school and high school, something happened that wasn't very happy," she said, lowering her head. "It changed my life."

Her father had brought her to be a part-time cook for the summer at a golf course where he was now working. The facility was overwhelmingly used and staffed by men. One evening Sijia was asked to keep an eye on a neighboring vendor's shop and was told that she could even use the shower. When she went to the back of the shop and slipped out of her clothes, her father's boss came in. "There was only one wall between us and where my dad was," she said. "I was crying but it was my dad's boss. I was scared, so I didn't scream." She was sixteen years old.

Reliable statistics on sexual assaults in China do not exist, but incidents like Sijia's are not uncommon. Tsun-Yin Luo, a professor at the Graduate Institute for Gender Studies at Shih-Hsin University in Taipei, estimates that fewer than one out of ten sexual assaults are ever reported in China.[2] "The patriarchal culture actually brings sexual violence to female victims," she told me. "Lots of victims of sexual assault feel ashamed of their victimization, and even if they don't feel ashamed, their family ensures that they feel ashamed."

Luo said that this culture disproportionally affects rural women, who do not have the same access to information about their rights as their urban counterparts. "Women in the countryside tend to be left behind," she said.

Over the following years, the man visited Sijia's family often. She became terrified whenever he walked in the door, but she never told her family what had happened. Eventually the golf course went out of business and she never saw him again. His mark would stay with her though.

In high school her attitude changed radically. She began to bully people and skip classes, but fortunately her studious habits had stuck and she managed to pass the *gaokao*, getting into a Xi'an film college where she could pursue her dream of becoming an actress.

While there she worked a gamut of part-time jobs to support herself, from selling clothes on the street to washing dishes. One job was at a high-end restaurant where she and another girl would stand in skirts and high heels to greet customers at the door as they entered. After a few months, her boss came to her and said he was scaling back. Only one of the two girls would be retained. "If you're together with me, I'll keep you," he told Sijia. She decided to quit.

During high school and her early college years, Sijia was haunted by what had happened at the golf course. She began painting her walls with images that she still does not quite understand. One depicted a clown crying next to an old man sitting on top of a jail. During this period she would sometimes cut herself and even attempted suicide four times by choking herself with a rope. But on each occasion she lost her nerve.

Later she began visiting a Buddhist master whom she had met during high school when her mother brought her to a temple to pray before an exam. She says that this source of inspiration slowly brought her out of her psychological torment. "Buddhism teaches you to accept your destiny," Sijia said. "In a former life, I owed someone a debt, so I need to get rid of my sins. I used to want revenge on that man, but now I'm at peace with it."

Both Buddhism and Christianity, though influenced heavily by local folk beliefs, have grown rapidly in rural China over the past two decades. In addition to the easing restrictions on organized religion, many attribute this trend to the shakeup of China's social order and the widespread need for spiritual coping mechanisms.[3] Sijia briefly contemplated becoming a Buddhist nun but eventually dropped the idea.

Later in college she began doing odd jobs on movie and TV sets. Then, in summer 2011, she was introduced to Peng Tao, the director preparing to make *The Cremator*. After reading the script, she persuaded Peng that her life and Xiuqiao's were virtually identical. Peng said he would give her a shot, but she would have to lose weight.

Over the next twelve days, Sijia managed to shed nearly twenty pounds through constant exercise and eating only one meal per day. At the time, she explained to me, she was motivated by money more than anything else. For several months she had been dating a man who had just bought a house and was worried about finances. He had often criticized Sijia for not having a steady income, so she thought the 12,000 yuan ($1,920) that she would earn from the film would prove her worth.

But the prospect of doing the film added further stress to a relationship already on the rocks. The man wanted the money she would receive but hated the fact that one scene would require nudity. The two fought constantly. Then, as Sijia was in the midst of her rapid weight loss, she found out that she was pregnant. "The guy had a good background," Sijia said. "Very different from mine. He went to good schools and got a law degree from one of Xi'an's best colleges. In his whole life he never had any setbacks."

Sijia reluctantly aborted the pregnancy. "I always thought that even though I wasn't a great person, at least I was a kind one," she said. "The abortion drove me completely mad. I wasn't punished by law, but deep in my heart I always consider myself a murderer."

When production began, Sijia was thoroughly depressed and the rapid weight loss only added to her stress. At one point in the film, Xiuqiao faints; Sijia said that it happened spontaneously during shooting because of her weak condition.

She also found herself almost completely surrounded by men. In Shaanxi, the birth ratio was more than 130 males for every 100 females.[4] The imbalance even extended into the afterlife, creating the black market for ghost brides depicted in the film.

Because no other young woman was available, Sijia unexpectedly had to act as the corpse. This entailed being zipped into a body bag, slid into a morgue's cold chamber, and shut into a coffin. She was furious about the assignment at first, but the complete isolation and feeling of death gave her a new perspective. "The moment I laid in the coffin, all outside sounds were gone," she said. "The only feeling I had was that I would live up to my life's potential."

Sijia was actually better off, in some respects, than most rural Chinese women. She was able to go to college and work in an industry that she found rewarding. Both of these opportunities have traditionally been unavailable to village women. Many rural residents still subscribe to a traditional saying: "Men belong in public, women belong at home" (*nanzhuwai, nüzhunei*).

An often-cited 2002 study found that, between 1995 and 1999, Chinese women bucked world trends by committing suicide at a 25 percent higher rate than Chinese men. Furthermore, rural suicides happened at three times the rate in urban areas, making rural Chinese women an especially vulnerable group.[5]

The study shocked the nation and led to dozens of media reports seeking to understand rural women's plight. These reports tended to portray a rigidly patriarchal countryside, where women were considered worthless except for child rearing and housekeeping. Due to this perceived uselessness, their families sold them off to abusive husbands and repressive in-laws.

These assessments were not entirely unfair. Chinese tradition dictates that when a couple marries, the woman joins the man's family. Because women were thought to have little economic potential, raising them entailed a cost that could be repaid only by their future husband. Thus, arranged marriages based on financial pragmatism were (and largely remain) common, causing women to be viewed as bought property and obligated to dutifully obey their husbands' family.

Researchers found that the main reasons for rural female suicides were indeed abusive husbands and overbearing in-laws, coupled with easy access to highly lethal pesticides. But a decade after the infamous study, suicide rates among this demographic group had plummeted. A newer study found that the annual suicide rate among rural women aged fifteen to thirty-four was just 3 cases per 100,000 people in 2011, down by over 90 percent from 37.8 cases per 100,000 in the late 1990s.[6] Research by Tsinghua University sociologist Jing Jun similarly found that the overall suicide rate among rural women in 2006 was about a quarter of what it had been two decades earlier.[7]

In interviews, researchers Jing Jun and Michael Phillips (who conducted the 2002 study) both cited urbanization as the primary factor for the drop. The proportion of rural workers employed away from home had reached 30 percent by 2011—more than quadruple what it was in the late 1980s—leaving many women separated from their husbands, in-laws, and pesticides for most of the year.[8]

Once kept powerless and financially dependent at home, China's migrant women were now in demand as maids, waitresses, and factory workers in the nation's booming cities. Through their migrant work, they pulled their families from abject poverty and flipped the family power dynamics, taking greater control of their lives. According to survey data collected by Professor Jing Jun, in 1990, 37 percent of rural women had their marriage decided entirely by their parents. By 2000, this figure had fallen to 16 percent.[9]

However, amid China's economic boom, rural areas have not kept up with cities and women still lag behind men. Disproportionate education investments and *gaokao* quotas in the cities have caused the proportion of rural students enrolled in college to drop. Only 5 percent of students from rural Shaanxi end up going to college, compared to 70 percent of students in urban areas.[10] And among rural families especially, resources tend to be directed toward boys, while girls are often expected to drop out of school early to support the family's males.[11]

As a result, rural women remain at the very bottom of China's growing wealth and power gaps. While annual per-capita income tripled for rural residents, from about 2,200 yuan ($352) in 2000 to 7,000 yuan ($1,120) in 2011, incomes in cities nearly quadrupled, from 6,300 to 24,000 yuan ($1,010 to $3,842), during the same period.[12] Again, rural women fared even worse. In 1990 they earned 79 percent of what their male counterparts received; by 2010, they were earning only 56 percent of men's compensation.[13] As in other societies, the large gaps between rich urban men and desperate rural women have left the latter group vulnerable to exploitation by the former.

When Sijia's restaurant boss held her job ransom for sexual favors, her only choices were to consent or quit. Even if a rural female worker wishes to fight back against sexual exploitation by an urban boss, she seldom has the legal awareness or financial resources to do so. Given this ever-present risk of sexual abuse, it is not surprising that many migrant women skip traditional labor altogether and go straight into sex work. With little education and rampant discrimination, some have little to rely on but their bodies.

For her book *Red Lights: The Lives of Sex Workers in Postsocialist China*, Yale ethnographer Zheng Tiantian spent two years documenting the lives of women who provide sexual services in the country's ubiquitous karaoke parlors. Zheng argued that the androgynous socialist conformity instituted under Mao stripped Chinese men of their masculinity, which they reclaimed by subjugating women once they gained the economic means to do so. "It seems that in the patriarchal state where resources are in the hands of males, what is left for females is to find a sexual niche—that is, to decorate an essentially male world," Zheng wrote. "In this patriarchal environment, it is not surprising that women have to use their looks and sexuality—the only accepted talents of women—to get ahead."[14]

For those who tire of grueling factory work or get frustrated by the glass ceiling at even the most menial jobs, sex work offers an escape that migrants often find too tempting to pass up. One estimate in 2000 put the number of prostitutes in China as high as 20 million (though other estimates have been far more conservative), with major migrant destinations like Shenzhen and Beijing hosting hundreds of thousands, overwhelmingly made up of rural women.[15] According to the same estimate, prostitution and related industries could represent anywhere from 6 to 12 percent of China's entire economy.

A young woman blessed with exceptionally good looks might become the mistress of a wealthy businessman or government official. Those unable to do so might end up as karaoke bar "princesses" who entertain, get fondled by, and occasionally go home with wealthy patrons. Or they might end up even further down the sex industry ladder, toiling in the back of a seedy massage parlor.

These thinly veiled brothels with pink lights and lingerie-clad "masseuses" in their windows can be found in nearly any neighborhood of every major Chinese city. In migrant meccas like the cities of the Pearl River delta, entire districts are full of them.

I once interviewed a twenty-five-year-old woman who worked at one of these establishments in Beijing. Her name was Yan, and she had come to the capital from a small town in central Hubei province after high school to make some money. She started out with a string of waitress jobs, earning far better pay than she could get back home, but the work was tiring, the hours long, and the customers and managers demeaning. When she was twenty-three, a hometown friend introduced her to a way that she could "make a lot of money with work that's not too tiring."[16]

As far as her family and boyfriend back home knew, Yan was still waitressing. But in reality, she was servicing three or four men per day at the massage parlor. After the owner got her cut, Yan usually took home around 10,000 yuan ($1,600) each month.

"It's not much, is it?" she asked with a smile. In fact, it was more than most educated urban Beijing women her age made. It was three times what she could make in a factory and more than both her parents and boyfriend earned combined.

"Of course I don't like it," she scoffed playfully when I asked how she felt about her work. "But it's alright." After a few months on the job, she said, she had gotten used to the sex, but was still struggling to adjust to the boredom of sitting around all day and night waiting for customers. In any case, though, she felt that this job beat waitressing.

Up to that point she had been lucky. She had not experienced any abuse from customers—most just did their business quickly and went on their way—and there was always a man on security detail in an adjacent room. Furthermore, the parlor had never been subject to a police crackdown as far as Yan knew. Like most such brothels, it was either under the protection of local authorities or deemed too insignificant to disturb.

Yan's experience is hardly indicative of all young migrants who decide to market their bodies. As Zheng Tiantian and other scholars have documented, abuse of prostitutes by both customers and pimps is tragically common. Without the law or any nearby family members to protect the sex workers, there is little recourse when things turn violent. And the periodic vice crackdowns that arise out of local power struggles or the need for a veneer of morality push the sex trade further underground and put women more firmly under the control of their handlers.[17]

Even rural women not involved in the sex trade are finding life a bit scarier, especially in regions like Shaanxi with high male surpluses. Numerous studies have linked China's growing gender imbalance to rises

Massage girls sit in a Shenzhen "barber shop" waiting for customers. (Photo: Chris DCmaster, Flickr: Barber shop, Bao'an, Shenzhen, China)

in abduction, trafficking, rape, forced prostitution, forced marriage, and enslavement.[18] In 2012 near Yang Sijia's hometown, thirty-seven members of a gang were busted for raping women and selling them into prostitution.[19]

Yan represents many young rural Chinese women of today—afforded very few options, yet possessing just enough tools to break free from the isolated existence into which they were born. Her ultimate goal was to learn English, emigrate to Canada, and buy a house—perhaps with her boyfriend if they got married, or perhaps not. Her time in cosmopolitan Beijing had left her with little desire to ever live in rural Hubei again. But at the same time, she was still a second-class citizen in the capital city, unable to reap the benefits of an urban *hukou* and forever priced out of home ownership by the astronomical housing prices.

Yan had romantic notions about Canada—that it was clean and egalitarian, with a high quality of life. Best of all, she had heard that even normal people like her could afford a nice house there. But the few jumbled phrases that she attempted to speak in English suggested that her plan was a long way from implementation. Probably it would never happen. But if she played her cards right and avoided serious trouble, maybe she would pull it off someday. The mere chance to escape the destiny of her patriarchal birthplace is something that generations of women before her lacked. Her work in the city left her objectified in many ways but empowered in others.

Of the many contradictions in contemporary China, the position of young rural women is among the greatest. By most measurable indicators—suicide rates, marriage opportunities, education levels, income—their situation has improved tremendously in recent years. Many are breaking the shackles of their rural upbringings and determining their own fates.

But by less measurable metrics—such as frequency of exploitation, psychological status, or power relative to men—it is less clear whether things are getting better or worse for them. The mass migration to cities has brought new socioeconomic opportunities, but it has also created its own unique hardships. Meanwhile, the growing surplus of men in the countryside makes the situation ever more precarious for the women left there. The exploitation of this precious minority grows along with the gender imbalance. It is hard to say whether the period of greatest bitterness for this group of women lies in the past or the future.

By the time shooting on *The Cremator* ended, Yang Sijia had broken up with her boyfriend and started spending time with one of the film crew members, whom she described as "kind and honest." He would soon have to return home to Beijing, but Sijia promised that when she finished school in December she would join him. "He didn't really believe me at first," she said. "But after all the bad things that had happened and the bad feelings while making the movie, I just wanted to get out of the area."

In true "eating bitterness" fashion, Sijia denied that her life is indicative of any wider trends, saying that she has just been unlucky and that her hardships are not an indictment of society. The last time I spoke with her, she was in Beijing with her boyfriend, working on film sets and occasionally acting. She said her favorite movie was Will Smith's *The Pursuit of Happyness* and that she hoped to eventually make her own films, which would portray people caring for one another. Overall, she was optimistic about her chances of being happy and that China would become a better place for people like her.

"I think you always have to have hope," she said. "My Buddhist mentor told me it's the heart that determines your environment. Good people will live in good places, and good places always have good people."

11

FINDING FAITH

On an autumn afternoon in 2011, a young mother in the southern Guangdong city of Foshan scampered to pull laundry inside as a storm brewed. In her haste, she lost track of her two-year-old daughter, Wang Yue. Only days later would surveillance camera footage reveal to her, and to the world, the sickening sequence of events that transpired next.

The little girl had wandered into a nearby alley as a large white van lurched forward, its driver chatting on his cell phone. Her head turned just in time to meet the oncoming headlight as it ran her over. The driver paused, then slowly ran over the girl again with the back tire before driving away.

Over the next few minutes, several people passed through the narrow road. One by one, they each skirted around little Yue, ignoring her as she lay battered and bleeding. A young woman and her own young daughter glanced down, but kept their brisk pace forward. Finally, a fifty-eight-year-old scrap peddler came upon Yue and shouted to alert her mother. In the seven minutes since she had been hit, little Wang Yue had been neglected by eighteen passersby.

The van driver allegedly (although this account has been disputed) explained his actions to a reporter before turning himself in, saying, "If she's dead, I may pay only about 20,000 yuan ($3,200). But if she's injured, it may cost me hundreds of thousands of yuan."[1] Little Yue succumbed to her injuries eight days later.

Similar incidents of voluntary manslaughter and heartless bystanders had grabbed attention in China for years, but the Foshan video's graphic nature shocked the nation into weeks of introspection. Academics, sociologists, and journalists from around the country pondered how China had so badly lost its way.

A few weeks later I met a twenty-one-year-old college student from Hefei named Chu Zhen who, like many young people at the time, had been keeping a close eye on the Wang Yue story. "I think Chinese almost don't have morals," he said. "In ancient China people had merits, but now more and more Chinese just care about money. Reform and Opening Up changed us. We don't know what's right."[2]

Legions of Chinese youth were feeling the same as Chu Zhen. For three decades after the foundation of the People's Republic, Chinese were taught to worship Mao, strive for Communism, and put the needs of the masses before personal interests. Sacrifice and humble living, they were told, were the marks of a model citizen. But when China's markets were opened, the socialist moral framework began to crumble along with the socialist economy.

Getting rich, which was previously a crime, suddenly became glorious. Those who continued to labor altruistically for the masses lost their revered status in the new society, while those who clawed and swindled their way to material fortunes were admired. Concepts of right and wrong were flipped on their heads.

In 2002, Hong Kong University professor Wang Xiaoying described this as China's "post-Communist personality," warning that free markets had taken hold without the emergence of a sustaining moral order. "Whatever the intrinsic flaws of capitalism as a social system, China's social problems seem to come as much from the failure to establish a viable capitalist social order," Wang wrote.[3]

Chu Zhen said that he used to feel lost in society. He was the only child in his family, and the tectonic societal shifts that had occurred between his parents' era and his own left a severe generation gap. "I grew up almost by myself; my parents were very busy and didn't have time to care about me," Chu said. "I used to be aggressive. I did a lot of bad things to my friends, parents, and people who cared about me. At that time I just wanted to find a belief."

In retrospect, gravitating to religion seemed inevitable for Chu. It was just a matter of something knocking over that first domino. For him it was the movie *Forrest Gump*. When one of his teachers screened the film, he was struck by a scene where Gump went on the *Dick Cavett*

Show to recount his trip to China. The host and fellow guest John Lennon found it hard to "imagine" that the Chinese do not practice religion. "We don't understand why Americans are surprised that Chinese don't have faith," Chu said. "We think that's very normal."

Wanting to experience what Americans apparently took for granted, Chu started going to church and Bible studies around campus. Within a few weeks, he was sold. "We sang songs, told stories. I found peace in my mind. I went again and again, and became a Christian."

Yang Fenggang, a Purdue sociologist and author of *Religion in China: Survival and Revival under Communist Rule*, told me that it is common for youth like Chu Zhen in today's China to feel this anomie. "Many people felt lost in this market transition," Yang said. "But then they somehow ended up at a church and realized Christianity provides a clear set of values and moral standards, and that it's good living a life where you know what you should and shouldn't do."[4]

China had fewer than a million Christians in 1949 before the Communist Party all but stamped out religion for the next three decades. A few years after it launched Reform and Opening Up, the Party reluctantly reopened the gates to faith, expecting that only elders clinging to "feudal superstitions" would trickle in to seize the newfound freedom. Instead, a flood poured through. According to government figures, which count only worshippers in state-sanctioned churches, there were roughly 24 to 40 million Christians in China by 2014.[5] But independent estimates accounting for unofficial worshippers put that number at anywhere from 70 million to over 130 million.[6]

According to Yang Fenggang, nearly every Chinese university now has a thriving Christian community. "When I talk with [Christian students] I find the atheist education is weak and they're more open-minded with nothing really holding them back from converting to a religion," he said. "Especially one that's perceived as modern and Western."

Though religion was tolerated after the economic reform of the 1980s, the Communist Party continued to actively discourage and often suppress it. In 2001, then-President Jiang Zemin called on cadres at all levels to cautiously accommodate believers, but also to guide religion toward adapting to socialist society and to promote atheism among the younger generation.[7] Official role models were to remain godless and inspired exclusively by socialism. But for young Chinese, that message rang hollower by the day.

In the months following little Wang Yue's death in Foshan, the country continued its bout of soul-searching. Numerous factors contributing to the attitudes displayed in this incident were cited. Many of these factors were by no means unique to China, but the hypothesis offered again and again was that a spiritual vacuum had emerged amid the excesses of capitalism. So the Communist Party responded by dusting off an old socialist icon.

Lei Feng had long been a symbol of altruism in China. The People's Liberation Army soldier, killed in an accident in 1962 at age twenty-one, had allegedly lived his life doing good deeds like cleaning his comrades' socks, shoveling manure for people's communes, and giving up his train tickets to those in greater need. Lei detailed his deeds in a diary that also conveniently documented his source of inspiration. "I have only one desire in my heart," read one entry. "I want to be whole-heartedly dedicated to the Party, socialism, and Communism."[8]

Today, most historians agree that Lei Feng's life story was at least partially (if not completely) fabricated by propagandists. But the legend lives on in Chinese education, to the extent that Lei Feng is a universally recognized symbol among Chinese youth.

Little Wang Yue's death occurred a few months before the annual "Learn from Lei Feng Day" on March 5. As China's moral decay and loss of empathy remained fervently discussed topics, the Communist Party went on a propaganda blitz promoting Lei Feng spirit. For weeks leading up to the holiday, billboards were erected, speakers delivered speeches at schools, and media ran Lei Feng–themed programs around the clock. One Chinese Central Television (CCTV) segment struck an almost religious tone, proclaiming, "The Lei Feng spirit has been a source of strength for the Chinese nation. The Lei Feng spirit is eternal."

In the end, the campaign fell flat. Weibo overflowed with cynical remarks lampooning Lei Feng and his irrelevance in modern China. At a time when socialism existed in name only and materialism prevailed, "Lei Feng spirit" was a hard sell. A few days after the holiday, even the Party mouthpiece *People's Daily* asked, "Is learning from Lei Feng now outdated?"[9]

During the campaign, one CCTV segment depicting "modern Lei Fengs" caught my eye. The subject was a lanky, bearded, forty-something American named David Deems. For the better part of two decades, Deems had taught in some of the very poorest parts of China. He always insisted that his schools cut his salary to the same dismal level as his Chinese colleagues and house him in the same rundown dorms. He wore old shoes with holes in them, kept only a backpack's worth of worldly possessions, and listed "serving the people" on the interests portion of his résumé.

It turned out that Deems had been the focus of numerous Chinese television segments over the years. But when I dug deeper still, I discovered something that all these programs had neglected to mention: his motivation came from his devout Christian faith. One young man from the northwestern province of Gansu blogged that Deems had inspired several of his college classmates to become Christians themselves. [10]

For a generation that increasingly sees its Communist leaders as hypocritical and corrupt, Marx offers very little in terms of inspiration for altruism. With the cult of Mao killed off before they were even born, young people looking for a moral code and something to believe in are turning their backs on socialist icons.

Shortly after "Learn from Lei Feng Day," I started attending a popular "English Corner" at a public square in Renmin University, where young Chinese practice speaking with foreigners. Every time I went, the biggest group by far congregated around a forty-one-year-old American missionary going by his Chinese name, a transliteration of "Hallelujah." Wearing a suit and tie adorned with a crucifix pin, he shouted into a belt-mounted megaphone and used an iPad to illustrate biblical lessons. "Marxism is a terrible system," he once told the group, contradicting everything they had ever been taught in school. "Marxism is the exact opposite of the Bible."

The crowd was receptive to the message, laughing in agreement the moment he chastised Marx. Other messages Hallelujah delivered—that abortion, belief in evolution, and Buddhist idol worship were evil—received a chillier reception. When he began to discuss the gift of speaking in tongues, he earned a more derisive round of laughter. "I think he's insane," one young man in the crowd said to me. "But I think he's a good person. Some people are insane but don't know it—like being drunk."

Most of the young people there seemed interested in Hallelujah chiefly for entertainment, but a few did appear moved. One girl came to the front and whispered into his ear, concerned that she had not yet been able to hear the Holy Spirit or speak in tongues herself. Another girl said she was becoming more interested in Christianity and coming to hear more every week.

When I spoke with Hallelujah a few weeks later, he claimed that about one-tenth of the people to whom he preaches actually become interested in Christianity—a number that would make any Western missionary envious.[11]

At the university where I taught in Nanjing, several of the other foreign teachers were Christian missionaries like Hallelujah, though they were subtler in their methods. Some would bring up Christian themes in class discussions or talk about their faith at English Corners.

A sign at the Renmin University public square where English Corner takes place. (Photo: Eric Fish)

One year at Easter, a teacher invited students to her home to watch a movie about the holiday, which turned out to be *The Passion of the Christ*. According to students, a few girls began crying during the bloody crucifixion scenes, and some later converted after the teacher told them that "Jesus did this for you."

By day these students would sit through tedious lectures in Marxism and socialist morality, playing along with lessons of a bygone era that even the instructors would acknowledge were hopelessly discredited. But by night, many would go to Bible studies with foreign teachers or study-abroad students. There they were treated to lessons about a supernatural deity who was always listening to their prayers and—perhaps more importantly—monitoring their sins.

The message and the messengers were appealing. The Christians offered biblical answers to the problems and moral quandaries that the students brought to them. Whereas they would often be brushed off when seeking guidance from their *fudaoyuan* or other school staff, the Christians became intimately involved in their lives. They would give dating advice, listen to the students' problems, and sometimes just provide a shoulder to cry on.

Such scenes were occurring in universities across the country, and by 2011 the central government had taken notice. That year the General Office of the powerful Central Committee circulated a secret document nationwide relaying concerns that foreign missionaries were "infiltrating" colleges and becoming too influential. The document was reportedly given only to municipal-level cadres with instructions to communicate the contents orally to lower officials.[12]

The document, which was later leaked, reflected an old Communist Party mentality that was still kicking strong. "Foreign hostile forces have put even greater emphasis on using religion to infiltrate China to carry out their political plot to westernize and divide China," it read. "The goal of foreign use of religion to infiltrate institutes of higher education is not just to expand religious influence but more to vie with us for our young people; our next generation."[13]

In a carrot-and-stick approach, the document offered guidance on how to forcibly stop "illegal religious activities" but also offered ways to counter the attractiveness of foreign missionaries, such as providing psychological counseling for troubled students and holding heart-to-heart talks in order to understand their problems.

But then the document zeroed in on what the Communist Party thought could best prevent students from exploring Christianity in the first place. "Launch thorough and meticulous political ideological education," it said. "Extensively launch activities for the study, teaching, publicizing, and popularization of core socialist values. Strengthen propaganda for and education in Marxist views on religion."

It is impossible to assess the document's effectiveness, as central government directives routinely go ignored by lower officials. But harassment of underground religious activities backed by foreigners had never been discontinued. Three months after the document was issued, a foreign missionary in northeastern China posted a blog entry stating that an illegal house church with which he worked had been raided by police. They detained several congregants and pressed four lines of questioning: what kind of religious group they were, where their money came from, what they were preaching, and what role the foreigners played. [14]

Incidents like this one were not unusual. Western Christians are often viewed as agents of imperialism like those who accompanied the violent foreign incursions of the nineteenth century.

Usually though, if illegal house churches do not have contact with foreigners and limit their gatherings to a few dozen people, they are left alone. One of my students, Sue (a pseudonym), told me about a house church near campus that she and many of her classmates attended on weekends. It had about 150 members, who came at different times to ensure that the number at any given service was not large enough to attract unwanted attention. It had been operating for six years without incident, although Sue felt that the police almost certainly knew about it. "If our church has too much communication with churches abroad or Western preachers, then maybe people who go there will be monitored by the government," she told me. "But there are too many churches like this; they can't ban them all." [15]

The students did not really need this clandestine gathering if all they wanted was Christian worship. There were state-sanctioned churches all over the city, including China's largest at the time, with room for five thousand people. I asked Sue why she and her classmates did not just go to one of these churches. "Their words and hymns will all be checked by the government," she answered. "There's a lot they won't approve of, so if we just listen to that we'll never grow."

I had walked into services at several official churches around China and could see why they might not be appealing to young people. Though large and beautiful, they tended to be crammed with retirees singing gentle songs and listening to restrained sermons.

When I moved to Beijing, I discovered the appeal of the alternative. As I rode the elevator in my apartment building one day, a girl in her twenties handed me a card for the house church on the floor just below mine. I asked if I was still welcome, given that I was an atheist and, even worse, a journalist. "Then you should definitely come," she laughed.

The "church" was a small studio apartment identical to my own. Situated in Beijing's Zhongguancun district, it was strategically situated between Peking, Tsinghua, and Renmin Universities. Twenty-five congregants showed up on the Sunday I attended, making it a very full house. Other than an American student, a middle-aged woman, and her young child, all were in their twenties, either professionals or students from nearby colleges. They stood chatting and eating snacks before the service started, enthusiastically welcoming each newcomer. A young woman from a nearby medical college told me that she had come to the church for several months before ultimately converting. "Finally, I felt Jesus as clearly as I see you right now," she said.

The forty-something preacher, named Brother Xin, took the pulpit before rows of tightly packed chairs. "Thank you for overcoming the obstacles to be here," he said. He leafed through the Bible, reading verses from the gospel of Mark on the faithless. His delivery gradually became more passionate and he occasionally pounded on the podium. "Many who go to church on Sunday are Christians; they have Christmas and Bibles," he exclaimed. "But they don't represent religion. They think they represent Christianity, but they don't know the heart of God. They still have Satan in them!"

After he spoke, a girl took out a guitar and everyone stood. The congregation belted out upbeat hymns in both Chinese and English as they swayed back and forth with their hands in the air. One young woman started crying as she sang.

Toward the end of the service, congregants were invited to the front to give personal testimonies. A few described hardships in their family or school and how faith was helping them through their challenges. One girl wept as she spoke of her sister, who she hoped would soon join her in converting. Several in the audience grasped each other's hands.

The outpouring of emotion was something I had never seen before in China, where people tend to hide their true feelings and weaknesses from strangers. Even family members commonly refrain from open displays of affection toward one another, but there was no such hesitancy in this church. Everyone referred to each other as brother and sister.

Sue related having had a nearly identical experience at her church in Nanjing. "When I began to have some contact with brothers and sisters in the church, they treated me just like family," she said. "Maybe my parents have the closest relationship with me, but they can't understand me or love me like this."

It was obvious what the state-sanctioned religious experience was missing. A firebrand like Brother Xin would never be approved to preach at an official church. Spontaneous testimony from congregants would also be out of the question. After a lifetime of struggling to communicate with parents of a very different generation and being educated in rigid Marxist dogma, these young people were finding in their underground church something that they could not find anywhere else: a community of unconditional love and acceptance.

Chu Zhen recalled that a similar experience in his house church was the biggest influence in his decision to convert. "Brothers and sisters were very kind to me," he said. "They cared about me and taught me how to love people. That was the biggest change."

Gerda Wielander, a researcher of Chinese religion at Westminster University and author of *Christian Values in Communist China*, argues that this concept of loving your neighbor is largely absent from traditional Chinese beliefs. "In Confucianism it's not universal," she told me. "It's hierarchical. The degree of compassion you have for somebody relates to how close you are on the hierarchy."[16]

Chinese sociologist Fei Xiaotong has described these hierarchical relationships as like the surface of a lake after a rock has been thrown in. The distance of each circle from the center represents social and emotional distance, with blood connections the closest, followed loosely by hometown people and then those with a similar social identity (rich, poor, urban, rural, white collar, blue collar). The further someone is outside the center circle, the more that person is either seen as a tool to benefit those closer to the center, or simply disregarded.[17]

This mentality has been frequently cited as an aggravating factor in the social ills plaguing China, from environmental degradation and endemic food safety problems to corruption and cases like little Wang Yue's.[18]

Wielander said that, to some extent, attitudes within the Communist Party have begun to shift from seeing Christianity primarily as a threat toward viewing it as a tool. "There's a fair amount of overlap between the government agenda and the Christian agenda," she said. "When you speak to [Chinese Christians] or look at the data, they all emphasize what good citizens they are and what good citizens they want to be, so there's a lot for the government to tap into there."[19]

In spite of ongoing crackdowns on house churches, some quarters of the government have paradoxically given signals of a warming to Christianity due to its moral, economic, and even political potential. "Christianity is seen as useful from the official point of view because it's not just about acting morally as an individual and being a good citizen. It's about the work ethic," Wielander said. She pointed out that the government seemed to be attracted to sociologist Max Weber's idea of the "Protestant work ethic" and to the argument that religion had curbed excesses of greed and corruption in Western market economies during the early stages of capitalist development.

A number of Chinese universities now have religious studies departments, and academics at all levels, including the government-backed Chinese Academy of Social Sciences, have published research on the positive contributions of Christianity in China. A foreign missionary who helped to build state-sanctioned churches told me that he was finding himself increasingly welcomed with open arms by local officials and even, on occasion, quietly encouraged to try converting locals.

In spite of this warming attitude, though, many quarters of the Communist Party remain deeply suspicious of Christianity and its potential for stirring up social upheaval.

In Beijing's Zhongguancun district, a literal stone's throw away from the small house church that I visited, the Protestant Shouwang church has regularly been shut down and its leaders arrested, forcing it to change locations more than twenty times. Started by a charismatic Tsinghua graduate in 1993, the church had grown to over one thousand members by 2011.[20] Then there is the Almighty God cult, which came to prominence in 2014 when five of its members bludgeoned a woman to death in a McDonald's for being an "evil spirit." The group, which is thought to have perhaps hundreds of thousands of members, believes that a forty-something Chinese woman is the reincarnate of Jesus Christ. Its ultimate stated goal is "to kill the Communist Party."[21] What worries the Chinese government most about such religious groups is their organizational power and the potential for wayward figureheads to lead their flocks in subversive directions.

Historical precedents give reason for such concern. The Catholic Church's role in the 1989 fall of Communist rule in Poland provides a cautionary tale for China's Communist leaders. Closer to home, the Falun Gong spiritual movement blindsided the Communist Party in 1999 when more than ten thousand of its members surrounded the Zhongnanhai leadership compound in Beijing, demanding an end to their repression (the government subsequently deemed Falun Gong an illegal cult and launched an aggressive crackdown that remains ongoing). Then there was Hong Xiuquan, the disillusioned nineteenth-century intellectual who decided he was Jesus Christ's younger brother. His small Taiping religious movement grew into a fourteen-year rebellion that left 20 million dead.

However, few scholars see much political threat from any modern Christian movement in China. "As long as they can worship freely, they tend not to criticize the government or policy," Yang Fenggang said. "Theologically they're evangelical but politically they're apolitical."

Some within the Communist Party even appear to be viewing religion more as a means to maintain control than as a way of losing it, as if Marx's idea of religion as "the opiate of the masses" may not necessarily be a bad thing. Peng Guoxiang, a Peking University professor of Chinese philosophy and religions, told me that this is nothing new in China. "Almost every emperor knew the power of religion," he said. "It is very possible that the authorities have started to rethink the function of religion and how to manipulate it skillfully, instead of simply trying to curb or even uproot its development."[22]

In 2014, President Xi Jinping said that "religion has much wisdom in encouraging human goodness," and an earlier report cited sources with ties to China's leadership as saying Xi was "troubled by what he sees as the country's moral decline and obsession with money."[23] But contrary to signals from some other high officials, he expressed hope that China's traditional beliefs of Confucianism, Buddhism, and Taoism, rather than

Christianity, would help to "fill a void that has allowed corruption to flourish."[24]

In spring 2014, several prominent churches and Christian crosses were torn down across Zhejiang province in the east, ostensibly in a campaign to demolish structures that violated zoning restrictions. But documents leaked to the *New York Times* revealed that only "overly popular" Christian locations were targeted.[25] Later that year, the government seemed to take another step back from the warming that had unfolded in previous years when it announced it would be establishing a unique Chinese Christian theology that "adapts to China's national condition" and is compatible with "the country's path of socialism."[26]

Conversely, other accounts have suggested that local officials in restive areas with large Muslim and Tibetan Buddhist populations have welcomed Christianity as a preferable alternative to the more politically volatile local religions.[27] Gerda Wielander commented that the Chinese government is no longer a unified monolith and that it comprises a wide range of opinions on what the roles of different religions should be. "Both Buddhism and Daoism are fairly otherworldly," she said. "They're more about how to escape from all this chaos and hide from this terrible world, whereas Christianity is very proactive. That can be a good thing for the government, provided it manages to channel this energy into projects on the government's agenda."

A few weeks after the Wang Yue incident, I sat down with my Christian acquaintance Sue, a few of her friends, and Chu Zhen to talk about faith in their lives. It appeared that through studying with foreign Christian missionaries, they had picked up some of the more controversial tenets of evangelical Christianity. Sue recommended a book to me "debunking" evolution and casually mentioned that homosexuality is a sin. However, most of their comments seemed inoffensive to, and sometimes even supportive of, the Communist Party line.

They all related how Christianity had given them a greater desire to help others. One young man discussed the aid work that he had done in rural Gansu province (where he also took the opportunity to proselytize whenever he could).

Unlike the rest of the young Christians in the group, one girl said she did not have any significant life problems before converting. She had gotten along well with her family and done well in school, so I asked why someone like her would be drawn to religion. "When people pursue materialism, maybe they'll have success," she replied. "But after they finish and they're alone, they'll find their earnings and material goods can't satisfy their empty heart."

She summarized an attitude that many successful young Chinese appeared to be displaying. Having found material comfort, they craved spiritual satisfaction. Some found it in endeavors outside religion, such as nature, sports, or secular volunteer work. But unlike these other outlets, religion is inescapably political. Regardless of the signs that the government was warming up to Christianity, there were still constraints. Government leaders had to be atheists, proselytism was illegal, and those who did not acknowledge that their church was subject to the authority of the Communist Party were in violation of the law.

I put these issues before the young Christians, but they appeared unconcerned so long as they could go on worshipping without harassment. "The Bible says we have to follow the rules of the government," Sue said. "We have to follow the rules but we should also have faith. It's not contradictory."

Chu Zhen dissented. "Socialism contradicts Christianity," he snapped. "The Party thinks God doesn't exist."

Sue shot back, "Their socialism isn't real socialism. It's Chinese socialism."

IV

Pushing Back

12

THE SOCIAL ACTIVISTS

It is probably fair to say no woman has ever taken more flak for walking into a men's room than Li Maizi.

In the run-up to Women's Day in 2012, the feminist college student was distressed by the one-to-one ratio of public restroom facilities for males and females. She believed that women's longer wait times necessitated legislation to enforce giving women twice as many toilets. Determined to correct the oversight, she organized demonstrations for true "toilet parity."

The "Occupy Men's Room" movement involved some twenty women who took over male public restrooms periodically over the course of an hour in Guangzhou and Beijing. Outside they distributed fliers and held signs with slogans like "Care for women, starting with toilets."

The two events were small and cheeky, causing no more trouble than a little embarrassment for a few men. Most onlookers just laughed it off and expressed support for the cause. Li Maizi did not figure that her action could draw the wrath of authorities. She could not have been more wrong.

"We didn't think it was sensitive," she laughed. "But I guess we can't gauge the risk since the government is so strange."[1]

When I met Li a year after her Occupy movement, I could not help but find it amusing that she had been considered a threat by China's vast "stability maintenance" apparatus. The petite twenty-four-year-old with miniature top hat could easily have been mistaken for a middle school student. Whether she was recounting one of her quirky demonstrations or the childhood beatings she had endured, she ended nearly every thought with a mischievous giggle.

Li was born in the rural outskirts of Beijing. She described her mother as a sweet and caring woman who had endured pain her entire life. Her father, on the other hand, she labeled a stubborn chauvinist.

According to Li, her parents had been forced to marry young after becoming pregnant with her. As a child, her father delivered fertilizer for a farming company, but he was exceptionally unpopular with his colleagues. He had narrowly failed the *gaokao* after high school and remained perpetually bitter about the peasant's existence to which that failure had relegated him. So when his company had to start laying off workers, he was one of the first to go. A few years later, he was offered his job back, but he was too proud to accept.

Li's mother picked up the slack, moving to a distant part of Beijing to work in a factory. Though she was bringing in the money and even continued to do the housework when she was home, her husband remained firmly in charge. His orders were nonnegotiable and any affront by his wife or daughter resulted in a beating. Li remembered getting thrashings for things as simple as writing with her left hand rather than her right.

She would go on to a top-tier college in Xi'an, where she became involved in activism and later set up a gender equality advocacy network. By 2013 the group consisted of some two hundred active volunteers around China, many of whom, like Li, had grown up experiencing domestic violence. They advocated for equal-rights legislation and highlighted discriminatory behavior in government and businesses. But the work that made them famous was their "performance art"—a term deliberately used to dodge the political sensitivity of "protest."

Their performances usually related to events that they considered discriminatory, and they were designed to garner wide attention on social media. On one occasion, they shaved their heads to protest some universities' practice of lowering admissions standards for boys in order to maintain a gender balance with higher-achieving girls. On another occasion, they went into action after the Shanghai subway authority addressed a groping epidemic on its trains by suggesting that women "have some self-respect" and not dress so provocatively. A few volunteers proceeded to board the subway wearing miniskirts, metal breast protectors, and signs saying "I can be slutty, but you can't get dirty."[2]

The girls frequently rallied against domestic violence, which is rampant in China. An official from the state-run All-China Women's Federation said that one-fourth of all Chinese women suffer abuse in their marriage; in a separate survey, half of Chinese men admitted to violence against their partners.[3]

Since 2001, China's marriage law had specifically prohibited "domestic violence," but it failed to lay out any legal recourse or even define what constituted abuse (though at the time of this writing, comprehensive domestic abuse legislation had been drafted and was awaiting approval by the National People's Congress).[4] As a result, police and courts remained hesitant to take on these cases and tended to push couples to reconcile. "Some women get abused for ten years, or even thirty years, because once she leaves her husband, she might lose her home and children," Li said. "That's the reason they don't leave."

On Valentine's Day 2012, Li and two other volunteers decided to call attention to the problem of domestic violence by wearing bridal gowns splattered with red paint to resemble blood. They marched down a crowded Beijing shopping street, holding signs and chanting slogans like "Love is not an excuse for violence." They jokingly chided couples holding hands, warning them to be vigilant against abuse.

The crowd was mostly receptive, but unlike their earlier performances, the subject matter made some people uncomfortable. A common saying in China reflects the traditional attitude: "Family ugliness must not be aired" (*jiachou buke waiyang*). To many Chinese men and women alike, beating is a normal part of marriage, and it certainly is not something to be discussed outside the home. "Many families had no humor," Li recalled. "There were even some chauvinists in China saying feminists are evil—that our group is evil."

As they marched down the street, they were confronted by *chengguan* (urban management officials) warning that they had not registered their three-person demonstration. The officers followed the women until they left.

The Occupy Men's Room demonstration a few days later was meant to address a less threatening gender-related issue that could gain broad support. After all, long bathroom lines for women also affect the men who accompany them. "In the beginning we thought it was very humorous," Li said.

Most people did see the humor. After the first event in Guangzhou, the movement went viral on Weibo and started getting international

Li Maizi holds a sign saying "Care for women, starting with toilets" during Occupy Men's Room. (Photo: Li Maizi)

attention. By the time the Beijing demonstration rolled around a week later, it was a media circus involving nearly every major domestic and foreign news outlet in the city. Li gave interviews under her "Li Maizi" public pseudonym, hoping that anonymity would keep her under the radar. It did not.

Perhaps it was all the foreign media attention focused on China's gender issues. Perhaps it was bad timing, as the National People's Congress would meet the following week. Or perhaps Li's ability to organize large groups for public demonstrations seemed threatening. She still is not completely sure why, but the Beijing event introduced her to the suffocating grip of China's "stability maintenance" apparatus.

"Stability maintenance" euphemistically refers to the country's vast internal security network, tasked with stamping out any hint of potential unrest. It includes multiple agencies and thousands of offices overseeing surveillance, censorship, police, special informants, community volunteers, and even contract thugs. The system began in the late 1990s and evolved into an extremely well-oiled machine in time for the 2008 Beijing Olympics. Since 2010, spending on the system has outstripped the country's entire military budget.[5]

The day of the Beijing Occupy performance, the propaganda department sent directives for media to stop covering the event. Then immediately after the demonstration, two plainclothes men escorted Li to their unmarked car. Only their badges, without names or numbers, identified them as police.

To Li's surprise, the men took her to a fancy restaurant and treated her to a feast. "The good thing is you can eat a big dinner," she giggled while recounting the story. "Stability maintenance has a big budget for this sort of thing, and the standard for people like me—the lowest, I think—is having to spend at least 600 yuan ($96) on the meal."

The officers kept her there for the rest of the day. They were subtle in their message at first, telling Li that she was a smart girl with a bright future ahead of her . . . provided that she avoided trouble. Eventually, they got to the point and warned her to cease her demonstrations, stop posting on Weibo, and stop giving interviews.

Later that evening, six marked police cars with ten uniformed officers pulled up to her parents' home in rural Beijing. They took Li's terrified father to a restaurant, lavishing the same 600-yuan banquet on him that his daughter had enjoyed. For him they even brought an offer to the table, saying that if he could get Li to discontinue her activities, they could arrange a cushy government job for her at the local Women's Federation. "If my family had something—such as if we owned a factory—they could just threaten to shut it down," Li speculated. "But my family had nothing to lose, so they offered me a job."

Li's father had always pushed her to try entering civil service and was disappointed and humiliated when she instead delved into feminist causes. But somehow, she now had a shortcut to his dream dangling right in front of her. After living a simple rural life for so long, he yearned to see his daughter enter the Golden Rice Bowl and improve the family's fortunes.

But Li did not bite. She continued giving interviews and kept posting on Weibo, so authorities stepped up the pressure. They showed up again and took her to their car, but there was no fancy dinner this time; just a brief session of "good cop, bad cop." They told her that defying their orders constituted a betrayal of "trust between friends." They also wined and dined her father a few more times, but it became clear that he had no power over her. She was already planning the next demonstration.

For Women's Day on March 8, 2012, she and her volunteers slated an action in front of a Beijing government building in opposition to invasive gynecological exams that female civil service applicants were forced to undergo. This time, though, the authorities were one step ahead of her. On the day when the demonstration was to happen, Li phoned a friend to make final preparations. Within half an hour, police showed up at her door. She would later realize that they had tapped her phone and hacked her e-mail.

Li was brought to the police station for a long interrogation, released, then awakened again early the next morning for another session. Finally, the police invoked leverage that Li could not ignore by calling her university in Xi'an, where she was still awaiting graduation. The vice-dean of her department and her *fudaoyuan* counselor were dispatched to retrieve her from Beijing. "My counselor was proud of me," Li said, "but told me I'd better stay at school and read more books."

The vice-dean told Li she needed to stay on campus and check in regularly, but she would be given a token work-study position paying 120 yuan ($19) per month that is usually reserved for students from low-income families. Li retorted, "How about I give you 120 yuan and you give me my freedom!"

But by this point, the harassment was finally starting to wear on her. She made a calculated decision to retreat to Xi'an, then continue her demonstrations in the more open-minded city of Guangzhou until the heat was off in Beijing.

Over the following months, authorities would still listen in on Li's phone calls and frequently called to check in, but she was largely left alone outside Beijing. I asked whether her Occupy Men's Room experience had hampered her in any way. "Sometimes it bothered me," she replied. "But this thing passed, and now I'll say it was just one period of my life. Sometimes I'm scared, but I have some peers backing me, so I'm not afraid of them."

In an earlier era, a rabble-rouser like Li Maizi could have been dealt with easily enough. The state could have held her entire future ransom, or simply scared her straight by dispatching her to a labor camp for a few years. But in today's information age, Li's network gave her a measure of security.

Still, the "Occupy" experience gave Li a stark reminder that she could push the envelope only so far. If political winds shifted or she somehow crossed a line and the Communist Party felt that its legitimacy had been questioned, it would not hesitate to bring the hammer down hard. China's labor camps and prisons house dozens of activists just as influential as Li who focused their efforts on more sensitive goals like democracy, Tibetan autonomy, or recognition for Falun Gong.

Li's case illustrated that even social movements pushing only slightly controversial agendas tend to irk the Communist Party. "I know what I do is a good thing," Li told me. "But it's hard to communicate with the government because they're biased against nongovernmental organizations. They think they always make trouble and are bad for society."

Contrary to most of the young people it governs, the CCP has been slow to embrace the rapidly emerging diversity in China. While uneasiness over the organizational power of nongovernmental organizations (NGOs) is one reason why groups like Li's get harassed, there is a bit more to the story.

Wei Xiaogang, a prominent Chinese gay-rights activist and filmmaker, told me that the government generally does not believe it has failed to give people any of the rights they need, and it certainly does not like being challenged. "I think they force people to think collectively," he said. "They want a very harmonious society. They want everyone to be the same as everyone else."[6]

Wei added that China's feminist movement in particular suffers because China's elder male leaders are uncomfortable with gender issues. Among the 204 leaders on the Communist Party's all-powerful Central Committee, only 10 were women as of 2014.[7]

In the same way that feminism challenges the traditional patriarchal culture of China, Wei's fight for lesbian, gay, bisexual, and transgender (LGBT) rights challenges the country's traditional family structure. For Li Maizi, both issues are near and dear to her heart and, in fact, closely linked to one another.

During her elementary and middle school years, Li realized that she was attracted to other girls. She thought that she must have some sort of illness. At the time, homosexuality was still classified as a psychiatric disorder in China and was never discussed in textbooks or media. But eventually Li went online and discovered that she was not alone. "In high school about three or four friends knew my sexual orientation," she said. "But at that time, I just didn't want others to know."

By the time Li entered college, homosexuality's social stigma had subsided enough that she fully embraced her sexuality and came out to everyone—except her parents. While homosexuality does not face the same degree of religious opposition in China as in many Western countries, it can be considered an affront to the Confucian notion of filial piety and continuing one's family line. Failing to marry and bear offspring in China is viewed as a slap in the face to one's parents.[8]

As with many social issues, the disparity in attitudes between older and younger generations can present just as big a barrier to progress as government resistance. Indeed, the two factors tend to be intertwined.

Xin Ying, a twenty-seven-year-old lesbian from Wuhan and program director of the Beijing LGBT Center, explained to me how this dynamic played out in her own family. She was active in high-profile public stunts to raise awareness for LGBT and gender issues, including Occupy Men's Room. But the demonstration that got her the most attention occurred when she invited reporters to watch as she and her girlfriend attempted to register for marriage at Beijing's Civil Affairs Bureau (where she was denied). After a picture of the couple kissing outside the bureau was splashed across newspapers, several family friends quietly mentioned it to her mother. "My mom said, 'You want me to go crazy! Why do you do such a disgusting thing?'" Xin recalled.[9]

However, nobody dared say anything to the family's patriarch. Xin's father was still under the impression that she was working for an environmental NGO. Despite all her high-profile advocacy for LGBT rights, she still could not discuss her sexuality directly with him. "Maybe when I become stronger, I can come out to him," she said.

Xin explained that this perceived threat to family stability is what irks the government most about the LGBT cause. "We all know families are sort of the unit of society," she said. "So if same-sex couples can get married, it kind of destroys the traditional concept of family. That's why the government gets so upset about this."

Though homosexuality has been perfectly acceptable on paper for more than a decade, authorities have continued to crack down on LGBT film festivals, parades, and clubs while censoring depictions of homosexuals in entertainment. The country has yet to enact an antidiscrimination law protecting LGBT individuals, let alone put gay marriage up for debate in the National People's Congress. In 2013, police in the central city of Changsha went so far as to throw a nineteen-year-old activist in jail for twelve days after he led a street rally against homophobia.[10]

Ironically, the government's attempt to maintain the status quo may be causing more harm than good to "family stability." Because of the intense social pressure to marry and bear children, Chinese homosexuals overwhelmingly enter heterosexual marriages. A University of Shanghai sexologist estimated that 90 percent of gay Chinese men marry unsuspecting straight women (compared to 15 to 20 percent in the United States).[11] Media periodically report disasters sprouting from these loveless and sexless marriages, ranging from bitter divorces to suicide.[12]

Many Chinese homosexuals have begun sidestepping these problems through "cooperative marriages," in which a gay man marries a lesbian with the understanding that it is all an act for the sake of family and career. This practice started gaining rapid popularity in the early 2010s, with matchmaking websites emerging to accommodate them. But these arrangements have their own problems—such as whether to have a child and how the family assets are divided—that tend to place a heavier burden on the woman. And even in these sham marriages, domestic abuse still occurs.

This is one reason why Li Maizi chose to focus primarily on women's rights. While LGBT issues are a major concern for her, she felt that gay men had greater political advantages. For example, they have been able to piggyback on the less sensitive HIV/AIDS prevention movement to get media attention and face time with government officials. Lesbians, however, have few avenues to raise their voice and even feel disrespected by male gay-rights activists. "I realized that if gender discrimination can't be wiped out in China, then there's no lesbian movement," Li said.

Like Xin Ying, Li was very hesitant to reveal her sexuality to her family. She finally worked up the nerve to tell her mother during college and was relieved to learn that she had already known for a decade. Her father was less accepting, though. He found out when documentary filmmakers accidentally let the secret slip while shooting at their home.

Even though well aware that his daughter was gay, he still pressured her to get married and have kids. She resisted and then went a step further by suggesting that if he had any interest in working, he could get paid to give speeches about having a lesbian daughter. The suggestion infuriated him. "Now he just doesn't ask about it," Li said. "I'm out of his control now. He used to beat me but now he can't. I'm grown up and can resist, so he just says I'm trash and other mean words."

When I spoke with Li, she was trying to persuade her mother to get a divorce, and for years had been pushing her to speak up for herself more. "But there's a generation gap," Li lamented. "My mom thinks there's no absolute gender equality."

Li said she sympathizes with women who do not fight back against abuse and discrimination. To some extent, she even sympathizes with men like her father, whom society educated to be the way they are. "But that's the reason I need to stand now," she added. "This society needs young people to speak out—to point out the fact that the genders in China are unequal. This is social advocacy and policy advocacy. Nature is very hard to change, but the policy is very easy to change."

Policy was indeed changing. It is impossible to know how much the changes are the result of campaigns like Li's, but it is hard to discount the connection.

Soon after the Occupy Men's Room protests, several major city governments began suggesting (and in some cases even legislating) that new buildings have more toilet facilities for women than for men.[13] Then, after the feminist volunteers targeted companies responsible for job advertisements that discriminated against women, several were fined by the Beijing government.

These successes motivated Li more than "stability maintenance" discouraged her. A few weeks before I met her in 2013, the Sichuan Supreme Court in Chengdu had upheld the death sentence for a woman who had killed her husband during a beating session after years of abuse at his hands. Li and the volunteers organized a petition to stop the execution and were even so bold as to protest outside the courthouse. But always mindful of the need to be strategic, they demonstrated on a day when court was not in session and police were not on hand. In the end, the execution was quietly canceled and the following year the sentence was completely overturned in a "landmark" case.[14]

While the Communist Party once appeared to be an omnipresent and all-powerful monolith, young people pushing for social change today have little memory of the bloodshed in Tiananmen. And today they are finding strength in numbers online. These changes have made the CCP seem a more vulnerable, though certainly still formidable, force to contend with. Youth activists are finding that, even if they threaten the Party by pushing for particular social changes, they sometimes get their wish rather than a prison sentence.

Still, young social activists like Li Maizi, though apparently growing in number, represent a tiny fraction of Chinese youth. "Most of my generation is afraid to speak up," she said. "They feel helpless and don't do anything. But I don't want to blame them because there's actually no real law that protects their rights."

Li points to worries that the government might use violence on students again if it felt threatened. The conformist education that numbs Chinese to activism is another problem. To express a different opinion is risky; to actively organize others to protest on behalf of that opinion is downright dangerous with little tangible benefit.

But to Li, the most compelling disincentive for youth to engage in political activity is that it presents a distraction from their primary pursuit: money. "If you can earn more money, you are successful," she said. "We don't educate people to chase their dreams; we just need to make more money. In China, we're just chasing GDP."

Li echoed the regrets often expressed over the lagging political consciousness of Chinese youth, saying that abstract social progress tends to be a low priority next to the many immediate pressures they face. "If you want to chase your dream, you'll have a low salary," she said. "You'll have no time to get a higher position. If you're a man, you must marry and you must have a house and a car. So it's big pressure. For me, it's very hard to ask the post-90s generation to chase their dreams."

Since graduating from college, Li had been working for a (technically illegal) gender equality NGO in Beijing with a paltry monthly income of 3,000 yuan ($480)—less than what most migrant laborers in the city made. Still, there was nowhere else she would rather be. "Places like Switzerland or Taiwan already have good gender equality—[they are] maybe thirty years ahead of us," she said. "Moving there would be nice, but there's not much I could do to help there. I love China; I just don't love the government."

"Change is step by step," Li continued. "But we must push it. Some people say there can't be absolute gender equality, so there's no point in fighting for it. But if you fight for something, it shouldn't be because you think it can be achieved. You should fight for it because it's right."

13

THE ENVIRONMENTALISTS

Nobody is quite sure who instigated what would become the largest "illegal" protest in China since 1989, but whoever it was launched something further-reaching than they ever anticipated.

It was the summer of 2007, and coastal Xiamen was preparing to build a massive petrochemical plant that promised to double the city's GDP. The plant had all the relevant government approvals to produce paraxylene (PX), a chemical used in everything from polyester to plastic bottles, but the environmental assessments had been illegally withheld from the public.

In late May, as local residents were complaining loudly about the controversial plant, an unidentified person circulated an explosive text message. "Once this extremely poisonous chemical is produced, it will be like an atomic bomb for the people of Xiamen," it read. "We will have leukemia and deformed babies. We want to live, we want to be healthy!"[1] The message, which was eventually forwarded to more than a million people, ended with a call for public protest on June 1.

The dangers mentioned in the text were exaggerated, and much of the worry came from an inaccurate rumor that PX was the same type of chemical responsible for a disastrous explosion in northeastern China two years earlier. Local television stations and newspapers undertook a propaganda blitz to dissuade people from these notions, but few trusted the state-controlled media. The government began to grow seriously worried about the possibility of people taking to the streets, especially on the eve of the June 4 Tiananmen Square anniversary. So leaders at

the very top of China's central government ordered the project sus-
pended. But this still was not enough.

On June 1, some ten thousand residents took to Xiamen's streets.
Marching past government buildings, they wore yellow ribbons and
held signs decrying the project's developer and the local Communist
Party chief. Temporary suspension of the project would not suffice—
they wanted it booted out of town forever. Anxious to prevent more
young students from joining in, the government dispatched paramilitary
forces to guard the gates of Xiamen University, but this move only
prompted protests to break out there.[2]

The demonstrations dispersed the following day, but the protesters
got their wish. The plant was moved out of the city altogether.

The Xiamen anti-PX movement, unprecedented in China, became a
catalyst for youth-driven environmental activism. In the following years,
comparably large "not in my backyard" protests would hit several more
cities while online movements against everything from air pollution to
soil contamination also took shape. It was the beginning of an awaken-
ing for tech-savvy, middle-class youth starting to demand more from life
than unrestrained economic growth.

One of these youth was Wei Hanyang. He was twenty-four years old
when I met him in 2013 in his hometown of Guangzhou, where he had
started an environmental NGO a few months earlier. "It's because of
the growth in civil awareness," he said of the protests that began with
Xiamen. "It also shows that the environmental sector isn't as sensitive as
other things. *People's Daily* and CCTV will even talk about it. That's
why I see potential here."[3]

Born to an upper-middle-class family, Hanyang spent his childhood
vacations traveling throughout the country with his parents, visiting
everything from the mountains of Tibet to the forests of Sichuan. "I
traveled to so many beautiful places," he recalled. "But I also saw a lot
of damage. I guess many people don't feel urgency about environmental issues because they haven't seen them and felt the problems."

China's "economic miracle" that saw thirty years of double-digit
GDP growth has left a legacy of environmental destruction that remains
unresolved. The statistics are frightening. About half of the rivers that
existed in China in 1990 have already dried up, and of those rivers and
lakes that remain, about 75 percent are "severely polluted."[4] Mean-

while, an estimated 20 percent of the country's arable land is contaminated, threatening an already scarce food supply.[5] The country's carbon emissions, already the highest in the world, are not projected to peak for another two decades.[6] All but a small handful of China's major cities fail to meet air pollution standards, and its countryside is dotted with over four hundred villages harboring abnormally high cancer rates.[7] The list goes on and on.

For Hanyang, the issue that first grabbed his attention was dams. Traveling to the upper Yangtze River, he saw hydropower projects ripping apart the serene forests and threatening to upend the surrounding people and wildlife.

Like most Chinese parents, Hanyang's wanted him to go into a stable and lucrative line of work. He agreed to follow in his father's footsteps and study finance and economics. In retrospect, it was a good choice. "I like economics because it tells me a lot about incentive schemes—why people do one thing but not another," Hanyang said. "That's highly related to environmental issues."

He studied at Hong Kong University, where he was exposed to information usually censored in mainland China, gaining a better sense of the economic and political factors contributing to the environmental crisis. But even on the mainland, many young Chinese have opportunities to learn about environmental responsibility during their college years. Clubs and startup NGOs have sprouted up on nearly every campus, with scores of students volunteering—some out of a real sense of civic duty, others seeking to boost their résumés. The first group with which Hanyang became involved was the China Youth Climate Action Network (CYCAN), a nationwide collaboration of college students originally formed to encourage energy efficiency in Chinese universities.

During this time, Hanyang revisited the issue that had awakened his environmental consciousness when a Hong Kong newspaper asked him to write about dam projects in southwest China. At the time, the region's three major river systems—the Nu, Mekong, and Yangtze—already had thirty-two major dams, but another hundred were under construction or proposed. An indefinite suspension of these projects, instituted by Premier Wen Jiabao in 2004 due to environmental concerns, appeared to be expiring as his term drew to an end in 2012. Developers and local officials licked their lips at all the hydropower potential and were keen to make up for lost time.[8]

What Hanyang found in his investigation of the construction projects shocked him. He saw the excavation of mountains, tainted waters, destroyed ecosystems, and sleepy villages along the river banks that would soon be submerged. "Few people know about the hydropower schemes," Hanyang said. "Almost no media talk about it."

In the 1990s and 2000s, the government had loudly boasted of its gargantuan Three Gorges project—the largest dam in the world—expecting that this engineering triumph would be a source of national pride. "But the result was that people were doubtful about it," Hanyang recalled. "Now they turn to a new strategy: keep a low profile. So [the level of] transparency is very bad."[9]

The experience showed Hanyang that, for any change to occur, public awareness of environmental issues was essential. To this end, he was inspired to set up his own NGO.

In 2002, China passed an Environmental Impact Assessment (EIA) law mandating that when the government is ready to approve a project its assessments must be disclosed to the public.[10] This is the law that was ignored in the Xiamen PX plant project. Hanyang noticed that, as with most such laws, enforcement was terrible. In many cases, projects were mentioned in fine print in obscure newspapers or on websites that

Wei Hanyang stands atop a dam on the upper Mekong River. (Photo: Wei Hanyang)

nobody actually read, allowing officials and developers to claim that they had satisfied the disclosure requirement with no public objections.

This strategy was used frequently in Hanyang's native Guangzhou and the rest of the Pearl River delta as new developments continued to sprout up in increasingly fragile areas. "The environmental capacity of this area is almost at the edge," Hanyang said. "But Guangdong still wants to push so much development. It's the GDP logic of the whole mainland."

The aim of Hanyang's new NGO, known as the Cross-Border Environment Concern Association (CECA), was to ensure proper public disclosure regarding these projects so that people could raise objections if they wished. In other words, it was intended to help achieve the aim of an existing ordinance. In many countries, Hanyang could have simply registered his new entity and gone straight to work. But the Chinese government, wary of grassroots organizations, made things more complicated.

Increasingly receptive to NGOs' assistance where official resources are stretched thin, the government has given the go-ahead to thousands of environmental NGOs over the past two decades. But registration remains a lengthy, precarious process involving numerous bureaus and years of patience. Chinese leaders still harbor fears that NGOs might allow people to more efficiently organize resistance against the government or be used by "hostile foreign forces" as a Trojan horse into China.[11] Even after getting approval, groups remain subject to restrictions on public fundraising, accepting foreign money, and setting up interprovincial branch offices that connect people from across the country. Because of these obstacles, many groups instead choose to register as a business under a special "civil nonenterprise" category. "This is a special word created by China," Hanyang explained with a laugh. "You just accept it."

Fortunately for him, the relatively progressive cities of Guangzhou and Shenzhen simplified the NGO process in 2012, allowing easier independent registration through a single bureau (similar reforms have since unfolded in other provinces as well). This was the final impetus he needed to launch his NGO.

Many others, though, are less fortunate. Beijing-based CYCAN, with which Hanyang remained affiliated, was still waiting for approval of its

NGO status after six years. This lack of formal approval made getting government support for projects difficult and left the organization vulnerable should someone in authority ever decide that CYCAN was a nuisance.

Li Lina, a post-80s Anhui native who worked with CYCAN and several other environmental organizations, described the love-hate relationship between these entities and the authorities. Often, certain quarters of the government are happy to collaborate with nonprofit groups; CYCAN had been praised and approached for dialogues by local environmental bureaus and China's powerful National Development and Reform Commission. But the security apparatus remained suspicious. Lina guessed that her group still could not get registered partly because some former members had been placed on a blacklist for publicizing cancer villages. "It depends on individuals," she said. "But these people just don't get why NGOs want to get involved. They think we might be a channel to criticize the government and only see us as opposition."[12]

At this stage, she and Hanyang both found it necessary to take a cooperative rather than antagonistic approach with the authorities and the companies causing environmental degradation. In a sea of powerful leaders and special interests, a small NGO with ambiguous legality stirring the pot too forcefully could put its members and its own existence at risk.[13] When I first reached out to Hanyang, he even downplayed the idea that he was an "environmentalist," saying that this was a loaded term in China. He simply described himself as working on very practical community problems.

Lina contrasted her work with the approach taken by Western NGOs like Greenpeace, which tend to take an adversarial approach with polluters. She called herself a "realist idealist"—keen to change things, but aware of the sociopolitical realities that mandate a slower transition from China's growth model. For her, the choices are to work within the government's terms or not at all.

At the same time, though, more antagonistic grassroots movements were achieving undeniable gains. When smog consumed Beijing in 2011, an Internet campaign prompted the local government to start publishing air pollution data.[14] In 2013, when the Ministry of Land and Resources declared national soil pollution data to be a "state secret," an online uproar eventually prompted the information's release.[15] Then there were the street protests. It is unlikely that officials ever would have budged on proceeding with lucrative chemical projects had the only resistance been a gentle nudge from small environmental groups.

"It raises strong questions among NGOs," Lina said. "Citizens are moving ahead while we're sort of lagging behind. As an NGO in China, you're constantly questioning what impact you can actually have."

Still, Lina stressed that achieving meaningful change requires more from young people than joining a one-time protest. A chemical plant in their backyard gets people involved for a day, but that does not do much for less visible issues that require sustained attention, like deforestation and ecosystem breakdown. However, far fewer young people are willing to make this sort of commitment.

Like Hanyang, Lina was also compelled to devote herself to the environment because of travel—in her case, a trip to Antarctica that she was awarded during college. "You see the most beautiful place in the world that's going to be destroyed by climate change," she recalled. "You gain a stronger heart for what you want to be and what you want to do."

She studied diplomacy and politics at Renmin University and later, as a graduate student, at Peking University—the quality of education that most young Chinese can only wish for. Upon graduation she accepted a lucrative job in sales and marketing for a foreign oil company. It was a dream come true for her family.

But Lina was unfulfilled, and she quit after eighteen months to go into NGO work, focusing on climate change and civic engagement. "My mom wasn't so happy about me quitting my job," she said. "Many families in China judge your job based on how much money you get. We had a big fight when I quit."

In the end, her mother relented after realizing that Lina's NGO salary was decent and that she could travel to international conferences. "That's good for her; she thinks it's fancy," Lina chuckled. "But some NGO employees have maybe half my salary. If I were there, it wouldn't be so easy for her to accept it."

Financial compensation is a key problem confronting civic-minded Chinese youth who might want to pursue careers in social advocacy. NGOs tend to be understaffed and underfunded everywhere in the world, and even more so when just obtaining official recognition is a great struggle. For bright young Chinese seeking to have a social impact, this means working long hours for low pay and low status—a

Li Lina during a trip to Antarctica. (Photo: Li Lina)

tough situation to accept in China's expensive cities. "For Germans, it's a matter of living a good life or better life," Lina said. "For us, it's life or death. I think in Beijing you need 4,000 yuan ($640) per month just to survive."

Over recent years Lina had watched with encouragement as the number of young people wanting to get involved with environmental initiatives grew rapidly. But many, after a short period of involvement, would say that their parents were pressuring them to leave environmentalism to do something more lucrative. "On one hand I sympathize with their choice, because it's not easy to make a living in China," she said. "But on the other hand, I feel it's a pity that they don't try more before they make this decision. Many give up on their first [NGO] job after graduation."

Lina lamented that most of her friends work only for money and live only for their lover, rather than finding some kind of greater purpose— be it environmentalism or something else. "The trip to Antarctica struck my heart so much that I couldn't ignore the deeper calling," she said.

"When I worked for [the oil company], I had this constant internal quarrel saying I needed to do climate change work."

Along with economic challenges, the lure of foreign lands also appears to be impeding youth involvement in Chinese environmentalism. The middle-class lifestyle and access to information that push young people to care more about their environment also enable them to go elsewhere if it is not to their liking. When Hanyang studied at Hong Kong University, there were three hundred mainland Chinese students in his program. These students were highly sought after—exactly the caliber of people needed in China's environmental sector, or in any other field for that matter. But upon graduation, only seven of the three hundred returned to the mainland.

Hanyang was one of the seven. He had plenty of opportunities in Hong Kong and a number of foreign countries. Even his parents felt he might be better off elsewhere. But in the end, he felt he could have the biggest impact in China.

This trend was hardly unique to his class. Great numbers of highly capable people have been leaving China, often citing environmental concerns as a major reason. In early 2013, Beijing experienced a so-called airpocalypse when air pollution levels reached twenty-five times the limit deemed safe by the World Health Organization. After this event and other periods of intense smog, agencies facilitating emigration reported spikes in business of as much as 300 percent. One agent who specialized in emigration to Australia told the *Global Times* that 80 percent of his customers cited pollution as their top concern, with education and the legal system the next two most frequent drivers.[16] A 2014 survey reiterated these trends when it found that 64 percent of wealthy Chinese were in the process of emigrating or said they planned to emigrate in the future.[17]

These issues have been covered extensively by Chinese media, which routinely warn of a brain drain and capital flight amounting to hundreds of billions of dollars each year. To Hanyang, though, the scariest implication is not necessarily the loss of money and talent, but what he labeled an "optimism outflow."

If China were an inescapable pool, he explained, then everyone would be motivated to fix its pollution and social justice problems. "But if these people have the choice to leave the pool, then they won't care anymore," he said. "If everyone grows up for the sole purpose of going abroad, that leaves your society in a very difficult dilemma."

Ironically, China's authoritarian system is frequently compared favorably to less efficient Western democracies on environmental issues. The centralized government's ability to quickly divert massive resources without resistance has indeed made it the world's top investor in green energy. But this investment has been likened to eating both Slimfast and KFC and calling it a diet. Alongside green energy initiatives, China is still increasing its consumption of coal as part of an overall strategy to satisfy its growing energy needs.

Furthermore, the central government is hardly as powerful as outsiders tend to assume. Special interests like the auto and oil industries exert tremendous influence on government decisions, and in many cases they play a dual role as regulators of the very same industries that they profit from.[18] Their state-owned nature makes the marriage of vested interests, money, and politics even closer than in the West. Untangling these webs requires a degree of political will that few Chinese leaders have demonstrated.

Even when the central government does enact good environmental policies, it has little power to enforce them all the way down the bureaucracy to the nation's tens of thousands of local governments, each with their own economic aims and vested interests. In his book *When a Billion Chinese Jump*, environmental journalist Jonathan Watts described how weak governance and pollution go hand in hand: "China's political system is neither dictatorship nor democracy. For the environment, it contains the worst elements of both. At the top, the state lacks the authority to impose pollution regulations and wildlife conservation laws, while at the bottom citizens lack the democratic tools of a free press, independent courts, and elections to defend their land, air and water."[19]

The dilemma facing the Communist Party today is how to balance the economic development that maintains its legitimacy along with mitigating the environmental costs also threatening that legitimacy. Educated, tech-savvy youth tend to acknowledge the benefits that China's rapid economic development has brought them, but they worry about the impact on their health and quality of life. "I admit even my family has benefited hugely from the economic development," Lina told me. "[My grandma] lives a happy life that she never could have imagined before. I'm not one who says all the development is crap and we shouldn't do it. But even though your family benefits, there are others who suffer."

In spite of China's green initiatives, blooming NGOs, and growing numbers of bold activists, things appear likely to get worse before they get better. Desertification continues to claim hundreds of square miles of land each year, threatening millions of farmers and even the capital city. Some fifty thousand new cars were sold every day in 2013 and the country's coal usage will soon surpass that of the rest of the world combined, keeping city skies black.[20] If present trends continue, China will lack one-fourth of the water it needs by 2030 as demand quickly outpaces supply.[21] The effect this will have on prices is a scary thought for all those already struggling to get by.

Given this potentially bleak future, it is not hard to see why many with the means are creating an exit plan for themselves. But for the vast majority of Chinese who stay, the unfolding environmental crisis will likely continue to cause more dissatisfaction and foment additional protests. If so, protesters may start finding authorities less accommodating than those in Xiamen.

In 2012, a student-led demonstration against a local copper plant in Shifang, Sichuan, involving tens of thousands of people turned violent. State media claimed that students rushed a government building and started overturning police cars. Riot police ended the fracas with batons and tear gas, leaving scores bloody and battered. Dozens were subsequently arrested (though the plant was ultimately canceled).[22]

In Maoming, Guangdong, in 2014, an anti-PX demonstration involving thousands also provoked a violent police reaction that, according to some accounts, may have left some dead. A local protester commented on Weibo, "All that's left now is a road to death. For our offspring, it's all worth it."[23]

Environmental demonstrations are nothing new in China. Ever since reforms began, there have been hundreds, if not thousands, of local protests each year against polluting developers and officials. The two factors that made Xiamen a turning point, though, were size and demographics. Quickly alerted through technology and easily moved into the streets by the collective excitement of their peer groups, young

Protesters at an anti-PX demonstration in Kunming, 2013. (Photo: Southbysoutheast.com)

students unencumbered by jobs and families were at the forefront of these urban protests.

As with fervent young protesters in any country, the novelty, adrenaline rush, and the excitement of a rebellious movement were probably just as instrumental in drawing people to the demonstrations as the environmental issues themselves. And given the misinformation and rumors that tend to precede these events, it is probably safe to assume that not all of the young participants were well informed about what they were protesting.

Regardless of their motivations and understanding, however, these demonstrations carry significance beyond the immediate environmental issues at hand. The fact that young people feel safe enough to take to the streets against authorities in such great numbers surely makes China's leaders lose sleep at night. It suggests that the fear tactics on which the Communist Party relies to keep firm control of the country's hotheaded youth are losing their luster.

Joshua Rosenzweig, a human-rights researcher who has chronicled dissent in China since 2002, told me that one of the unintended consequences of the state-induced amnesia regarding the bloodbath of 1989 might be that post-80s and post-90s youth have a relatively benign view of the Communist Party. "I do think that there's a generational factor in terms of recognizing the state's ability or willingness to use violence against the people," he said.[24]

For Chinese youth who have grown up largely unaffected by political upheaval while taking basic freedoms and economic security for granted, worrisome quality-of-life issues are beginning to outweigh the diminishing might of Big Brother. "Popular expectations about good and clean governance, transparency, participation, etc. will most likely continue to outpace the authorities' willingness and ability to accommodate them," Rosenzweig said. "Continued conflict is inevitable, and I wouldn't rule out another massive show of force at some point in the future."

As we sat outside a Beijing coffee shop, Lina spoke of how young NGO workers like herself and the bolder groups of grassroots activists were complementing one another to push things in the right direction. "What I do helps me understand how important this generation is and how important this country is," she said. "By nature, we won't be ignored by the world or history."

However, she constantly worries whether it will be enough. She invoked a common phrase that was popular under Mao: "People will triumph over nature" (*rendingshengtian*). "That's why a lot of people think we can make it," she said. "But frankly, I'm worried because of China's size and cumulative power. Scientists say there's a tipping point that we can't come back from."

Lina paused and looked upward as she quietly trailed off in an unfinished thought. "But as an environmentalist, if I believe that . . ."

Hanyang expressed a similar uncertainty about China's future that he would rather just not think about. Like Lina, all he can do is play his small role and hope that enough people like him can guide the country through the unprecedented challenges threatening to spiral out of control. When I asked about the Communist Party's ability to lead the nation through these challenges, he reiterated that he was committed to working within the system and helping to better enforce existing laws.

"But to some extent there are some big issues inherent in the system itself," he admitted. "If we don't overthrow it, perhaps some problems can never be settled."

14

THE JOURNALISTS

On the night of July 23, 2011, one of China's sleek new bullet trains barreled through Wenzhou, Zhejiang, with 558 passengers. Several miles away, lightning had struck a metal signaling box, bringing a separate train with over a thousand people to a halt on the track ahead. By the time the conductor noticed it looming large through his windshield, it was too late. The crash threw four coaches off a 65-foot-high viaduct, killing forty.

In the immediate aftermath, authorities clung to the standard response: cover up and downplay. Propaganda directives were sent to media outlets with strict instructions not to question or elaborate on official reports, but instead to promote "great love in the face of tragedy."[1]

But many suspected what would eventually be confirmed: the accident was not just the result of bad weather. Untrained railway workers and faulty communication systems sprouting from corruption and overzealous development at the Ministry of Railways were also at fault.[2]

Web censors tried to prevent critical discussion by social media users, but it was hopeless. "When a country is so corrupt that one lightning strike can cause a train crash . . . none of us are exempt," read one of the most retweeted Weibo messages. "China today is a train rushing through a lightning storm . . . we are all passengers."[3]

Less than twenty-four hours after the accident, workers were told to halt rescue operations. Soon afterward, a video of backhoes attempting to break apart and bury one of the train coaches surfaced. It appeared that officials were literally trying to bury the story. Even more dramatically, hours after the rescue search was called off, a two-year-old baby was discovered alive in the wreckage. At a subsequent press conference, a hapless railways spokesman told noticeably angry reporters that it was simply "a miracle."[4]

Authorities were widely ridiculed and condemned online, and attempts to censor the debacle only magnified it. In one fell swoop, the government had struck a powerful blow against its own credibility. It was one of the first major incidents in which microblogs shattered the Party's monopoly power over the public narrative.

The widely available information circulating online opened the door for more aggressive traditional media coverage. In defiance of a second propaganda directive to cease all critical reporting, the *Economic Observer* (EO) newspaper printed an eight-page feature one week after the accident, including a scathing commentary. "Yiyi, when you've grown up and started to understand this world, how should we explain to you everything that happened on July 23, 2011?" it said, speaking to the two-year-old child who had been found. "They called your survival a miracle, but how do we explain it to you: When respect for life had been trampled, caring forgotten, responsibility cast aside, the fact that you fought to survive—what kind of miracle is this? . . . Now, Yiyi, on behalf of you lying there on that sickbed and those lives buried in the ground, people are refusing to give up on finding the truth. Truth cannot be buried."[5]

A year after this incident, I applied for a job at the *Economic Observer*. The paper had started in 2001 as one of a very small handful of privately owned national newspapers. It hoped to become a Chinese equivalent to the *Financial Times,* and over the years it had indeed built a reputation for investigative journalism and challenging the Party line. Most notably, in 2010, EO deputy editor Zhang Hong took an unprecedented step in Chinese media history when he organized thirteen other newspapers to run a joint editorial calling for the government to abolish the *hukou* residence system. For this action, the government subsequently saw that he was "removed" from his job (though in reality he continued working under another title).

EO hired me as one of just two foreigners on its staff, and I quickly found the newspaper to be a breath of fresh air compared to the state-owned papers I had come into contact with. The journalists were young—mostly of the post-80s generation—fiercely intelligent, and hardly constrained in their thinking by the Party line. There was one major drawback they faced though. Their peers in state media were relatively sheltered by their state-owned status; EO reporters challenged authorities at their own risk.

As with any Chinese paper, self-censorship by reporters was critical. In a few prominent areas, such as Tiananmen, Falun Gong, and ethnic tensions, a clear line of demarcation told reporters where they could not go, but on most topics the line was blurry and always moving. Frequent directives from propaganda officials indicated items not to discuss, but this list was by no means all-inclusive. The resulting guessing game usually caused reporters to be overly cautious, but sometimes it led them unintentionally into taboo territory.

During my first month at the paper, two such transgressions occurred. The first came when the worst rainstorm in fifty years hit Beijing, causing catastrophic flooding that overwhelmed the city's unseen infrastructure (the inadequacy of which remains in stark contrast to the glitzy showcase buildings thrown up for the Olympics). The local government announced an official death toll of thirty-seven, then revised it to seventy-nine after heavy criticism. But for reporters on the ground, the numbers still did not quite add up.

Officials in a village popular with tourists on the city outskirts claimed that no deaths had been recorded there. But the EO found that locals were aware of three people who were swept away and still missing. The paper printed the story, renewing public skepticism about the overall death toll. Similar stories had frequently been written after previous disasters without retribution. But this one proved to be a major miscalculation.

After the story appeared, Beijing authorities seized copies from newsstands and local officials paid a visit to the EO office. Though in practice the paper was nationally circulated and headquartered in Beijing, it was officially licensed only as a local paper headquartered in Shandong. Such clerical matters are routinely ignored until they become convenient tools for authorities. Citing this technical violation, the Beijing government officials said that the paper had to shut down and get out of town.

It turned out that the critical article had come at a very bad time, because several high-ranking Beijing officials, including the city's mayor, were expecting promotions at the upcoming 18th Communist Party Congress.

News of the shutdown was leaked to foreign media, and eventually management negotiated a truce with officials to stay open. As a precautionary measure, the *"Economic Observer"* sign on the building was removed and replaced with one for the company's marketing arm, thereby suggesting that nothing was headquartered there and that no laws were being flouted.

But the paper soon angered another group of authorities when it reported that the corruption-ridden Ministry of Railways would soon be broken up and absorbed by separate entities. The roughly two million people employed within the railway system became concerned about their jobs, and the ministry was furious. EO was threatened with clo-

The entrance to *Economic Observer's* headquarters after Beijing authorities threatened to shut the paper down. The *Economic Observer* sign has been replaced with characters for the paper's advertising branch. (Photo: Eric Fish)

sure once again and slapped with a fine. The young reporter who had written the piece was "removed" and stripped of her journalist accreditation (she kept working under a pseudonym and was ultimately vindicated when the ministry was broken up the following year).

The two incidents made reporters aware that it was a very sensitive time. At the upcoming 18th Party Congress, most of the Politburo would be overturned and power would be transferred to Xi Jinping. An EO editor summoned all journalists for a meeting, warning them to be very careful for the next few months. Until the congress was over, the paper was to stay focused on economics.

Just in case any reporters had not gotten the message, they received one more not-so-subtle warning. A few days before the congress began, a few mysterious men in army fatigues entered the building and conspicuously walked through each department.

Journalists throughout the country were feeling similar pressures. Across town, Liu Zhiyi, the *Southern Weekend* intern who had gone undercover at Foxconn, was also feeling the pinch. "The time around the 18th Party Congress was a holiday for journalists," he laughed.[6]

Liu had become a journalist by accident after poor scores on his high school math exams prevented him from pursuing an information technology career. But in retrospect, he feels that it was a blessing in disguise. "When I went into [journalism], I felt very happy," he said. "You start feeling maybe there are problems you can stop."

By 2012, at age twenty-three, he was interning for *Caixin*, a respected independent financial magazine. Although he was still finishing his studies at Tsinghua University, his Foxconn reports had convinced editors that he was ready for the big time. He was sent to cover stories that might put even veteran reporters on edge.

In Inner Mongolia, he reported that a mine dump with millions of tons of metal waste powder was contaminating groundwater, affecting three thousand farmers and potentially harboring a radioactive threat. Local propaganda officials tracked him down during his research, but only after he had obtained nearly all the information he needed.

That did not mean he would be able to publish, though. Inner Mongolia's Party secretary at the time was up for promotion to the Politburo at the upcoming 18th Party Congress. The story was shelved for several months until after he had left. "The media environment is just like a stock market," Liu said. "Sometimes better, sometimes worse, but the main character has never changed."

A few months later, Liu was intercepted during an investigation of Shandong cancer villages. "That happens almost every time I report," Liu laughed. "You can only guess when and where." Police escorted him to the train station and got him a ticket back to Beijing, but they stopped at the gate. Liu went inside, waited a bit, and then walked right back out to continue reporting.

His whole trip to Shandong was a game of cat-and-mouse. Liu's phone was easy to track, and he had to use his ID card to check in at every hotel. Inevitably, someone would come banging on his door. "Eventually you feel tired and a little scared," he said. "You need a hard heart."

In the days leading up to the 18th Party Congress, the chokehold on media reporting apparently proved too much for some journalists. In 2008, Shanghai-based reporter Jian Guanzhou of the *Oriental Morning Post* had exposed the state-owned dairy company Sanlu's responsibility for tainted milk powder in one of China's largest ever food safety scandals. But by September 2012, he had had enough. "I've been at the *Oriental Morning Post* for ten years, during which I have poured the most precious years of my youth, my sorrow, my dreams and feelings into the purest of ideals," Jian wrote on Weibo. "Now my ideal is dead, so I'll get going. Take care, brothers!"[7]

Over the coming months, several other famous reporters would take the same step—some forced out after provocative reporting, others departing voluntarily after becoming frustrated by the moral compromises their job entailed. In 2011, a study showed that over 40 percent of China's investigative journalists wanted to change careers.[8] Wang Keqin, the EO's most prominent investigative journalist, reflected on Weibo about the rapidly deteriorating media environment. "It's getting colder," he said. "The winter is approaching."[9] He probably did not realize how right he was.

But as these veteran reporters were leaving the field, wide-eyed young journalism school graduates were coming up to take their place. In 2013 I met Shen Nianzu, a spunky twenty-three-year-old Fujian native hired by EO straight out of college. Contrary to Liu Zhiyi, she had known from the beginning that she wanted to be a journalist. "I never thought of doing anything else," she told me.[10]

During her sophomore year of college, she pulled strings so she could take the unusual step of starting a full-time internship in lieu of her required classes. She started at *Southern Weekend*, the Guangzhou-based paper known for its liberal bent. Shen worked for free at its Beijing bureau and lived among the "rat tribe" in a basement apartment. She described life there as "horrible" but regarded the opportunity as "precious." After doing another six-month internship at EO, she joined the paper full-time and wrote stories highlighting official privilege and corruption. "The propaganda department calls often," she laughed. "And it's always my fault. I always make trouble."

Every few months, we would take on a fresh batch of Chinese college students as interns in the English Department. When Shen Nianzu described how she had gotten into journalism, she sounded a lot like our interns at their first interviews. They came from some of China's best schools and were rabid social media followers, unindoctrinated and full of idealism. When we asked why they wanted to work at EO, they would inevitably mention Wang Keqin.

Wang, forty-eight years old, was one of China's leading investigative reporters. His most prominent achievements included unearthing a Henan AIDS epidemic caused by unsanitary blood donation schemes and exposing a major securities fraud racket run by local mafia. He had butted heads with both "black society" (gangs) and "red society" (officials), getting threatened with prison and death at various times.[11] For the elite, he was a nuisance and a threat. For those at the bottom, he was often the last hope. Occasionally, downtrodden commoners from the provinces whose grievances had been rebuffed by the government bureaucracy would wander into EO, asking where they could find "Teacher Wang."

For the aspiring reporters who had grown up glued to social media and addicted to discovering the truth behind the Party line, Wang represented an ideal to strive for. Sadly, I would have to give several of them their first disillusioning revelation about Chinese journalism.

After the Beijing flood story and a separate report on local media censorship that had drawn the ire of propaganda officials, EO felt under pressure. Wang's investigative department, which had written the stories, was stripped bare and eventually Wang himself was pushed out.

On his last day, he packed up two tons of case papers from petitioners who had come to him with their stories. "The things stacked here are misery, blood and tears," he wrote on Weibo. "But I've always seen them as treasures. They go with me wherever I go. I can throw away my furniture, but these cannot be discarded!" [12]

In the following days, I had to inform intern applicants who had yet to hear the news that their idol had been unceremoniously kicked to the curb by the very same paper he had inspired them to join. For several weeks, I could not help but feel embarrassed and conflicted about working there. Several of the Chinese reporters felt the same way. But it was hard to place too much blame on the higher-ups. It was just another battle in the war that they were constantly fighting with authorities. They had to carefully decide when to attack and when to retreat so they could fight another day.

It was these kinds of moral compromises that could wear on a journalist fast. For Shen Nianzu, the wide-eyed idealism she had harbored about changing the country through journalism quickly dampened. "Gradually, I feel I'm just a small person changing little things—I can't change the whole structure," she told me. "I have no hope that the ruling class will change." She looked up at me and laughed. "Why did you come from a democracy to such a nation?"

But politics was not the only source of stress. Surveys have identified reporters as the least desirable job category for a marriage partner in China. [13] The low pay, long and erratic hours, and inherent instability of the job make getting by a constant struggle. Not surprisingly, when opportunities to supplement income present themselves, more than a few reporters indulge.

Usually these supplements came in the form of "transportation fees" of a few hundred yuan when public-relations professionals were seeking coverage of their companies' events or product launches. I learned from a higher editor that accepting such payments was against EO policy, but most reporters seemed to view it as a perfectly normal part of the job.

Things sometimes appeared to go a step further when articles started resembling corporate advertisements. On occasion, management would send a company-wide e-mail informing employees that a certain journalist and his or her editor had been fined for "unprofessional reports." The fines could be as much as 1,000 yuan ($160), but the public humiliation was worse.

Accepting bribes in exchange for giving positive coverage or with-holding negative coverage was ubiquitous in China. One former editor-in-chief of a popular Chinese magazine proclaimed in 2014 that China's media had entered an "age of corruption."[14] This practice had even spawned a cottage industry of fake reporters who blackmail company bosses, threatening to cover embarrassing incidents and demanding payoffs. For real reporters, the allure of bribes was constant. But turn-ing them down and refusing to play by the rules of powerful corporate interests could get downright scary.

After EO published an unflattering article about a Chongqing real-estate company, a group of burly thugs with shaved heads showed up at the office looking for the reporter (who was tipped off and escaped before they could find his desk). Likewise, a television reporter I knew in Nanjing who did exposés on unscrupulous businesses would routine-ly receive threats and was once even sent an envelope containing a bullet. This reporter eventually gave up journalism in favor of hosting a cheesy Japanese-style obstacle-course TV show.

As with officialdom or any other Chinese profession vulnerable to corruption, journalists frequently faced the dilemma of whether to do what was righteous and extremely dangerous or swallow their pride and accept a stack of cash. During Wang Keqin's heyday in the early 2000s, making the righteous choice may have been a tad easier. In those years, which some have charitably deemed a "golden age" of investigative journalism in China, commercial watchdog papers like EO were al-lowed to thrive and reporters became bolder.[15] But then in 2003, the stability-minded Hu Jintao took over China's presidency. In the follow-ing year, new regulations on cross-provincial reporting attempted to rein in the media's growing annoyance of those in power.[16]

Zhang Hong, my former boss at EO and the editor behind the 2010 joint *hukou* editorial, told me that this was what began a gradual tight-ening of the press that would unfold for the next decade and beyond. "Even three years ago [journalism] was regarded as a good job," Zhang told me in early 2014 after he had left EO for the Hong Kong–based *South China Morning Post*. "You could still have influence and respect, and the payment wasn't bad."[17]

Zhang commented that the crunch on traditional papers brought about by the Internet was squeezing out jobs and lowering salaries while tightening restrictions were creating a media brain drain. "Journalism is just a job," he said. "The overall environment is becoming more materialistic and realistic. Passion isn't the driving force."

I asked why he himself had gotten into the field. "Sometimes I was idealistic," he replied. "I wanted to change society for the better and change the country for the next generation, but nothing changes. You just get frustrated."

I protested, reminding him of the waves he had created with the 2010 *hukou* joint editorial. "But what changed?" he asked, before answering his own question. "Nothing changed, it made no difference. People with dignity and passion get driven out of the newspaper business."

In late 2012, the 18th Party Congress came and went without incident, but any hopes that the media environment would relax were dashed when Xi Jinping further tightened the already ironclad grip on reporters. The following summer, he made his stance on the issue clear. "We must adhere to the Marxist view of journalism," he said in a speech. "We must communicate positive energy. We have to make sure the front of the Internet is firmly controlled by people who are loyal to Marxism, loyal to the Party, and loyal to the people."[18]

The "Marxist view of journalism" has three basic tenets: support Communist Party principles, criticize the "bourgeois concept of free speech," and maintain the correct "guidance of public opinion."[19] Soon after Xi's speech, it was announced that the three hundred thousand reporters working for state-owned media would be required to undergo a two-day Marxist journalism refresher course and pass a test. Propaganda Ministry officials would also be put in charge of top-tier journalism schools to ensure implementation of the required subject matter.[20] But as with all such top-down initiatives, it was hard to tell how effective the program was at the local level.

When I studied journalism at Tsinghua University, my Chinese classmates usually laughed off my questions about the concept of "Marxist journalism." One professor suggested that it might more accurately be called "nationalist journalism," but that was becoming a harder sell in an increasingly internationally oriented China.

The dean of the Tsinghua journalism school at the time, Liu Binjie, held a dual role as head of the General Administration of Press and Publication—China's chief censorship agency for print publications.

But like a growing number of journalism schools in the country, Tsing-hua had also started hiring foreign professors who had worked for Western media outlets. As a result, my Chinese classmates would listen to a professor from the state propaganda apparatus in one class and then study ethics with an American *Bloomberg News* reporter in the next. Students would debate questions like whether a journalist should be loyal to their country or their readers first, and attitudes among Chinese and foreigners were not so dissimilar.

The head of my journalism program, Shi Anbin, had taught for years in the United States before coming to Tsinghua, where he also trained government spokesmen. He agreed with Zhang Hong's assessment that young journalists today lack the idealism of his generation. "I would say most of them who choose journalism still have some ambition to change society," he opined. "But if you balance materialist and spiritual aspects, materialism wins out."[21]

Indeed, when my Chinese classmates looked for work after graduation, benefits trumped ideology. One student went from interning at *Bloomberg* to working for *People's Daily*. Another started at the official government news agency Xinhua, only to move to *Caixin* a few months later. Shi said this frequent pattern is one reason why he aims to expose students to both Marxist journalism and the Western philosophy of "professional" journalism. This way, no matter where they ended up, young reporters could better push things in a positive direction. "If they write something for *People's Daily,* they can also distill something from the *New York Times*," he said. "And those who work for *Caixin* will also have an idea of Marxist journalism so they know where the bottom line is."

Shi conceded that, with the drop in idealism and the Internet-induced upheaval in the news industry, newspapers were struggling. But he saw this as an opportunity to develop a new form of investigative journalism. When I spoke with him in early 2014, he was appealing to the Ministry of Education to require a course in "netizen [i.e., Internet citizen] journalism" for all university students, not just aspiring journalists. "I believe that in the future everyone will be a journalist," he said.

In many ways, that future had already arrived. After microblogs widely drew attention to the 2011 Wenzhou train crash, a new era of information dissemination that circumvented state censors was ushered in, with Weibo leading the charge. Over the following year, a series of officials fell after being exposed online—some by professional journalists, but others by ordinary citizens. In one especially damning incident, local Shaanxi officials gave a twenty-two-year-old woman a forced abortion after she had failed to pay a 40,000 yuan ($6,385) fine for violating the one-child policy. Officials then proceeded to place the dead seven-month-old fetus on the bed beside the woman.[22] Family members snapped a picture and posted it on Weibo, where it was forwarded some forty thousand times among enraged netizens. The officials involved were later fired, and the incident also exposed the widespread practice of forced abortion, of which many Chinese were previously unaware. It stirred a national debate about the one-child policy in which several major newspapers participated.

But the social media event that would shake the Communist Party harder than any other came at the beginning of 2013, when *Southern Weekend* tried publishing a New Year's editorial calling for constitutionalism. The original version never appeared. *Southern Weekend* reporters alleged that, in a break from the norm of working with editors on changes, Guangdong propaganda chief Tuo Zhan had unilaterally altered the editorial, turning it from a biting social commentary into an error-riddled puff piece glorifying the Communist Party. For *Southern Weekend* reporters fed up with increasingly overbearing censorship, it was the final straw. They publicly demanded Tuo Zhan's dismissal and threatened to go on strike.

The reporters were not rejecting censorship in general or demanding a free press. They just opposed particularly egregious intrusions. But their modest appeal sparked much more ambitious demands from public supporters.

Actress Yao Chen, who had 31 million Weibo followers, and actor Chen Kun (with 27 million followers) chimed in with messages of support for the paper, followed by dozens of other major public figures. Across the country, hundreds of college students uploaded pictures of themselves—most of them with their faces shown—holding placards that read "Let's go *Southern Weekend!*"[23] In an open letter, eighteen students at Guangzhou's Sun Yat-sen University wrote, "It is because we have yielded that power has become unbridled and wanton; it is because we have been silent that the Constitution has become a rubber stamp. Our yielding and our silence have not brought a return of our freedom and our radiance. Quite the opposite, they have brought the untempered intrusion and infiltration of rights by power."[24]

Perhaps the most remarkable show of support was the hundreds of young people who gathered outside *Southern Weekend*'s Guangzhou offices to protest. Some wore Guy Fawkes masks and signs demanding freedom of speech. One read, "If I don't stand up today, I won't be able to stand up tomorrow."[25]

As Guangdong authorities debated their response, protesters were tacitly allowed to stay. But in an attempt at intimidation, police walked around the demonstration taking pictures of participants. When one officer lifted his camera to capture a young woman's face, she raised two fingers to her cheek in a "V for victory" sign.

As the events unfolded, I was shocked by the fearlessness of the young protesters. It was not just another demonstration over environmental issues or land requisitions. They had a lot to lose by calling publicly for press freedom and very little tangible benefit to gain. They still represented a very small sample of Chinese youth, but they were a segment few people realized existed yet.

But in hindsight, the evolution of attitudes did not seem so strange. When I had first arrived in China five years earlier, the young people with whom I spoke usually defended the country's censorship system, echoing the Party line with comments like "If the truth were revealed, China would collapse" or "Poor people must support the leaders if we're to keep developing. They wouldn't if the media could criticize the leaders." Since the outbreak of microblogs, I was hearing such comments less often. One incident at a time, China's youth were gradually realizing that the country's press and speech restrictions did not just cover up abstract embarrassments. They hid petty corruption, tainted food, avoidable accidents, pollution, and unjust land grabs—injustices that could be prevented in the future if reported.

But in the end, whatever inspiration the event yielded slowly evaporated. *Southern Weekend*'s stand fizzled out in a negotiated truce with officials. The protesters went home, and soon the editor thought to have sparked the conflict with propaganda authorities was replaced. In late 2013 the paper shocked many when it inexplicably provided testimony that helped authorities to prosecute activists accused of "disturbing public order" by organizing protests of support.[26]

Still, the event's resolution might be seen as an improvement over the past. A decade earlier, in 2003, the Guangdong-based *Southern Metropolis Daily* had embarrassed provincial officials with reports on detention camps and SARS; two of its editors were slapped with lengthy prison sentences on trumped-up charges. "In the old days they'd just get rid of you completely, destroy you," Zhang Hong told me. "Now they just get someone else to do the job."

Throughout 2013, the Xi Jinping–led Communist Party continued a media crackdown that extended online. That year, the Supreme People's Court also ruled that "spreading rumors" on the Internet could result in up to three years in prison. On the surface, this ruling appeared to address a legitimate problem, since destructive false rumors did indeed run rampant on Weibo and other platforms. In one case, a pharmaceutical company lost one billion yuan ($160 million) in market value after a television actress with 26 million Weibo followers retweeted a doctor's false claims that the company's medicine had been proven toxic.[27] However, one of the first "rumormongers" arrested under the law was a sixteen-year-old boy in western China who questioned a police ruling that a local man had jumped to his death.[28] Over the following months, influential bloggers who spoke out against authorities were reined in through account deletions and even, in some cases, arrests on unrelated charges.[29] This ratcheting up of controls was accompanied by a raft of new restrictions on traditional media. In 2014, China was ranked 175th out of 180 countries on the World Press Freedom Index, just behind Iran and Vietnam.[30]

But even amid this clampdown, China was on an irreversible course of de facto democratization of permissible speech. Young people coming of age on social media were growing intolerant of official deception and less frightened of speaking up. The curtain had been pulled back on the once-mighty monolith, exposing a deeply insecure network of vulnerable bureaucrats. Though the journalism sector was going through ups and downs (mostly downs), young people continued to use social media to tug on the boundaries of permissible speech, making it easier for those within the professional media apparatus to push from the inside.

On its twelfth anniversary in April 2013, the *Economic Observer* ran an editorial reflecting on the role of media in modern China. "In an era where the Internet can penetrate every aspect of life, there are more and more channels for gaining information," it read. "But the difference between a responsible media and simple disseminators of information always lies in the fact that media must have social responsibility and the courage to confront lies. Media sees reporting facts as its fundamental mission. . . . Needless to say, sometimes the media must also keep silent. Silence is a kind of attitude. Just continuing to exist is often a difficult commitment to make. But it is a valuable one, because as long as you are still here, you will always have the possibility to speak out— even when it means suffering for doing so."[31]

The summer after the 2013 *Southern Weekend* protest, Liu Zhiyi graduated from Tsinghua and accepted his first full-time job at the paper. I asked him how he felt about embarking on a career in such a restrictive and uncertain environment. "Sooner or later the system will be changed," he said. "But I think it's later, not sooner."

He paused and cracked a smile. "But I don't even look for the destination, I just enjoy the trip."

15

GENERATIONS

Every Friday evening, at the main square of Beijing's Renmin University, hundreds of Chinese urbanites show up for English Corner. Between tall trees and lush bushes that enclose the stone grounds, students, teachers, professionals, dissidents, nationalists, foreigners, evangelists, and lonely singles all come together. A desire to practice English ostensibly unites them, but other motives abound.

The weekly gathering is perhaps the biggest of its kind in the capital, and some have dubbed it an unofficial "free speech zone" because of the wealth of topics discussed.[1] When I arrive and a group congregates around me, the first question is inevitably "Where are you from?" followed immediately by "What do you think of China?"

"America" and "It's complicated," I reply. A lengthy political discussion typically ensues.

In the late 1980s, across town, college students from around the city would assemble on another patch of land sheltered by brush. On a small hill in Purple Bamboo Park, hundreds gathered each Sunday morning, primarily to improve their English skills. But the discussions invariably turned to politics, a subject more comfortably broached in a foreign language.

Around that time, cities across the country had similar informal gatherings—in parks, classrooms, and public squares—where youth discussed the ills that had taken hold in their once-great country. They were eagerly picking up where their grandparents and great-grandparents had left off seven decades earlier, when China was emerging from imperial rule. Back then, youth lamented that an antiquated culture and a lack of democratic tools were keeping the country weak. The "New Culture Movement" culminated with a nationalistic uprising on May 4, 1919, as students lashed out at what they considered weak and corrupted leaders who had stood by idly as foreign powers handed Chinese territory to Japan in a post–World War I treaty.

The movement would eventually break into sparring factions—including Marxists who would go on to found the Communist Party—before sputtering out completely. When the CCP eventually came to power, it monopolized the legacy of May 4th and, for a generation, silenced all political ideas other than its own.

When Mao's iron-fisted rule ended after three decades, the nation agreed that change was long overdue. The message of Reform and Opening Up was touted, but with no clear roadmap as to how far change would extend. Throughout the late 1970s and 1980s, many of the ideas set aside after the New Culture Movement were picked up again and calls for reform grew louder, spilling out into the streets on many occasions. It was an era of openness and discussion that the country had not seen for more than half a century. But these discussions did not always pan out as they have been popularly romanticized.

Some of the first stirrings of the 1989 Tiananmen movement began four years earlier in, of all places, Japan. It was a period when the island nation was flooding China with aid loans and investment, partly as a means to access the alluring Chinese market and its natural resources. It was a time when China was hardly in a position to reciprocate and capitalize on the Japanese market. Amid soaring inflation, many Chinese resented this uneven economic exchange and felt it was the result of their government officials selling out the country for their own benefit. [2]

The final straw then came in August 1985 when Japanese Prime Minister Yasuhiro Nakasone visited a shrine for war martyrs that included some convicted of war crimes against China. Young Chinese cried foul. For years there had been isolated pockets of protest against restrictive university policies and conditions like poor food, overcrowded dormitories, and nighttime power cutoffs. [3] But with this incident, students were emboldened to take on bigger issues. Signs were put up at universities railing against Japan and the domestic leaders cozying up to it. One poster read "Commemorate the [Chinese] martyrs" and "Overthrow the corrupt cadres."[4]

On the September 18 anniversary of Japan's invasion of Manchuria, against the orders of school officials, hundreds of college students marched to Tiananmen Square to protest.[5] Over the next several months, more student protests erupted that were ostensibly aimed at Japan, though more and more voices critical of the Chinese government and official privilege were joining in.[6] Another demonstration was slated for Tiananmen Square in December of 1985 to mark the fiftieth anniversary of the 1935 December 9th Movement, where thousands of Chinese students had protested the Kuomintang government for its failure to resist Japanese aggression and its unwillingness to secure freedom of speech, press, and assembly. This time around, however, the students never made it to the square. Authorities succeeded in stopping them, but that success was fleeting.[7]

Over the next two years, protests continued at universities across the country that increasingly conflated antiforeign slogans with those against local corruption and authoritarianism. Gradually, they tilted almost completely toward political reform at home.[8] The protests spread to over 150 campuses across China (sometimes spilling back into Tiananmen Square and around local government bureaus) with some attracting tens of thousands of participants.[9] In 1987, Communist Party Chairman Hu Yaobang was pushed out of his position for taking a tolerant stance on the protests—a move that would come back to haunt the Communist Party.

In December 1988, nationalism again led to cries for democratic reform. That month in Nanjing, a brawl broke out after African students were prevented from bringing Chinese women through the gates of their university to attend a dance. In previous years, several large-scale racially motivated brawls had broken out at universities around China, often due to relations between African men and Chinese women.[10] And going back nearly a decade, Chinese students had frequently expressed resentment over what they saw as special treatment being bestowed upon foreign students in the form of better food and accommodations.[11]

In the immediate aftermath of the Nanjing incident, false rumors spread that Chinese women had been kidnapped, a Chinese security guard had been killed, and that officials were shielding the African murderers. [12] It implied an infuriating indication of China's weakness.

The story was not true, but the issues it represented struck a nerve for the students who were becoming increasingly aware of the corruption and privilege around them. They wanted to stand up and defend their country's dignity, but once again (as they saw it) they were thwarted by bought-off officials and an unjust legal system.

Students took to the streets of Nanjing by the thousand, besieging the foreign student dormitory and marching toward a railway station where Africans were thought to be headed, all while intermittently singing the Chinese national anthem. The protests were mostly directed at the alleged African perpetrators, with slogans like "Down with the black devils." [13] But their attention soon encompassed those thought to have shielded the foreigners. Slogans like "Protect human rights" slid into the chants, as did calls for political and legal reform. [14] The news spread to other cities, where local students joined what had started as a nationalistic anti-African protest. [15] Then, with the death of the popular reformist leader Hu Yaobang four months later, the volume of calls for change was cranked up. Years of "patriotic" protests had laid the foundation for the largest one of all in 1989.

The Tiananmen movement tends to be remembered as an anti-Communist rebellion aimed at installing electoral democracy. But of course, the reality was much more complex.

In China, democracy is a more abstract concept. It encompasses the will of the people, the rule of law, public accountability of leaders, and basic freedoms, but not necessarily direct national elections or a tripartite separation of powers. Most of the Tiananmen protesters were calling simply for substantive reform within the existing system. They wanted an overhaul, not an overthrow.

The Tiananmen protest itself was incoherent. There was no clear list of grievances. Many of the demands were contradictory. For the average participant, names of so-called student leaders like Chai Ling and Wu'er Kaixi meant very little, or nothing at all. These leaders had their own power struggles and quickly broke into factions, often adopting the same elitist and authoritarian tendencies as those they were railing against in the government. [16] Whatever control they had over the movement was confined to very small pockets of it. There were too many divergent demands for anyone to exert any meaningful leadership.

The movement spontaneously galvanized multiple segments of Chinese society, some of which were not otherwise politically active. Students complained of poor university conditions and overbearing restrictions on their personal lives. Workers felt they were not getting their share of the spoils from economic growth. Journalists wanted more press freedom.

At the same time though, the various groups shared several common concerns: rising prices, the difficulty of eking out a living, an unfair employment landscape, endemic nepotism, and official corruption. Democratic tools like transparency, the rule of law, and media freedom were viewed as ways of addressing these problems. Students overwhelmingly agreed with these vaguely defined ideas in principle, and they had been primed by the smaller protests that had taken shape in previous years. When they saw a major social movement brewing around them, the excitement pulled throngs of people into the streets who cared very little about politics. For a few weeks, a patchwork of ideas and desires could be aired openly and, it seemed, safely.

But the euphoria was short-lived. The subsequent crackdown halted the era of openness in its tracks, and once again a movement that had begun as a unified celebration of liberal ideas descended into factionalism, with the Communist Party emerging as the big winner. Hardliners used Tiananmen to justify tighter control and purge their liberal opponents within the Party.

But even though the liberal ideas took a beating, they were not dead. They just retreated back to their niches. As Beijing remained under martial law, with PLA troops swarming the city and rounding up "counterrevolutionaries," college students returned to Purple Bamboo Park. One month after the suppression, a *Chicago Tribune* reporter visited and was immediately inundated with questions. "Does your country allow political demonstrations?" "Do soldiers use bullets on people in your home?" "What do you think about our country now?" "How can I get a visa from your embassy?" One young man who had studied in the United States told the reporter that they were down, but not out. "It's all we have now, this corner," he said. "One day they will take it away, but there will always be more corners, more talk to keep the fire burning."[17]

He was right on all counts. That October, police officially banned people from gathering in the space. But even though many of their classmates had been mowed down by machine guns or thrown in prison in the preceding months, students remained defiant. They continued meeting by the dozen, brushing off plainclothes police who tried to shoo them away. [18]

Eventually, though, Beijing's biggest English Corner had to move. It carried on at Renmin University where, miraculously, it has remained ever since. [19]

Plainclothes police are still known to circulate throughout the Renmin square and listen in on conversations, but for the most part people can say what they want. Each time I went, I was impressed by the young people's knowledge of their country and mine. One high school student recited passages from the American Declaration of Independence. Another talked in depth about the palace intrigue behind the Bo Xilai scandal that saw one of China's twenty-five most powerful leaders purged in 2012.

On one occasion, I spoke with half a dozen college students who expressed their admiration of the US electoral process. "But I think China would implode if we tried that," one young man said with a smirk. "And actually, if we asked for it, we'd be shot. It's just something we can dream about."

"Of course you think that," a sixty-something man huffed from outside the circle. Then he turned to me, with a flippant finger aimed at the students. "Their whole generation is like that—brainwashed and useless." To everyone's amusement, the old man, who professed having been the victim of unspecified "political troubles" in earlier years, went on haranguing the "useless" youth.

The situation felt like a real-time editorial cartoon of prevailing attitudes both within and outside China. Domestically, China's millennials are viewed as brain-dead moochers, unappreciative of the hardship that earlier generations endured. Abroad, the contrast is even starker. The Tiananmen generation is perceived as brave, idealistic, rebellious, and willing to lay down their lives for democracy. The post-Tiananmen generation, however, is made up of brainwashed materialists, unwilling to fight for anything aside from a BMW or Louis Vuitton bag.

With all the social change that has transpired since Tiananmen, it is tempting to compare today's youth unfavorably to those of the 1980s. In the days leading up to the Tiananmen crackdown's twenty-fifth anniversary in spring 2014, many foreign journalists in Beijing took this approach by reporting students who expressed either ignorance or ambivalence toward the incident. Many of the reports, which usually failed to account for how the presence of a foreign reporter might have influenced responses on the sensitive topic, tended to portray naïve youths who had been manipulated into complacent views.

But when I broached the topic of Tiananmen with young people with whom I had already spent time building rapport, I often found fairly well-informed and nuanced opinions. "I really feel sorry for those students," one twenty-eight-year-old man at Renmin University told me. "But politically speaking, maybe it was necessary." Another post-80s man agreed. "Things look different once it becomes history," he said. "[Tiananmen] looks bad, but maybe there were some good things. Chinese really want stability above all else."

The grand bargain of authoritarian capitalism that emerged after Tiananmen has served most of the country very well. The subsequent twenty-five years was a period of stability and growth that China had not experienced in centuries. In some cases, young Chinese whom I have encountered have even aggressively defended what the government did at Tiananmen, given how uncompromising and factionalized the protestors were—though these people usually do not understand how unnecessarily violent and indiscriminate the massacre was. More often though, they say it is just not worth dredging up the past if it might stir things up in the present. Bringing up the memories of Tiananmen could only hurt them personally and threaten the grand bargain nationally, so it is pointless to do so. It is better to just enjoy the gains and tolerate the Party that has so far proven it can provide stability. It may not be a great government, but it is preferable to an unknown and potentially chaotic alternative.

This attitude and the promise of China's return to greatness carried the country through the 1990s and 2000s. The Communist Party successfully suppressed any group that could potentially replace it, while at the same time convincing the populace that their choice was simple: the current path of stable growth or chaos. But now, the political environment is gradually regressing and the allure of economic growth is being dwarfed by associated social and environmental problems. The Communist Party's ability to provide "stability" becomes more questionable by the day, and the concerns of youth are growing remarkably similar to those voiced at Tiananmen.

In September 2012 I headed to the Japanese embassy in Beijing, where reports had said that thousands of Chinese had gathered to protest the intensifying Diaoyu Islands dispute. When I arrived, packs were marching in circles with banners while taking turns throwing bottles, eggs, and rocks at the embassy. At the same time, images of vandalized Japanese cars and destroyed shops were emerging from around the country. Along with the photos of thousands congregated at major protest sites, they gave the impression that China was rabidly jingoistic. The government's "Patriotic Education," aimed at whipping up popular support on the back of anti-Japanese nationalism, had worked all too well.

But by attending a protest personally I also saw a slightly different picture. The motivation of a few hundred people decked out in patriotic garb was not in doubt; their loud shouts and intense glares at the embassy showed that they meant business. But even their anger was not all directed at Japan. Some began chanting "Down with Chinese traitors!" exhorting the corrupt government to develop a backbone and defend China. They were echoing slogans from the 1919 May 4th movement, the 1935 December 9th Movement, the 1985 anti-Japan protests, as well as the anti-African protests of 1988.

Meanwhile, the majority of the reported "thousands of protesters" stood on the periphery, their crossed arms and amused chuckles at chants like "Little Japan, fuck your mother" betraying a more passive role in the activities. I asked a twenty-six-year-old man on the sidelines why he had come. "I think it's cool," he replied with a grin.

More than a year later, a twenty-nine-year-old man on a train offered a similar recollection of why he attended the demonstrations. "I thought I might never get the chance to see a protest again," he said. "I thought it would be interesting."

He explained that, naturally, he sided with China on the Diaoyu Islands dispute and agreed in principle with standing up to Japan's actions, "but to be honest, I don't really have any strong feeling about Japan."

I had heard similar accounts from a few Chinese friends in the weeks after the protests. Their anger at Japan's actions and their general disdain for its historical transgressions were real. But that was not what drew them to "protest." For them, it was more about the novelty, unity with peers, and a sense of patriotic duty. The demonstrations were something they had never seen and might not see again. It appeared patriotic, unifying, and politically safe to join in, so they did. But that does not mean they were necessarily enamored of nationalism, as many assumed. A survey conducted in five major cities the following spring found that those who thought military force should be on the table as an option to deal with Japan were in the minority (41 percent); a majority advocated compromise (57 percent) or United Nations arbitration (62 percent). Even more surprisingly, it found that people among China's post-90s generation were less likely than older generations to advocate sending in troops in territorial disputes, casting doubt on the idea that the post-Tiananmen youth have been made more nationalistic than those of 1989.[20]

As tensions with Japan were heating up in the autumn of 2012, someone posted an online poll on Weibo asking, "If your child were born on the Diaoyu Islands, what nationality would you pick for him/her: Japan, Taiwan, Hong Kong, or the mainland?"

The poll was unscientific and its sample was disproportionally composed of the young middle-class urbanites who most heavily frequent Weibo, but the results were telling nonetheless. In the nine hours during which the post was up before censors took it down, Taiwan had drawn the most votes with 40 percent. Hong Kong and Japan followed, leaving mainland China in last place with just 15 percent. One user wrote, "Sigh. I picked Taiwan, but in fact I love this country. Just that I feel it doesn't love me."[21]

Post-80s Chinese journalist Helen Gao reflected on the survey results: "The same Chinese nationalism that drives citizens to stand up for their native land when outside forces challenge it could also sharpen their pain when they observe the depressingly wide gap between China as it is and China as they wish it could be."[22]

In the 1995 documentary *The Gate of Heavenly Peace*, several of the Tiananmen protest leaders looked back on the grievances that had led to their involvement. "Hu Yaobang was an incorruptible official," said worker Han Dongfang, contrasting him with other leaders. "He didn't have bank accounts overseas. His children did not hold high positions because he was the head of the Communist Party." Feng Congde, one of the student leaders, offered a different complaint: "No matter how hard you worked you couldn't get anywhere."[23]

In talking with scores of young Chinese over the past several years, I have heard these same statements repeated ad nauseum in various forms. Official privilege is universally recognized, as is the growing gap between the haves and have-nots. In the summer of 2014, Peking University announced results of a study that drove home just how much wealth had accumulated among the elite. It found that the richest 1 percent of Chinese households controlled a full one-third of the nation's wealth.[24] An earlier survey asked Chinese what they felt were "very big problems." The top three answers were rising prices, corrupt officials, and the rich–poor gap.[25]

Chinese do not need the media to inform them about corruption. Evidence of it is everywhere—in their companies, their schools, their hospitals, and even the air they breathe. One 2014 survey found that among forty-four countries, Chinese said more than anyone else that they feel it is necessary to pay bribes to get ahead in life.[26] The economic growth that pacified the Tiananmen generation is growing less impressive for the post-Tiananmen millennials who treat economic security as a given. More of them are demanding the right to uncensored information, a clean environment, and the freedom to speak up when wronged. To their annoyance, the government is instituting these rights too slowly, and even rolling them back in many cases.

As we have seen, this annoyance manifested itself in major public protest in 2013, for the first time since Tiananmen, when hundreds showed up at *Southern Weekend*'s office calling for press freedom. Their action seriously challenged prevailing assumptions that this generation was not willing to stick its neck out for lofty ideals.

Later, some touched on an even more sensitive subject. In June 2014, civil-rights lawyer Pu Zhiqiang was arrested with several others while attending a private memorial for the Tiananmen crackdown's twenty-fifth anniversary. In response, a dozen students uploaded pictures of themselves to Weibo, holding a sign with Pu's likeness. "We are the post-90s, you say we are immature, we are rebellious, we are wild. But we are definitely not brain-dead!" it said. "We are the post-90s, in

fact we are passionate, we are rising, we are ready to take on responsibility. Therefore we support Pu Zhiqiang!"[27]

Shortly after these pictures started circulating online, I got in touch
with Liao Minyue, the twenty-one-year-old design student who had
organized the campaign. To her surprise, many young students were
willing to show their faces in support of the cause, and even more e-
mailed to express their quiet support.

In her younger days, Liao had been a star student and a leader in the
Communist Party Youth League, but later she publicly jettisoned all
affiliation with the CCP. Paradoxically, her father worked in the Public
Security Bureau and her mother, Liu Ping, was a member of the New
Citizen's Movement, an activist group that advocated wealth disclosure
for government officials (the two had long since divorced). Before the
Pu Zhiqiang online campaign, Liao had been outspoken on issues like
asset disclosure and constitutionalism. Her activities had gotten her
"invited to tea" with authorities, and two companies where she interned
had warned her that she would be fired unless she ceased her activism.
"At the beginning, I was scared but later the fear evaporated because I
know what I do is just," she told me. "China's current law system clearly
isn't independent. Police, lawmakers, and courts belong to one family. I
don't want my parents living in a social system without law, and I don't
certainly don't want the same situation to remain for my generation and
even my kids' generation."[28]

She explained that she was an anomaly among her peers for her
outspokenness, but she recognized more and more post-90s youth developing a consciousness for injustice. "One improvement over the past
is that young people are willing to talk about topics that they wouldn't
have dared breach years earlier," she said, citing discussion of the Tiananmen Square crackdown as an example. "Post-90s have a much stronger desire to learn and innovate, and they're willing to bypass the constrained education to learn the real history. So I think there is great
hope for post-90s to promote democracy and constitutionalism."

Today, many people believe that modern Chinese youths' supposedly
materialistic and nationalistic attitudes preclude an event like Tiananmen from happening again. But for all their differences, the Tiananmen and post-Tiananmen generations have a lot more in common
than is commonly recognized.

Several student protests took place in the 1980s (and even the 1970s), but all were broken up before they could metastasize into anything larger. Arguably, one of the most significant factors that set 1989 apart was a prolonged rift between liberals and hardliners at the top of the Communist Party leadership. That rift allowed the demonstrations to go on relatively undisturbed and permitted the media to advertise them to the rest of the country, propelling them to the point where it seemed safe and cool to join. The core of vocal activists was joined by droves of citizens who, like many of the 2012 anti-Japan protesters, agreed with the cause in principle and considered themselves patriotic but did not see themselves as especially political or emotionally invested in the action.

Between the anti-Japan protests, the environmental demonstrations, and the outpouring of support for *Southern Weekend* in recent years, it is not hard to see the same potential in Chinese youth today. The key difference is that the Communist Party has invested heavily in ensuring that this potential is never again leveraged.

Days after I spoke with Liao Minyue, her mother was sentenced to six and a half years in prison on trumped-up charges for her activism with the New Citizen's Movement. Liao herself was summoned by authorities and forced to forfeit her passport. Having learned from Tiananmen and the collapse of the Soviet bloc several months later, the Party now presents a united front in public and aggressively stomps out any slight spark that could grow into opposition.

But perhaps an equally compelling factor keeping young Chinese from taking to the streets en masse is that, in spite of the constant crackdowns on a relatively small pool of dissidents, most people feel freer than ever before. Zhang Lijia, a Beijing-based writer who organized a worker protest in Nanjing during the Tiananmen movement, compared her generation to post-90s youth. "We were in a small cage," she told me. "There's still a cage today, but for many people it's gotten so big that they often don't even notice it."[29]

In 2011 China's most famous post-80s blogger, Han Han, similarly wrote a post entitled "Speaking of Revolution" that summed up how people of his generation feel. "If you ask the average man or woman in the street if they are free, they generally feel that they are," he wrote. "And if you ask them whether they need justice, the prevailing view is that so long as they personally don't suffer injustice, that's sufficient. It's not everyone who regularly experiences unfair treatment, so they won't identify with efforts to seek justice and freedom for others. In China it's very hard to formulate a demand that has collective appeal. So it's not a question of whether a revolution is needed or not, it's a question of whether it can possibly happen. My view is: it's neither possible nor necessary. But if you ask me whether China needs more substantial reform, my answer is: absolutely."[30]

Rather than a single massive demonstration calling on the government to reform, China's millennials will more likely push and pull on the system from ten thousand directions, very gradually—one minor conflict and issue at a time. On the whole, most twenty-something Chinese youth are neither the liberal revolutionaries that many want them to be nor the sheep that many imagine them to be.

Still, it would be foolish to rule anything out in China. After Xi Jinping took power in 2012, he began a ruthless crackdown on corruption that reached officials previously thought to be untouchable, and it had effects beyond what anybody in the West expected. It was massively popular with the public, leading to a prolonged honeymoon period for Xi. Public cynicism cooled and the protest movements that appeared to have been building up under Hu Jintao ebbed.

But just as instrumental in achieving these effects may have been Xi's other, less publicized, campaign. While he was cracking down on corruption, he also began a far-reaching crackdown on dissent and a culling of religious, social, and environmental activities that had been tacitly tolerated in prior years. It sent a chill through the circles of would-be activists.

Xi's anticorruption campaign, while unprecedented in its scope, differed little from all those that had preceded it. It relied not on grassroots reporting of corruption or independent courts enforcing the rule of law, but on selective purges. It remains to be seen whether the drive can continue to support Xi's popularity and pay dividends to the Communist Party's legitimacy without introducing more basic political reforms. Over the coming years, China's list of demographic, socioeconomic, and environmental woes are set to trend upward, and it seems unlikely that the public's tolerance and inhibitions will move any direction but downward. If rising grievances and shrinking patience among an increasingly affluent and vocal populace were to intersect with some sort of sudden catalyst that cast doubt on the CCP's ability to lead, it is not hard to imagine another youth-led political movement taking shape.

Any predictions about how China's hundreds of millions of millennials will shape their country are risky, but one thing is almost certain: like youth around the world, they will not sit back idly and accept the status quo inherited from their parents.

At the main stadium of Tsinghua University on a humid September afternoon, thousands of new freshmen approach in army fatigues. It is the end of their three weeks of *Junxun* military training.

PLA marching music blares over the speakers as the students pour through the gates in companies of 170. At the front, the tallest boy hoists up a red flag with his classmates following behind, eyes locked forward as they clumsily try to keep their steps in line. Several of the shortest girls in the back scamper to keep up, breaking the perfect synchronization.

Crowds of parents and curious locals line the bleachers and peek through the stadium's fence as an announcer shouts, "Make sure to practice the good thoughts, good behavior, and good habits you learned during *Junxun* in your future study and life!"

Finally, the last platoon settles into standing formation. The announcer says that military training is "one of the holiest tasks given by the People's Republic of China." After a few more exhortations about the importance of national defense and character building through *Junxun*, the performances begin. At one point, sounds of machine-gun fire and cannons are blasted from the speakers as plumes of smoke are released. Students fall to the ground and crawl forward, simulating the fog of war.

Finally, the atmosphere lightens and students take a seat. A series of university officials and military officers give speeches, often cracking jokes to the smiling students. "These twenty days of training have been unforgettable," says one of the PLA instructors. "If we did anything wrong, please forgive us. Now I would like to use a salute to say good-bye to the teachers and students, and may our friendship last forever!"

With that, the PLA instructors all stand and march off to the buses waiting to return them to base. Many of the girls (and several of the guys) begin crying as they watch their officers depart.

As the festivities were winding down, I approached a group of girls to ask how they view their generation relative to the common stereotypes. Eighteen-year-old Zhang Xiaonan from Heilongjiang responded with an almost defensive tone. "People discriminate against us and say we're spoiled only children," she said. "In fact, the post-90s are very independent and have many traditional spirits. Many things are changing, so we're also changing."[31]

When I suggested that foreigners may regard the endless drills and patriotism lessons in *Junxun* as part of a broader power play aimed at keeping their generation in line, eighteen-year-old Li Hao from Hebei scoffed. "That's a kind of discrimination. There are differences between countries. They see the same thing, but their impression is opposite."[32]

As if to prove her point, the closing ceremony drew to a close with school officials leading the students in one last revolutionary song. In contemporary China, who the song is directed against and who best champions its ideals remain ambiguous. Nevertheless, the girls smiled and sang along:

> Unity is strength.
> It's harder than iron,
> Stronger than steel.
> Toward the fascists open fire.
> Death to all nondemocratic systems!
> Toward the sun.
> Toward freedom.
> Toward a new China.

NOTES

PREFACE

1. Lim, Louisa. *The People's Republic of Amnesia: Tiananmen Revisited*. New York: Oxford University Press, 2014, 99.

2. Tang, Didi. "25 Years On, Tiananmen Barely Known to China Youth." Associated Press (Beijing), June 2, 2014. http://bigstory.ap.org/article/25-years-tiananmen-barely-known-china-youth.

3. Twenge, Jean M. *Generation Me: Why Today's Young Americans Are More Confident, Assertive, Entitled—and More Miserable Than Ever Before*. New York: Free Press, 2006.

4. Guo, Zhang, Ping Yang, and Wang Wei. "Do Not Frown When You See Post-90s." *Chinese Education and Society* 44, nos. 2–3 (2011): 65–69; Tong, Luding, and Marietta College. "The Young and the Restless: Grappling with the Young Chinese Consumer's Mindset." *Global Conference on Business and Finance Proceedings* 9, no. 1 (2014): 58–59.

5. "蒋方舟：我的清华体验" [Jiang Fangzhou: My Tsinghua Experience]. *Financial Times*, April 26, 2011. Accessed October 2, 2014. http://www.ftchinese.com/story/001038263?full=y.

I. BOOT CAMP

1. "Freshmen Fall In!" *Global Times*, September 10, 2009. Accessed November 13, 2013. http://www.globaltimes.cn/content/732227.shtml.

2. Pan, Kai. "Military Training for China's University Students" (video). CNReviews (blog), September 5, 2009. Accessed November 13, 2013. http://

cnreviews.com/life/society-culture/military-training-china-university-students-video_20090905.html.

3. Yang, Fenggang. Telephone interview by author, November 2011.

4. Yang, Yi. "Tiananmen Square Protest and College Job Placement Reform in the 1980s." *Journal of Contemporary China* 17, no. 7 (2014): 965–81.

5. Zhao, Dingxin. *The Power of Tiananmen State-Society Relations and the 1989 Beijing Student Movement*. Chicago: University of Chicago Press, 2001.

6. Vogel, Ezra F. *Deng Xiaoping and the Transformation of China*. Cambridge, MA: Belknap Press of Harvard University Press, 2011, 600.

7. *The Gate of Heavenly Peace* (documentary). Long Bow Group Inc. 1995. Transcript, http://citationmachine.net/index2.php?reqstyleid=0&stylebox=10.

8. WuDunn, Sheryl. "Chinese College Freshmen to Join Army First." *New York Times*, August 15, 1989.

9. Mason, David, and Jonathan Clements. "Tiananmen Square Thirteen Years After: The Prospects for Civil Unrest in China." *Asian Affairs* 29, no. 3 (2002): 166.

10. World Bank 2014 Data; Yeung, Wei-Jun J. "China's Higher Education Expansion and Social Stratification." *Asia Research Institute Working Paper Series* 199 (2013): 3.

11. Yang, Wanli. "At 97m and Growing, China Has Most Outbound Tourists." *China Daily*, January 9, 2014. Accessed October 1, 2014. http://www.chinadaily.com.cn/china/2014–01/09/content_17224806.htm.

12. Larsson, Milene. "Vice Meets Cui Jian" (interview, podcast video). Vice, August 27, 2008. Accessed February 23, 2014. http://www.vice.com/vice-meets/cui-jian.

13. "How Will China's Tech-Savvy, Post-90s Generation Shape the Nation?" CNN, July 19, 2010. Accessed November 13, 2013. http://www.cnn.com/2010/TECH/social.media/07/18/china.post90s.generation/.

14. "Rachel." Interview by author, Beijing, August-September 2011. Some quotations first appeared in Fish, Eric. "March of the Freshmen." *Foreign Policy*, November 10, 2011. http://www.foreignpolicy.com/articles/2011/11/10/march_of_the_freshmen.

15. Volkin, Michael. Telephone interview by author, August 2011. First quoted in Fish, "March of the Freshmen." For further reading see Volkin, Michael C. *The Ultimate Basic Training Guidebook*. New York: Savas Beatie LLC, 2005.

16. Grossman, Dave. *On Killing: The Psychological Cost of Learning to Kill in War and Society*. Boston: Little, Brown, 1995.

17. PLA Lieutenant. Interview by author, Beijing, October 2011.

18. "教育部关于在高级中学开展学生军事训练若干问题的意见" [Opinions from the Ministry of Education on Issues Relating to High School Student Military Training]. Ministry of Education of China, 2002. http://www.moe.gov.cn/publicfiles/business/htmlfiles/moe/s3289/201001/xxgk_81140.html.

19. Lim, Louisa. *The People's Republic of Amnesia: Tiananmen Revisited*, 107–8. New York: Oxford University Press, 2014.

20. "30th Statistical Report on Internet Development in China." Beijing: China Internet Network Information Center, 2012.

21. Guo, Baogang. *China's Quest for Political Legitimacy: The New Equity-Enhancing Politics*. Lanham, MD: Lexington Books, 2010.

22. Guo, Baogang. Telephone interview by author, September 2011. First quoted in Fish, "March of the Freshmen." For further reading see Guo, *China's Quest for Political Legitimacy*.

23. "90后女大学生军训戴耳环涂指甲引热议" [Female Post-90s Students Wearing Earrings and Painted Nails for Military Training Cause Heated Discussion]. news.163.com, September 19, 2008. Accessed October 7, 2014. http://news.163.com/08/0919/04/4M674J3A00011229.html.

24. "Female Post-90s Students Wearing Earrings." Comments Section. 163.com.

25. Zhang, Guo. "大学新生体质差引关注 基础教育'摧残'成主因" [Education 'Devastated,' Freshmen Cited Poor Health Concerns as the Main Reason]. *China Youth Daily*, September 17, 2012. Accessed November 13, 2013. http://news.yunnan.cn/html/2012–09/17/content_2405675.htm.

26. Li. Interview by author, Beijing, September 2011; Fish, "March of the Freshmen."

27. Zhang, Zhuo. "中国高校开展军训20年 近七成大学生称很有价值" [After 20 Years of Military Training, Nearly 70 Percent of College Students Find It Worthwhile]. *China Youth Daily* and Sina, September 26, 2005.

28. Davis, Becky. "Violence at Chinese High School Raises Questions about Mandatory Military Training." *New York Times*, August 28, 2014.

29. Davis, "Violence at Chinese High School."

30. Gang, Guo. Telephone interview by author, September 2011; Fish, "March of the Freshmen."

31. Wang, Xiaoying. "The Post-Communist Personality: The Spectre of China's Capitalist Market Reforms." *China Journal* 47 (2002): 1–17.

2. THE TEST

1. "考生出考场后得知母亲12天前去世" [After Exam, Test Taker Learns Mother Died 12 Days Prior]. news.163.com, June 10, 2012. http://news.163.com/photoview/00AP0001/24302.html.

2. Schmitz, Rob. "The Damaged Generation." *Marketplace*, June 6, 2011. Accessed October 28, 2014. http://www.marketplace.org/topics/chinopoly/damaged-generation.

3. Wu, Hongchao. "Analysis on the Reasons and Countermeasures for Educational Corruption." Huazhong Normal University, 2006.

4. Levin, Dan. "A Chinese Education, for a Price." *New York Times*, November 21, 2012. Accessed December 12, 2013. http://www.nytimes.com/2012/11/22/world/asia/in-china-schools-a-culture-of-bribery-spreads.html?pagewanted=all&_r=0&gwh=0C0DC14DF90D43513B24FF7F1EA652BF.

5. Beaton, Jessica. "The Worst of the 2010 Gaokao Essays." CNN, June 25, 2010. Accessed December 12, 2013. http://travel.cnn.com/shanghai/life/worst-2010-goakao-essay-312786.

6. Kracke, E. A. "Region, Family, and Individual in the Chinese Examination System." In *Chinese Thoughts & Institutions*. Chicago: University of Chicago Press, 1967.

7. Zhao, Yong. "The Emperors' Game." In *Who's Afraid of the Big Bad Dragon: Why China Has the Best (and Worst) Education System in the World*. Hoboken, NJ: Wiley, 2014.

8. Zhao, Yong. Telephone interview by author, September 2014; for further reading see Zhao, *Who's Afraid of the Big Bad Dragon*.

9. Branigan, Tania. "China Jails Teachers and Parents for Hi-tech Exam Cheating." *The Guardian*, April 3, 2009. Accessed December 12, 2013. http://www.theguardian.com/world/2009/apr/03/china-jails-exam-cheats.

10. Zheng, Jinran. "Gaokao Ghostwriters to Face Punishment." *China Daily*, June 18, 2014. Accessed June 20, 2014. http://usa.chinadaily.com.cn/china/2014-06/18/content_17595912.htm.

11. Beaton, Jessica. "10 Million Chinese Students, Metal Detectors and Danish Fishermen: It's the Gaokao." CNN, June 8, 2010. Accessed October 7, 2014. http://travel.cnn.com/shanghai/life/957-million-chinese-students-only-one-things-matters-week-gaokao-919014.

12. Moore, Malcolm. "Riot after Chinese Teachers Try to Stop Pupils Cheating." *The Telegraph*, June 20, 2013. Accessed December 12, 2013. http://www.telegraph.co.uk/news/worldnews/asia/china/10132391/Riot-after-Chinese-teachers-try-to-stop-pupils-cheating.html.

13. Melcher, Tom. "White Paper No. 4." Zinch. http://www.washcouncil.org/documents/pdf/WIEC2011_Fraud-in-China.pdf.

14. Gallagher, Brendon. "China Disqualifies Marathon 'Cheats.'" *The Telegraph*, January 22, 2010. Accessed December 12, 2013. http://www.telegraph.co.uk/sport/othersports/athletics/7051158/China-disqualifies-marathon-cheats.html.

15. "Exam Questions Remain." *China Daily*, September 9, 2014. Accessed October 7, 2014. http://usa.chinadaily.com.cn/opinion/2014–09/09/content_18563951.htm.

16. Fu, Yiqin. "China's Unfair College Admissions System." *The Atlantic*, June 19, 2013. Accessed December 12, 2013. http://www.theatlantic.com/china/archive/2013/06/chinas-unfair-college-admissions-system/276995/.

17. Wing, Kam, and Li Zhang. "The Hukou System and Rural-Urban Migration in China: Processes and Changes." *China Quarterly* 160 (1999): 818–55.

18. Luard, Tim. "China Rethinks Peasant 'Apartheid.'" BBC News, November 10, 2005. Accessed October 11, 2014. http://news.bbc.co.uk/2/hi/asia-pacific/4424944.stm.

19. Fu, "China's Unfair College Admissions System."

20. All-China Women's Federation Data, 2013.

21. Chuankai. Interview by author, Jinan, March 2013.

22. "上大学网百所中国虚假大学警示榜" [100 Fake Chinese Universities Warning List]. Shangdaxue, June 26, 2103. Accessed January 12, 2014. http://www.sdaxue.com/top/87.html.

3. THE UNIVERSITY

1. "普通高等学校辅导员队伍建设规定: 教育部令第24号" [Fudaoyuan in Colleges and Universities: Ministry of Education Order No. 24]. The Ministry of Education of China, 2006. Accessed October 8, 2014. http://www.moe.edu.cn/publicfiles/business/htmlfiles/moe/moe_621/201001/81843.html.

2. Li, Baoyuan. E-mail interview by author, March 2013.

3. "How Many Students Get a Tertiary Education?" In *Education at a Glance 2010: OECD Indicators* (OECD, 2010), 72.

4. "Government Refutes Reports of High College Dropout Rate." Xinhua, October 22, 2011. Accessed December 16, 2013. http://english.people.com.cn/202936/7623669.html.

5. Qiu, Jane. "Publish or Perish in China." *Nature* 463 (2010): 142–43.

6. Yang, Rui. Interview by author, Hong Kong, November 2013. For further reading see Yang, Rui. "Corruption in China's Higher Education System: A Malignant Tumour." *International Higher Education* 39 (2005): 18–20.

7. "Chinese Education Evaluators Are Passing Failing Schools." Seeing Red in China (blog), April 7, 2011. Accessed October 7, 2014. http://seeingredinchina.wordpress.com/2011/04/07/chinese-education-evaluators-are-passing-failing-schools/.

8. Sang, Guoyuan. E-mail interview by author, March 2013.

9. Shen, Nianzu. "'倒'在工地上的大学校长们" ['Downfall' College Presidents Who Fell During Construction]. *Economic Observer*, June 1, 2013. Accessed December 16, 2013. http://www.eeo.com.cn/2013/0601/244833.shtml.

10. "Tarnished Halls." *Global Times*, December 5, 2013. Accessed December 16, 2013. http://www.globaltimes.cn/content/830189.shtml.

11. "Tarnished Halls."

12. "Qingdao Teacher Fired after Inebriated Student Falls to Her Death." eChinacities, November 23, 2012. Accessed December 16, 2013. http://www.echinacities.com/news/Qingdao-Teacher-Fired-After-Inebriated-Student-Falls-to-Her-Death?cmteditid=.

13. Sun, Li, and Meidong Hu. "Behavior beyond Classes." *China Daily*, July 29, 2014. Accessed August 20, 2014. http://www.chinadaily.com.cn/2014–07/29/content_17945686.htm.

14. "China to Promote Equality in Education." Xinhua, November 15, 2013. Accessed December 16, 2013. http://news.xinhuanet.com/english/china/2013–11/15/c_132892157.htm.

15. Yang, Rui. Interview by author. For further reading see Xia, Jin, and Bin Feng. "Analysis of the Reasons and Countermeasures for Academic Corruption." *Chinese Education and Society* 40, no. 6 (2007): 95–105.

16. Ministry of Education Group. 思想道德修养与法律基础 [Morality and the Basis of Law], 6th ed. Higher Education Press, 2013.

17. "2010年考研政治答案部分选择题试题和答案" [2010 Political Exam Multiple Choice Questions and Answers]. kaoyan.hjenglish.com, January 1, 2010. Accessed November 8, 2013. http://kaoyan.hjenglish.com/detail/93558/.

18. Wang, Ji. Interview by author, Beijing, August 2011.

19. Simpson, Peter. "China's Vice President Orders More Thought Control over Students." *The Telegraph*, January 5, 2012. Accessed December 16, 2013. http://www.telegraph.co.uk/news/worldnews/asia/china/8995123/Chinas-vice-president-orders-more-thought-control-over-students.html.

20. "Document 9: A China File Translation." *China File*, November 8, 2013. Accessed December 16, 2013. http://www.chinafile.com/document-9-chinafile-translation.

21. Holley, David. "China Acts to Curb West's Influence: Regime Seeks Controls on Universities, Foreign Media." *New York Times*, July 16, 1989. Accessed December 16, 2013. http://articles.latimes.com/1989–07–16/news/mn-5937_1_foreign-media.

4. THE PATRIOTS

1. Fairclough, Gordon. "Chinese Dismayed by Tales of Tibet Violence." *Wall Street Journal*, March 25, 2008. Accessed July 14, 2014. http://online.wsj.com/news/articles/SB120638214966859837?mod=tff_main_tff_top.

2. Miles, James. Interview by CNN. "Transcript: James Miles Interview on Tibet." CNN, March 20, 2008. http://edition.cnn.com/2008/WORLD/asiapcf/03/20/tibet.miles.interview/.

3. "Timeline of Tibetan Protests in China." CNN, January 31, 2012. http://edition.cnn.com/2012/01/31/world/asia/tibet-protests-timeline/.

4. Zhang, Yiqian. "Correspondent Calling." *Global Times*, December 13, 2012. Accessed October 13, 2014. http://www.globaltimes.cn/content/750063.shtml.

5. Ye, Jun. "Lhasa Riot Reports Show Media Bias in West." *China Daily*, March 22, 2008. Accessed October 13, 2014. http://www.chinadaily.com.cn/china/2008–03/22/content_6557738.htm.

6. Xu, Nengyu. "一个'四月青年'的创富情怀" [An 'April Youth' Passion for Wealth and Public Goods]. *China Youth Daily*, May 10, 2010. Accessed October 13, 2014. http://zqb.cyol.com/content/2010–05/10/content_3221681.htm.

7. "CNN Statement on Tibet Coverage." CNN, March 28, 2008. Accessed September 14, 2013. http://edition.cnn.com/2008/US/03/28/tibet.statement/.

8. Graham-Harrison, Emma. "Disabled Torch Bearer Becomes Chinese Hero." ABC News, April 11, 2008. Accessed October 13, 2014. http://abcnews.go.com/International/story?id=4634434.

9. Branigan, Tania. "Chinese Nationalists Hit at Carrefour over Tibet." *The Guardian*, April 20, 2008. Accessed September 14, 2013. http://www.theguardian.com/world/2008/apr/21/china.france.

10. Tang, Jie. "2008! China Stand Up! 2008, 中国，站起来!" Recorded April 17, 2008. http://www.youtube.com/watch?v=MSTYhYkASsA.

11. "Foreign Ministry Spokesperson Qin Gang's Regular Press Conference on March 27, 2008." Ministry of Foreign Affairs of the People's Republic of China, March 28, 2008. Accessed September 14, 2013. http://www.fmprc.gov.cn/eng/xwfw/s2510/2511/t419160.htm.

12. Yang, Lijun, and Yongnian Zheng. "Fen Qings (Angry Youth) in Contemporary China." *Journal of Contemporary China* 21, no. 76 (2012): 637–53.

13. Rao, Jin. Interview by author, Beijing, March 2013.

14. Deng, Xiaoping. "Address to Officers at the Rank of General and above in Command of the Troops Enforcing Martial Law in Beijing." June 9, 1989. Accessed September 14, 2013. http://english.peopledaily.com.cn/dengxp/vol3/text/c1990.html.

15. Wang, Zheng. *Never Forget National Humiliation: Historical Memory in Chinese Politics and Foreign Relations*. New York: Columbia University Press, 2012, 99.

16. Wang, *Never Forget National Humiliation*, 48.

17. Wang, *Never Forget National Humiliation*, 101.

18. Shao, Xiaoyi, and David Stanway. "China Dismisses Japan Plan to Buy Disputed Islands." Reuters, July 8, 2012. http://www.reuters.com/article/2012/07/08/us-china-japan-islands-idUSBRE86701A20120708.

19. Smith, Sheila. "Why Japan, South Korea, and China Are So Riled Up over a Few Tiny Islands." *The Atlantic*, August 16, 2012. Accessed October 13, 2014. http://www.theatlantic.com/international/archive/2012/08/why-japan-south-korea-and-china-are-so-riled-up-over-a-few-tiny-islands/261224/.

20. "Confrontation Will Be Huge Mistake for Japan." *Global Times*, September 13, 2012. Accessed September 14, 2013. http://www.globaltimes.cn/content/732890.shtml.

21. "China Struggles to Curb Anger as Protesters Denounce Japan." Reuters, September 16, 2012. Accessed October 13, 2014. http://www.reuters.com/article/2012/09/16/china-japan-idUSL3E8KG02T20120916?type=marketsNews.

22. Chen, Ming. "砸车者蔡洋生存碎片" [Surviving Fragments of Cai Yang the Car Smasher]. *Southern Weekend*, October 11, 2012. Accessed August 18, 2014. http://www.infzm.com/content/81726.

23. Okudera, Atsushi. "Mother Says Arrested Chinese Protester Influenced by Anti-Japanese Dramas." *Asahi Shimbun*, October 24, 2012. Accessed September 14, 2013. http://ajw.asahi.com/article/asia/china/AJ201210240070.

24. Chen, "Surviving Fragments."

25. Chen, "Surviving Fragments."

26. Lam, Oiwan. "China: Protesters Arrested for Human Rights Banner at Anti-Japan Rally." *Global Voices*, September 17, 2012. Accessed September 14, 2013. http://globalvoicesonline.org/2012/09/17/china-protesters-arrested-for-carrying-wrong-banner-at-anti-japan-rally/.

27. Weiss, Jessica Chen. *Powerful Patriots: Nationalist Protest in China's Foreign Relations*. New York: Oxford University Press, 2014.

28. Weiss, Jessica Chen. Telephone interview by author, September 2014. For further reading see Weiss, *Powerful Patriots*.

29. Qiu, Zhenhai. "未来三年需有突破性的改革" [The Need for Breakthrough Reform over the Next Three Years]. *Southern Weekend*, October 11, 2012. Accessed October 13, 2014. http://www.infzm.com/content/99587.

30. Chubb, Andrew. "'War Is Good, It Reshuffles the Cards': Qiu Zhenhai's Taxi Ride." Southseaconversations, April 20, 2014. Accessed May 14, 2014.

http://southseaconversations.wordpress.com/2014/04/20/war-is-good-it-reshuffles-the-cards-qiu-zhenhais-taxi-ride/.

31. Chubb, Andrew. E-mail interview by author, May 2014. For further reading see Chubb, Andrew. "Chinese Public Opinion on Maritime Territorial Issues: Attention, Context, Government Performance, Policy, Confidence, Certainty and National Identity." Perth USAsia Centre, 2014.

5. FACTORY TOWN

1. Chung, Olivia. "Foxconn Suicide Toll Mounts." *Asia Times*, May 22, 2010. Accessed January 14, 2014. http://www.atimes.com/atimes/China_Business/LE22Cb01.html.

2. Liu, Zhiyi. "与机器相伴的青春和命运——潜伏富士康28天手记" [Youth and Fate Accompanied by Machines—Notes from 28 Days Undercover at Foxconn]. *Southern Weekend*, May 25, 2010. Accessed October 11, 2014. http://www.infzm.com/content/44881.

3. Uken, Cindy. "High Country Crisis." *Billings Gazette*, November 25, 2012. Accessed January 14, 2014. http://billingsgazette.com/news/state-and-regional/montana/montana-s-suicide-rate-leads-the-nation/article_b7b6f110–3e5c-5425-b7f6–792cc666008d.html.

4. Fan, Fumin. Interview by Qian Dong. "央视《新闻1+1》:富士康'七连跳'谜团" [CCTV 'News 1+1' Mystery of Seven Foxconn Jumpers]. CCTV, May 12, 2010. http://view.news.qq.com/a/20100513/000001.htm.

5. Liu, "Youth and Fate."

6. Zhang, Moran. "China's Urbanization Pace to Slow, So Will Growth." *International Business Times*, February 27, 2014. Accessed March 19, 2014. http://www.ibtimes.com/chinas-urbanization-pace-slow-so-will-growth-1558120.

7. Yao, Kevin. "China's Migrant Worker Pay Growth Nearly Halved in 2012." *Reuters*, May 27, 2013. Accessed January 14, 2014. http://articles.chicagotribune.com/2013–05–27/business/sns-rt-us-china-economy-migrantsbre94q03a-20130526_1_migrant-workers-national-bureau-shanxi.

8. Chan, Anita. "The Culture of Survival: Lives of Migrant Workers through the Prism of Private Letters." In Perry Link, Richard Madsen, and Paul Pickowicz, eds., *Popular China: Unofficial Culture in a Globalizing Society*. Boulder, CO: Rowman & Littlefield, 2002, 163–88.

9. Chan, "The Culture of Survival."

10. "White Collar Workers Lose Out as Factory Wages Rise in the Pearl River Delta." China Labor Bulletin, March 9, 2011. Accessed October 7, 2014.

http://www.clb.org.hk/en/content/white-collar-workers-lose-out-factory-wages-rise-pearl-river-delta-0.

11. Liu, Zhiyi. Interview by author, Beijing, October 2012.

12. Liu, "Youth and Fate."

13. Liu, "Youth and Fate."

14. Chan, Jenny, Pun Ngai, and Mark Seldon. "The Politics of Global Production: Apple, Foxconn and China's New Working Class." *New Technology, Work and Employment* 28, no. 2 (2013): 104.

15. Wan, William. "Foxconn Riot in China Seen as Likely to Recur." *Washington Post*, September 26, 2012. Accessed January 14, 2014. http://www.washingtonpost.com/world/asia_pacific/foxconn-riot-in-china-unlikely-to-be-the-last-experts-say/2012/09/25/1e6828b8–071c-11e2-afff-d6c7f20a83bf_story.html.

16. Sunflower Women Workers Centre. "The Sexual Harassment of Women Factory Workers in Guangzhou." November 25, 2013. Accessed January 14, 2014. http://www.clb.org.hk/en/sites/default/files/Image/research_report/sexual harassment survey sunflower centre.pdf.

17. Liu, "Youth and Fate."

18. Liu, Peng. Interview by author, Shenzhen, November 2013.

19. Huan, Cheng. Interview by author, Shenzhen, November 2013.

20. Chiang, Yilin, Emily Hannum, and Grace Kao. "It's Not Just about the Money: Motivations for Youth Migration in Rural China." *Asia-Pacific Education, Language Minorities and Migration Network Working Paper Series*: 20.

21. Anderlini, Jamil. "Chinese Labour Pool Begins to Drain." *Financial Times*, January 18, 2013. Accessed January 14, 2014. http://www.ft.com/intl/cms/s/0/ad1e00e6–6149–11e2–957e-00144feab49a.html?siteedition=intl.

22. Ngai, Pun, and Huilin Lu. "Unfinished Proletarianization: Self, Anger, and Class Action among the Second Generation of Peasant-Workers in Present-Day China." *Modern China* 36, no. 5 (2010): 493–519.

23. Barboza, David. "In China, Unlikely Labor Leader Just Wanted Middle-Class Life." *New York Times*, June 13, 2010. Accessed January 14, 2014. http://www.nytimes.com/2010/06/14/business/global/14honda.html?pagewanted=all&gwh=DD8C13B15F71965960FF251580828907&gwt=pay.

24. Cheng, Qijin, Feng Chen, and Paul Yip. "The Foxconn Suicides and Their Media Prominence: Is the Werther Effect Applicable in China?" *BMC Public Health* (2011). http://www.biomedcentral.com/1471–2458/11/841.

25. Moore, Malcolm. "'Mass Suicide Protest at Apple Manufacturer Foxconn Factory." *The Telegraph*, January 11, 2012. Accessed January 14, 2014. http://www.telegraph.co.uk/news/worldnews/asia/china/9006988/Mass-suicide-protest-at-Apple-manufacturer-Foxconn-factory.html.

26. Chan, Anita. Telephone interview by author, January 2014. For further reading see Chan, Anita. "Die Internationale Gewerkschaftsbewegung, Arbeitskonflikte und Aussichten auf Tarifverhandlungen in China" [The Trade Union Movement, China's Labour Protests and Prospects for Collective Bargaining]. In *Arbeitskampfe in China* [Labour Conflicts in China]. Vienna: Promedia Druck- Verlagsgesellschaft, 2013.

27. Lau, Kevin, and Stephen Green. "China's Rising Wages in Quest for Rural Workers Reach a Critical Milestone." *The Nation*, May 29, 2013. Accessed January 14, 2014. http://www.nationmultimedia.com/business/Chinas-rising-wages-in-quest-for-rural-workers-rea-30207052.html.

28. "Floating Population Records Decrease." *Global Times*, April 23, 2012. Accessed January 14, 2014. http://english.peopledaily.com.cn/90778/7795378.html.

29. China Labor Bulletin. "Searching for the Union: The Workers' Movement in China 2011–13." February 20, 2014. Accessed February 21, 2014. http://www.clb.org.hk/en/content/searching-union-workers%E2%80%99-movement-china-2011-13-0.

30. Boehler, Patrick. "Q&A: Strikes Peak in China with New Generation of Interconnected Blue-Collar Workers." *South China Morning Post*, August 13, 2014. Accessed August 20, 2014. http://www.scmp.com/news/china-insider/article/1572050/qa-strikes-peak-china-new-generation-interconnected-blue-collar.

6. THE ANTS

1. "New Grads Crowd Tightening Job Market." *Global Times*, May 28, 2013. Accessed January 11, 2014. http://www.globaltimes.cn/content/784976.shtml.

2. Liu, Geng. Interview by author, Beijing, September 2013.

3. Gan, Li. "Findings from the China Household Finance Survey." Texas A&M University and Southwestern University of Finance and Economics (2012). Accessed January 14, 2014. http://chfs.swufe.edu.cn/upload/files/Report-English-Sep-2012–2.pdf.

4. Naughton, Barry. *The Chinese Economy: Transitions and Growth.* Cambridge, MA: MIT Press, 2007, 186–87.

5. Breslin, Shaun. "The Politics of Chinese Trade and the Asian Financial Crises: Questioning the Wisdom of Export-Led Growth." *Third World Quarterly* 20, no. 6 (1999): 1179–99. doi:10.1080/01436599913352.

6. Yang, Dali. *Remaking the Chinese Leviathan: Market Transition and the Politics of Governance in China.* Stanford: Stanford University Press, 2005, 84.

7. Pei, Minxin. "Will China Become Another Indonesia?" *Foreign Policy* no. 119 (1999): 94–108.

8. Wang, Qinghua. "Crisis Management, Regime Survival and 'Guerrilla-Style' Policy-Making: The June 1999 Decision to Radically Expand Higher Education in China." *China Journal* no. 71 (2014): 132–52, 145.

9. Wang, "Crisis Management," 150.

10. "国家教委计划建设司纪宝成司长访谈录" [Interview with Ministry of Education Chief of Development and Planning Ji Baocheng]. *China Higher Education* no. 1 (1999): 7–11.

11. Yuan, Guofang, and Qingling Yang. "China's Dramatic Enlarged Enrollment to Higher Education: A Double-edged Sword." Paper presented at the 56th Annual Conference of the Comparative and International Education Society, Caribe Hilton, San Juan, Puerto Rico, 2012.

12. Minzner, Carl. "China's Higher Education Bubble." *China File*, September 3, 2013. Accessed January 14, 2014. http://www.chinafile.com/china-s-higher-education-bubble.

13. Yong, Zhao. Telephone interview by author, March 2013.

14. Guo, Weidong. "On the Reform of China's NCEE since 1977." PhD diss., Hebei University, 2008.

15. Waldmeir, Patty. "China's University System Faces Criticism for Being Unfit for a Modern Economy." *Financial Times*, October 7, 2014. Accessed October 16, 2014. http://www.ft.com/intl/cms/s/2/07c0aa44–283b-11e4–9ea9–00144feabdc0.html#axzz3GLietgTZ.

16. Roberts, Dexter. "A Dearth of Work for China's College Grads." *Businessweek*, September 1, 2010.

17. Lian, Si. 蚁族 [Ant Tribe]. Guilin: Guangxi Normal University Press, 2009.

18. "Ant Army Colonizes Suburbs." *Global Times*, January 20, 2010. Accessed October 16, 2014. http://www.globaltimes.cn/content/499907.shtml.

19. Wang, Huazhong. "'Ants' Feel the Bite of Being Forced Out." *China Daily*, June 2, 2010. Accessed January 14, 2014. http://www.chinadaily.com.cn/china/2010–06/02/content_9919814.htm.

20. MyCOS Institute. *2012 年中国大学生就业报告* [Chinese College Graduates Employment Annual Report 2012]. Beijing: Social Sciences Academic Press, 2012.

21. Feng, Sue. "Eight Questions: Lian Si, Author of *Ant Tribe*." *Wall Street Journal*, December 21, 2010. Accessed January 14, 2014. http://blogs.wsj.com/chinarealtime/2010/12/21/eight-questions-lian-si-author-of-ant-tribe/.

22. Feng, "Eight Questions."

23. Sun, Zhen, and Huang Huang. "83.5% 受访者感觉身边很多年轻人想拼爹" [83.5% Believe Their Peers Hope to Join the Competition of Family

Background]. *China Youth Daily*, August 16, 2013. Accessed October 23, 2014. http://zqb.cyol.com/html/2013–08/16/nw.D110000zgqnb_20130816_2–08.htm.

24. Li, Yu, and Weiting Wu. "90 后"的就业现实" [Post-90s Employment Reality]. *Economic Observer*, sec. Nation, June 24, 2013.

25. Tianya. "这个时代'寒门在难处贵子,'也许不服，不干" [In This Era 'A Poor Family Can No Longer Become Noble,' Perhaps Think It Is Unfair, Quit]. Last modified March 8, 2013. http://bbs.tianya.cn/post-funinfo-4011358–1.shtml.

26. Sheehan, Matt. "China's Funemployed Grads 'Gnaw on the Old.'" *Huffington Post*, September 26, 2014. Accessed November 4, 2014. http://www.huffingtonpost.com/2014/09/26/china-funemployment-youth_n_5886800.html.

27. Branigan, Tania. "Chinese Cash-for-Jobs Scam Netted £8m." *The Guardian*, May 20, 2013. Accessed January 14, 2014. http://www.theguardian.com/world/2013/may/20/chinese-cash-for-jobs-scam.

28. Li, Peilin. 社会蓝皮书：2014年中国社会形势分析与预测 [Society of China Analysis and Forecast (2014)]. Beijing: Chinese Academy of Social Sciences, Social Sciences Documentation Publishing House, 2013.

29. "China Hit-and-Run Driver Sentenced to Six Years in Jail." BBC News, January 30, 2011. Accessed October 16, 2014. http://www.bbc.co.uk/news/world-asia-pacific-12317756.

30. Rothwell, James. "Bo Guagua: The Student Playboy Whose Lavish Lifestyle Could Be His Downfall—As Father Bo Xilai Faces Prosecution." *The Independent*, September 10, 2013. Accessed October 16, 2014. http://www.independent.co.uk/student/news/bo-guagua-the-student-playboy-whose-lavish-lifestyle-could-be-his-downfall--as-father-bo-xilai-faces-prosecution-8807074.html.

31. Page, Jeremy. "Children of the Revolution." *Wall Street Journal*, November 26, 2011. Accessed January 14, 2014. http://online.wsj.com/news/articles/SB10001424053111904491704576572552793150470.

32. Market and Media Research Center of Peking University. "90 后毕业生饭碗报告" [Post-90s Graduate Job Report]. 2014. http://sta.ganji.com/att/project/2014/90/index.html.

33. Bland, Ben. "Young Chinese Shunning Factory Jobs, Says Foxconn Founder." *Financial Times*, October 7, 2013. Accessed January 14, 2014. http://www.ft.com/intl/cms/s/0/6f1576be-2f5a-11e3–8cb2–00144feab7de.html?siteedition=intl.

34. Walsh, Jon. "Why the Chinese Are the World's Most Stressed." *Wall Street Journal* Video. Regus. September 27, 2012. http://www.wsj.com/video/

why-the-chinese-are-the-world-most-stressed/
6A78DE82–72D6–4F21–8A30–6150D8D4B0C6.html.

35. Ipsos. "Global Attitudes on Materialism, Finances and Family" (2013). http://www.ipsos-na.com/news-polls/pressrelease.aspx?id=6359.

36. Grey, Judith. "24-Year-Old Ogilvy Employee Dies from 'Overwork.'" *Business Insider*, May 15, 2013. Accessed October 16, 2014. http://www. businessinsider.com/24-year-old-om-employee-dies-of-heart-attack-from-overwork-2013–5.

37. Chen, Xia. "China Has Fewest Paid Vacation Days in World." China.org.cn, August 2, 2011. Accessed October 16, 2014. http://www.china.org.cn/china/2011–08/02/content_23125687.htm.

38. Gan, Li. "Income Inequality and Consumption in China." Texas A&M University and Southwestern University of Finance and Economics, 2013. http://international.uiowa.edu/files/international.uiowa.edu/files/file_uploads/incomeinequalityinchina.pdf.

39. "Why Generation Y Yuppies Are Unhappy." Wait, But Why? (blog), September 9, 2013. Accessed January 15, 2014. http://waitbutwhy.com/2013/09/why-generation-y-yuppies-are-unhappy.html.

40. Wu, Yun. "让我们'占领长安街'吧!" [Let's 'Occupy Chang'an Avenue!']. DWNews, October 12, 2011. Accessed January 15, 2014. http://opinion.dwnews.com/news/2011–10–12/58207487.html.

41. Mackinnon, Mark. "Growing 'Occupy' Movement Makes China Nervous." *The Globe and Mail*, October 26, 2011. Accessed January 15, 2014. http://www.theglobeandmail.com/news/world/worldview/growing-occupy-movement-makes-china-nervous/article618621/.

42. Du, Guiyong. 中国网络社会心态报告 [China Social Psychology Network Report]. Fudan University Communication and National Governance Research Center, 2014.

43. Lin, Meilian. "Crowded Rat Race." *Global Times*, May 29, 2013. http://www.globaltimes.cn/content/785277.shtml.

44. Feng, "Eight Questions." Lian, Si. "蚁族2:谁的时代" [Ant Tribe II: Whose Time]. CITIC Publishing House, 2010.

7. THE GOLDEN RICE BOWL

1. August, Oliver. *Inside the Red Mansion: On the Trail of China's Most Wanted Man*. Boston: Houghton Mifflin, 2007.

2. Beech, Hannah. "Smuggler's Blues." *Time*, October 14, 2002. Accessed January 18, 2014. http://content.time.com/time/world/article/0,8599,2056114,00.html.

3. Hite, Brittany. "Chinese Grads Still Eager to Nab Government Jobs." *Wall Street Journal*, November 27, 2013. Accessed January 18, 2014. http://blogs.wsj.com/chinarealtime/2013/11/27/chinese-grads-still-eager-to-nab-government-jobs/.

4. "China's Civil Servants: Aspiring Mandarins." *The Economist*, December 16, 2010. Accessed October 17, 2014. http://www.economist.com/node/17732957; Roberts, Dexter. "In China, a 'Golden Rice Bowl' for Civil Service." *Businessweek*, October 26, 2012. Accessed October 16, 2014. http://www.businessweek.com/articles/2012–10–26/in-china-a-golden-rice-bowl-for-civil-service.

5. Xue, Bai, Zhang Zhongju, and Hua Dan. "关于大学生考公务员热及考试动机问题的调查研究" [Survey Research on Motivation of College Students Takes Civil Service Examination Tide Countermeasure]. *Hubei Social Science* 96, no. 1 (2010): 21–23; Zhai, Jiaoyi. "公务员职业吸引力深析" [Analysis on Graduates' Preference for the Civil Service]. *Public Administration Review* 19, no. 1 (2010): 27–42.

6. Tian, Guoliang. "高官腐败案例的启示" [Inspiration of High Official Corruption Cases]. Study Times, 2013.

7. Han, Yong. "Graft Breeds Graft." *News China Magazine*, September 2013. Accessed October 18, 2014. http://www.newschinamag.com/magazine/graft-breeds-graft. For further reading see Ren, Jianming, and Zhizhou Du. 腐败与反腐败理论、模型和方法 [Corruption and Anticorruption Theory: Models and Approaches]. Beijing: Tsinghua University Press, 2009.

8. Lim, Benjamin. "China's Xi Purging Corrupt Officials to Put Own Men in Place: Sources." Reuters, April 16, 2014. Accessed April 17, 2014. http://www.reuters.com/article/2014/04/16/us-china-corruption-xi-insight-idUSBREA3F1UT20140416.

9. Beech, "Smuggler's Blues."

10. Party Building Institute of the Communist Party Organization Department. 关于提高选人用人公信度的调研报告 [Research Report on Increasing Public Confidence in the Selection and Appointment of Cadres]. Communist Party Organization Department, 2014.

11. Moore, Malcolm. "Chinese Students Flock to Join the Communist Party." *The Telegraph*, August 9, 2013. Accessed January 18, 2014. http://www.telegraph.co.uk/news/worldnews/asia/china/10234401/Chinese-students-flock-to-join-the-Communist-Party.html; "China Communist Party 'Exceeds 80 Million Members.'" *BBC News*, June 11, 2011. Accessed October 18, 2014. http://www.bbc.co.uk/news/world-asia-pacific-13901509.

12. "中国少年先锋队章程" [Chinese Young Pioneers Charter]. National People's Congress, 2005. http://61.gqt.org.cn/sxd/200905/t20090512_239909.htm.

13. Fang, Ye. "大学名利场" [University Vanity Fair]. *Economic Observer*, sec. Lifestyle, September 12, 2012.

14. Jiang, Tao, and He Peixun. "入党申请书" [Application to Join the Party]. Hubei TV and Wuhan Steel Group. http://v.youku.com/v_show/id_XNjA0NDMwOTY=.html.

15. Chen, Xiaohui, and Chen Xingjun. "试论加强大学生入党动机教育" [On Strengthening Education of Motives to Join the Party among University Students]. *Journal of Yanan College of Education* 36, no. 2 (2002): 5.

16. Roberts, Dexter. "In China, a 'Golden Rice Bowl' for Civil Service." *Businessweek*, October 26, 2012. Accessed January 15, 2014. http://www.businessweek.com/articles/2012–10–26/in-china-a-golden-rice-bowl-for-civil-service; Li, Raymond. "Harder Than Ever to Find Prized Civil Service Job in China." *South China Morning Post*, November 5, 2013. Accessed October 17, 2014. http://www.scmp.com/news/china/article/1348306/civil-service-recruitment-speed-dating-applicant-admits.

17. Guo, Gang. "Party Recruitment of College Students in China." *Journal of Contemporary China* 14, no. 43 (2007): 371–93.

18. "学者建议将中共正式党员数量缩编3000万左右" [Scholars Suggest Downsizing Communist Party by 30 Million Members]. news.ifeng.com, May 18, 2003. Accessed October 18, 2014. http://news.ifeng.com/shendu/rmlt/detail_2013_05/18/25451326_0.shtml; Yuen, Lotus, trans. "Communist Party Membership Is Still the Ultimate Resume Booster." *The Atlantic*, May 29, 2013. Accessed January 19, 2014. http://www.theatlantic.com/china/archive/2013/05/communist-party-membership-is-still-the-ultimate-resume-booster/276347/.

19. Sanderson, Henry. "China's Communist Party Reports First New Member Drop in Decade." *Bloomberg News*, June 30, 2014. Accessed October 18, 2014. http://www.bloomberg.com/news/2014–06–30/china-s-communist-party-reports-first-new-member-drop-in-decade.html.

20. Ford, Peter. "How to Ensure a Movie Becomes a Blockbuster in China? Trickery." *Christian Science Monitor*, July 11, 2011. Accessed January 18, 2014. http://www.csmonitor.com/World/Global-News/2011/0711/How-to-ensure-a-movie-becomes-a-blockbuster-in-China-Trickery.

21. Lam, Oiwan. "China: Mixed Reactions to Communist Party Movie Epic." *Global Voices*, June 17, 2011. Accessed October 18, 2014. http://globalvoicesonline.org/2011/06/17/china-mixed-reactions-to-communist-party-movie-epic/.

22. Lim, "China's Xi Purging."

23. "'禁令年' 近八成公务员未收礼" [80 Percent of Officials Stop Taking Gifts Amid Ban]. *Beijing News*, January 9, 2014. Accessed January 15, 2014. http://www.bjnews.com.cn/feature/2014/01/09/301118.html.

24. Ranasinghe, Dhara. "Tough Times for Luxury Retail in China." CNBC, June 19, 2014. Accessed October 18, 2014. http://www.cnbc.com/id/101771742#.

8. THE ENTREPRENEURS

1. Yikai, Wang. "Will China Escape the Middle-Income Trap? A Politico-economic Theory of Growth and State Capitalism." University of Zurich (Job Market Paper), (2013): 34.

2. Xinhua. "Youth Urged to Contribute to Realization of 'Chinese Dream.'" May 4, 2013. Accessed May 14, 2014. http://news.xinhuanet.com/english/china/2013–05/04/c_132359537.htm.

3. Cohen, David. "Xi Jinping's Chinese Dream." *The Diplomat*, December 12, 2012. Accessed May 12, 2014. http://thediplomat.com/2012/12/xi-jinpings-chinese-dream/.

4. Shi, Yuzhi. "中国梦区别于美国梦的七大特征" [Seven Reasons Why the Chinese Dream Is Different from the American Dream]. *Seeking Truth*. Central Party School/Central Committee of the Communist Party of China. May 20, 2013. Accessed June 9, 2013. http://www.qstheory.cn/zz/zgtsshzyll/201305/t20130520_232259.htm.

5. Flannery, Russell. "Forbes China 30 Under 30: Meet 30 Young Entrepreneurial Disruptors in China." *Forbes*, March 11, 2013. Accessed October 18, 2014. http://www.forbes.com/sites/russellflannery/2013/03/11/forbes-china-30-under-30-meet-30-young-entrepreneural-disruptors-in-china/.

6. Shi, Kaiwen. Interview by author, Beijing, September 2013.

7. Lardy, Nicholas R. *Markets over Mao: The Rise of Private Business in China*. Institute for International Economics, 2014.

8. Zhang, Chunwei. "逐鹿打车APP" [Guru Taxi App]. *Economic Observer*, May 31, 2013, 41.

9. Fukuyama, Francis. *Trust: The Social Virtues and the Creation of Prosperity*. New York: Free Press, 1995.

10. Wang, Junxiu, and Yiyin Yang. 中国社会心态研究报告 *(2012–2013)* [Blue Book of Social Mentality Annual Report on Social Mentality of China (2012–2013)]. Beijing: Social Sciences Academic Press, 2013.

11. Rothstein, Bo, and Dietlind Stolle. "How Political Institutions Create and Destroy Social Capital: An Institutional Theory of Generalized Trust." Paper prepared for the 98th Meeting of the American Political Science Association, Boston, 2002.

12. White, Steve. Interview by author, Beijing, January 2014.

13. Zhang, Linxiu, Eli Pollak, Ross Darwin, Mathew Boswell, and Scott Rozelle. "Are Elite University Graduates Aiding China's Transition to an Innovation-based Economy? Results from a Career Choices Survey among Would-be Innovators in China and the USA." *Asia-Pacific Journal of Accounting and Economics*, no. 1 (2013): 58–69.

14. "China Becomes Largest Source of Overseas Students." Xinhua (Beijing), August 3, 2013. Accessed May 15, 2014. http://www.chinadaily.com.cn/china/2013-08/03/content_16868063.htm.

15. Bao, Beibei. "How Internet Censorship Is Curbing Innovation in China." *The Atlantic*, April 22, 2013. Accessed October 18, 2014. http://www.theatlantic.com/china/archive/2013/04/how-internet-censorship-is-curbing-innovation-in-china/275188/?single_page=true.

16. *The Economist*. "Vivek Wadhwa: Chinese Innovation Is a 'Giant Scam.'" FORA.tv, 2012. Accessed May 15, 2014. http://fora.tv/2012/03/28/An_Economist-Style_Debate_on_Global_Innovation/Vivek_Wadhwa_Chinese_Innovation_is_a_Giant_Scam.

17. Bell, Steve. Interview by author, Beijing, January 2014.

18. "Chinese Consumers: Doing It Their Way." *The Economist*, January 25, 2014. Accessed May 15, 2014. http://www.economist.com/news/briefing/21595019-market-growing-furiously-getting-tougher-foreign-firms-doing-it-their-way.

19. "Steve Jobs Biography Sells Out in China." *Silicon Republic*, October 27, 2011. Accessed May 23, 2014. http://www.siliconrepublic.com/digital-life/item/24246-steve-jobs-biography-sells.

9. THE LEFTOVERS

1. "Kathy." Interview by author, Beijing, December 2013.

2. Qian, Yue. "Marriage Squeeze for Highly Educated Women? Gender Differences in Assortative Marriage in Urban China." Master's thesis, Ohio State University, 2012.

3. Hong Fincher, Leta. *Leftover Women: The Resurgence of Gender Inequality in China*. London: Zed Books, 2014.

4. Hong Fincher, *Leftover Women*, 8.

5. National Bureau of Statistics. 2000 and 2010 National Census data.

6. Shanghai Municipal Civil Affairs Bureau 2012 data.

7. Xinhua. "Official Vows China Will Correct Gender Imbalance." May 24, 2012. Accessed May 15, 2014. http://news.xinhuanet.com/english/china/2012-05/24/c_131608451.htm.

8. Chen, Youhua. 中国和欧盟婚姻市场透视 [A Look at the Marriage Market in China and Europe]. Nanjing: Nanjing University Press, 2004.

9. Yang. Interview by author, Huanghua, October 2012.

10. Jin, Xiaoyi, Lige Liu, Yan Li, Marcus Feldman, and Shuzhuo Li. "'Bare Branches' and the Marriage Market in Rural China: Preliminary Evidence from a Village-Level Survey." *Chinese Sociological Review* 46, no. 1 (2013): 83–104. doi:0.2753/CSA2162-0555460104.

11. "China Warned on Gender Imbalance." BBC, August 24, 2007. Accessed May 15, 2014. http://news.bbc.co.uk/2/hi/asia-pacific/6962650.stm.

12. Hvistendahl, Mara. *Unnatural Selection: Choosing Boys over Girls, and the Consequences of a World Full of Men.* New York: Public Affairs, 2011, 28.

13. Mazur, Allan, and Joel Michalek. "Marriage, Divorce, and Male Testosterone." *Social Forces* 77, no. 1 (September 1998): 327.

14. Wright, Robert. *The Moral Animal.* New York: Pantheon, 1994, 100.

15. Edlund, Lina, Hongbin Li, Junjian Yi, and Junsen Zhang. "Sex Ratios and Crime: Evidence from China." February 6, 2009. Accessed May 15, 2014. http://igov.berkeley.edu/sites/default/files/Sex%20ratios%20and%20crime.pdf.

16. Hudson, Valerie M., and Andrea M. den Boer. *Bare Branches: The Security Implications of Asia's Surplus Male Population.* Cambridge, MA: MIT Press, 2004, 208.

17. Hudson, Valerie, and Andrea M. den Boer. "Surplus Males: The Dangers of Asia's Preference for Sons." *New York Times*, May 13, 2004. Accessed May 15, 2014. http://www.nytimes.com/2004/05/13/opinion/13iht-edhudson_ed3_.html.

18. Chin, Josh. "State TV Host Offers Advice on How to Throw Out 'Foreign Trash.'" *Wall Street Journal*, May 18, 2012. Accessed October 19, 2014. http://blogs.wsj.com/chinarealtime/2012/05/18/state-tv-host-offers-advice-on-how-to-throw-out-foreign-trash/?mod=WSJBlog.

19. Jin et al., "Bare Branches and the Marriage Market."

20. Liu, Lige, Xiaoyi Jin, Melissa Brown, and Marcus Feldman. "Male Marriage Squeeze and Inter-Provincial Marriage in Central China: Evidence from Anhui." *Journal of Contemporary China* 23, no. 86 (2014): 351–71. doi:10.1080/10670564.2013.832541.

21. Numbeo. "Property Prices Index for Country 2014." Last modified 2014. http://www.numbeo.com/property-investment/rankings_by_country.jsp.

22. Survey and Research Center for China Household Finance, Southwestern University of Finance and Economics. 2012. http://www.chfsdata.org/detail-19-26.html.

23. Wei, Shang-Jin, and Xiaobo Zhang. "The Competitive Saving Motive: Evidence from Rising Sex Ratios and Savings Rates in China." National Bureau of Economic Research working paper, June 2009.

24. Hong Fincher, *Leftover Women*, 7.

25. Deere, Carmen, and Cheryl Doss. "The Gender Asset Gap: What Do We Know and Why Does It Matter?" *Feminist Economics* 12, nos. 1–2 (2006): 39.

26. Hong Fincher, *Leftover Women*, 16.

27. Survey and Research Center for China Household Finance. *China Household Finance Survey.* Southwestern University of Finance and Economics, 2013.

28. Hong Fincher, *Leftover Women*, 102.

10. EATING BITTERNESS

1. Yang, Sijia. Interview by author, Beijing, January 2013. Some quotations first appeared in Fish, Eric. "'Eating Bitterness': Hardship and Opportunity for Rural Women in China." *The Atlantic*, May 17, 2013. http://www.theatlantic.com/china/archive/2013/05/eating-bitterness-hardship-and-opportunity-for-rural-women-in-china/275978/.

2. Luo, Tsun-Yin. Telephone interview by author, April 2013. For further reading see Luo, Tsun-Yin. "Marrying My Rapist?! The Cultural Trauma among Chinese Rape Survivors." *Gender and Society* 14, no. 4 (2000).

3. He, Guanghu. "Religion and Hope: A Perspective from Today's China." *The Humanities Study.* Chinese Academy of Social Sciences, 2003. Accessed October 20, 2014. http://bic.cass.cn/English/InfoShow/Article_Show_Forum2_Show.asp?ID=273&Title=The+Humanities+Study&strNavigation=Home-%3EForum&BigClassID=4&SmallClassID=8.

4. Wei, Xingzhu, Lu Li, and Therese Hesketh. "China's Excess Males, Sex Selective Abortion, and One Child Policy: Analysis of Data from 2005 National Intercensus Survey." *British Medical Journal*, 2009. Accessed December 16, 2013. http://dx.doi.org/10.1136/bmj.b1211.

5. Phillips, Michael, Xianyun Li, and Yanping Zhang. "Suicide Rates in China, 1995–99." *The Lancet*, no. 9309 (2002): 835–40.

6. Wang, Chong-Wen, Cecilia Chan, and Paul Yip. "Suicide Rates in China from 2002 to 2011: An Update." *Social Psychiatry and Psychiatric Epidemiology* 49, no. 6 (2014): 929–41.

7. Jing, Jun. Interview by author, Beijing, April 2013. For further reading see Jing, Jun, Xueya Wu, and Jie Zhang. "农村女性的迁移与中国自杀率的下降" [Rural Female Migration and a Decrease in China's Suicide Rate]. *China Agricultural University Journal of Social Sciences Edition* 27, no. 4 (2010).

8. Jing, Jun. Interview by author; Phillips, Michael. Telephone interview by author, April 2013.

9. Jing, Jun. Interview by author.

10. Stanford University and Chinese Academy of Science. "Understanding the Education Gap in Rural China." Stanford University Freeman Spogli Institute for International Studies. Accessed October 20, 2014. http://fsi.stanford.edu/research/understanding_the_education_gap_in_rural_china.

11. Brown, Philip, and Albert Park. "Education and Poverty in Rural China." *Economics of Education Review* 21 (2002): 523–41.

12. China National Bureau of Statistics, 2013.

13. "Gender Income Gap Continues to Widen." *China Daily*, May 16, 2013. Accessed May 18, 2014. http://english.people.com.cn/90882/8245636.html.

14. Zheng, Tiantian. *Red Lights: The Lives of Sex Workers in Postsocialist China*. Minneapolis: Regents of the University of Minnesota, 2009, 29.

15. Zhong, Wei. "透视中国的'性产业'" [A Close Look at China's 'Sex Industry']. *Lianhe Zaobao* (Beijing), October 2, 2000.

16. Yan. Interview by author, Beijing, April 2013.

17. Zheng, *Red Lights*, 74–84.

18. Jin, Xiaoyi, Lige Liu, Yan Li, Marcus Feldman, and Shuzhuo Li. "'Bare Branches' and the Marriage Market in Rural China: Preliminary Evidence from a Village-Level Survey." *Chinese Sociological Review* 46, no. 1 (2013): 83–104. doi:0.2753/CSA2162-0555460104.

19. "Shaanxi Police Arrest 37 for Rapes, Abductions." *Shanghai Daily*, August 22, 2012. Accessed December 16, 2013. http://www.china.org.cn/china/2012-08/22/content_26308198.htm.

11. FINDING FAITH

1. "Toddler's Survival Unlikely." *China Daily*, October 17, 2011. Accessed May 19, 2014. http://china.org.cn/china/2011-10/17/content_23641415.htm.

2. Chu, Zhen. Interview by author, Nanjing, November 2011. Some quotations first appeared in Fish, Eric. "China's 'Come to Jesus' Moment." *Foreign Policy*, February 15, 2012. Accessed November 1, 2014. http://www.foreignpolicy.com/articles/2012/02/15/china_christian_awakening.

3. Wang, Xiaoying. "The Post-Communist Personality: The Spectre of China's Capitalist Market Reforms." *China Journal*, no. 47 (2002): 1.

4. Yang, Fenggang. Telephone interview by author, August 2011. For further reading see Yang, Fenggang. "Lost in the Market, Saved at McDonald's: Conversion to Christianity in Urban China." *Journal for the Scientific Study of Religion* 44, no. 4 (2005): 423–41.

5. Chen, Boyuan. "China Has 23–40 Million Christians." China.org.cn, August 6, 2014. Accessed October 20, 2014. http://china.org.cn/china/2014-08/06/content_33161694.htm.

6. "Christianity in China: Sons of Heaven." *The Economist*, October 2, 2008. Accessed October 20, 2014. http://www.economist.com/node/12342509.

7. Overmyer, Daniel. "Religion in China Today." *China Quarterly* 174 (2003): 307–16.

8. Schell, Orville. *Mandate of Heaven: The Legacy of Tiananmen Square and the Next Generation of China's Leaders.* New York: Simon & Schuster, 1995, 246.

9. "Is Learning from Lei Feng Now Outdated?" *People's Daily Online*, March 8, 2010. Accessed May 19, 2014. http://news.xinhuanet.com/english2010/indepth/2010-03/08/c_13201861.htm.

10. "约瑟的彩衣的博客" [Joseph's Technicolor Dreamcoat Blog] (blog). "我认识的丁大卫：一个爱主的美国基督徒在东乡办教育" [I Know David Deems: An American Christian with Love for the Lord Teaching in Dongxiang]. February 2, 2010. Accessed May 19, 2014. http://blog.sina.com.cn/s/blog_4d87d8e20100hvqh.html.

11. "Hallelujah." Interview by author, Beijing, May 2012. Some quotations first appeared in Fish, Eric. "Missionaries in the Middle Kingdom." *Economic Observer*, October 12, 2012. Accessed November 1, 2014. http://www.eeo.com.cn/ens/2012/1012/234521.shtml.

12. Wan, William. "Chinese Leaders Still Suspicious of Religion, Party Document Shows." *Washington Post* (Beijing), December 19, 2012. Accessed May 23, 2014. http://www.washingtonpost.com/world/asia_pacific/chinese-leaders-still-suspicious-of-religion-party-document-shows/2012/12/18/706637f6-4856-11e2-ad54-580638ede391_story.html.

13. Wan, "Chinese Leaders Still Suspicious."

14. *The Gospel in China* (blog). "Police Situation Update—Released." August 9, 2011. Accessed May 23, 2014. http://gospelinchina.com/2011/08/08/571/.

15. "Sue." Interview by author, Nanjing, November 2011.

16. Wielander, Gerda. Interview by author, Beijing, August 2011 and April 2014. For further reading see Wielander, Gerda. "Beyond Repression and Resistance: Christian Love and China's Harmonious Society." *China Journal* 65, no. 1 (2011): 119–39.

17. Fei, Xiaotong, Gary G. Hamilton, and Zheng Wang. *From the Soil, the Foundations of Chinese Society: A Translation of Fei Xiaotong's Xiangtu Zhongguo, with an Introduction and Epilogue.* Berkeley: University of California Press, 1992.

18. Zhang, Lijia. "How Can I Be Proud of My China If We Are a Nation of 1.4bn Cold Hearts?" *The Guardian*, October 22, 2011. Accessed October 21, 2014. http://www.theguardian.com/commentisfree/2011/oct/22/china-nation-cold-hearts.

19. Wielander. Interview by author. Some quotations first appeared in Fish, "China's 'Come to Jesus' Moment."

20. Aikman, David. "Beijing's Theology of Repression." *Wall Street Journal*, July 11, 2011. Accessed October 21, 2014. http://online.wsj.com/news/articles/SB10001424052702304760604576428260216373754.

21. Moore, Malcolm. "Inside China's Most Radical Cult." *The Telegraph*, August 21, 2014. Accessed September 3, 2014. http://www.telegraph.co.uk/news/worldnews/asia/china/11046155/Inside-Chinas-most-radical-cult.html.

22. Peng, Guoxiang. E-mail interview by author, January 2012.

23. "把祖国的新疆建设得越来越美好" [Xinjiang Construction of the Motherland Getting Better and Better]. *People's Daily*, May 4, 2014. Accessed May 30, 2014. http://politics.people.com.cn/n/2014/0504/c1024-24968469.html.

24. Lim, Benjamin K., and Ben Blanchard. "Xi Jinping Hopes Traditional Faiths Can Fill Moral Void in China: Sources." *Reuters*, September 29, 2013. Accessed May 23, 2014. http://www.reuters.com/article/2013/09/29/us-china-politics-vacuum-idUSBRE98S0GS20130929.

25. Johnson, Ian. "Church-State Clash in China Coalesces around a Toppled Spire." *New York Times* (Wenzhou), May 29, 2014. Accessed May 31, 2014. http://www.nytimes.com/2014/05/30/world/asia/church-state-clash-in-china-coalesces-around-a-toppled-spire.html?hp&_r=0.

26. Wang, Hongyi. "China Plans Establishment of Christian Theology." *China Daily*, August 7, 2014. Accessed October 20, 2014. http://www.chinadaily.com.cn/china/2014-08/07/content_18262848.htm.

27. Kaiman, Jonathan. "Going Undercover, the Evangelists Taking Jesus to Tibet." *The Guardian*, February 21, 2013. Accessed October 20, 2014. http://www.theguardian.com/world/2013/feb/21/going-undercover-christian-evangelists-tibet.

12. THE SOCIAL ACTIVISTS

1. Maizi, Li. Interview by author, Beijing, March 2013.

2. Gao, Jing. "Shanghai Metro Blames Sexual Harassment on Women's Immodest Clothing: Netizens' Reaction." *Ministry of Tofu*, June 26, 2012. Accessed May 23, 2014. http://www.ministryoftofu.com/2012/06/shanghai-

metro-blames-sexual-harassment-on-womens-immodest-clothing-netizens-reaction/.

3. "Quarter of Chinese Women Suffer Domestic Violence." Xinhua (Beijing), November 26, 2013. Accessed May 23, 2014. http://www.chinadaily.com.cn/china/2013-11/26/content_17133231.htm; Wang, Xiangxian, Gang Fang, and Hongtao Li. *Research on Gender-Based Violence and Masculinities in China: Quantitative Findings*. Institute of Sexuality and Gender Studies at Beijing Forestry University and the Anti-Domestic Violence Network, with support from UNFPA China and Partners for Prevention, 2013.

4. Standing Committee of the Ninth National People's Congress. *Marriage Law of the People's Republic of China*. 2001. http://www.npc.gov.cn/englishnpc/Law/2007-12/13/content_1384064.htm; "China Mulls Family Abuse Law." Xinhua, November 25, 2014. Accessed November 25, 2014. http://news.xinhuanet.com/english/china/2014-11/25/c_133813641.htm.

5. Forsythe, Michael. "China's Spending on Internal Police Force in 2010 Outstrips Defense Budget." *Bloomberg*, March 6, 2011. Accessed May 23, 2014. http://www.bloomberg.com/news/2011-03-06/china-s-spending-on-internal-police-force-in-2010-outstrips-defense-budget.html.

6. Wei, Xiaogang. Interview by author, Beijing, March 2013.

7. Tatlow, Didi. "Why Do Men Dominate Chinese Politics? Because They're 'Just Too Superb.'" *New York Times*, March 13, 2014. Accessed May 23, 2014. http://sinosphere.blogs.nytimes.com/2014/03/13/why-do-men-dominate-chinese-politics-because-theyre-just-too-superb/?_php=true&_type=blogs&_php=true&_type=blogs&_r=1&.

8. Neilands, Torsten, Wayne Steward, and Kyung-Hee Choi. "Assessment of Stigma Towards Homosexuality in China: A Study of Men Who Have Sex with Men." *Archives of Sexual Behavior* 37, no. 5 (2008): 838–44.

9. Xin, Ying. Interview by author, Beijing, August 2013.

10. Jiang, Steven. "In China, Activists Fight for Gay Marriage." CNN (Shangfang), n.d. Accessed June 30, 2013. http://edition.cnn.com/2013/06/27/world/asia/china-gay-rights-jiang.

11. Balenieri, Raphael. "Taboos Push China's Gay Men to Wed Women." Al Jazeera, April 1, 2013. Accessed October 21, 2014. http://m.aljazeera.com/story/2013319931339528103.

12. Hu, Qingyun. "Gay Husband Committed No Fraud: Court." *Global Times*, January 8, 2013. Accessed October 21, 2014. http://www.globaltimes.cn/content/754400.shtml.

13. "China's 'Occupy' Toilet Protests Spread." *Agence France Presse*, February 24, 2012. Accessed November 7, 2014. http://newsinfo.inquirer.net/150969/chinas-occupy-toilet-protests-spread.

14. Boehler, Patrick. "Death Sentence Overturned in 'Landmark' Chinese Domestic Violence Case." *South China Morning Post*, June 24, 2014. Accessed October 21, 2014. http://www.scmp.com/news/china-insider/article/1539450/death-sentence-overturned-landmark-chinese-domestic-violence-case?page=all.

13. THE ENVIRONMENTALISTS

1. Landsberg, Mitchell. "China City Gets the (Text) Message." *Los Angeles Times*, June 1, 2007. Accessed October 23, 2014. http://articles.latimes.com/2007/jun/01/world/fg-china1.

2. Geall, Sam. *China and the Environment.* London: Zed Books, 2013, 149.

3. Wei, Hanyang. Interview by author, Guangzhou, November 2013.

4. Hamlin, Kevin. "China Coal-Fired Economy Dying of Thirst as Mines Lack Water." *Bloomberg*, July 24, 2013. Accessed May 23, 2014. http://www.businessweek.com/printer/articles/556406?type=bloomberg.

5. Wu, Wensong. "Quality of Arable Land 'Worrying.'" *China Daily*, April 18, 2014.

6. McGrath, Matt. "China's Experts Divided over Carbon Emissions Peak." BBC News, June 5, 2014. Accessed October 23, 2014. http://www.bbc.com/news/science-environment-27538716.

7. Wang, Qian. "Big Cities Fail to Meet Air Standards." *China Daily*, March 9, 2014. Accessed October 23, 2014. http://www.chinadaily.com.cn/china/2014npcandcppcc/2014-03/09/content_17333356.htm; Watts, Jonathan. "China's 'Cancer Villages' Reveal Dark Side of Economic Boom." *The Guardian*, June 6, 2010. Accessed October 23, 2014. http://www.theguardian.com/environment/2010/jun/07/china-cancer-villages-industrial-pollution.

8. Chen, Yong, and Liangbing Xie. "找回'失去的五年'" [Making Up for the 'Lost 5 Years']. *Economic Observer*, December 31, 2010, 11.

9. For further reading see Lee, Yuen-Ching. "Global Capital, National Development and Transnational Environmental Activism: Conflict and the Three Gorges Dam." *Journal of Contemporary Asia* 43, no. 1 (2013): 102–26.

10. The Standing Committee of the Ninth National People's Congress. *Environmental Impact Assessment Law of the People's Republic of China.* 2002. http://api.commissiemer.nl/docs/os/sea/legislation/china_s_ea_legislation_03.pdf.

11. Cao, Siqi. "Guangzhou OKs Foreign Cash for NGOs." *Global Times*, November 7, 2014. Accessed November 12, 2014. http://www.globaltimes.cn/content/890525.shtml.

12. Li, Lina. Interview by author, Beijng, September 2013.

13. For further reading see Van Rooij, Benjamin. "The People vs. Pollution: Understanding Citizen Action against Pollution in China." *Journal of Contemporary China* 19, no. 63 (2010): 55–77.

14. Larson, Christina. "How the Internet Is Powering the Fight against Beijing's Dirty Air." *The Guardian*, April 10, 2012. Accessed October 23, 2014. http://www.theguardian.com/environment/2012/apr/10/internet-beijing-dirty-air-pollution.

15. Chin, Josh, and Brian Spegele. "China Details Vast Extent of Soil Pollution." *Wall Street Journal*, April 17, 2014. Accessed October 20, 2014. http://online.wsj.com/articles/SB10001424052702304626304579507040557046288.

16. Yang, Jingjie. "Smog Pushes Emigration." *Global Times*, February 27, 2014. Accessed May 29, 2014. http://www.globaltimes.cn/content/845032.shtml.

17. Hurun Report, and Visa Consulting Group. "中国投资移民白皮书" [China Investment Immigration White Paper]. 2014. http://up.hurun.net/Humaz/201406/20140606132055085.pdf.

18. See Van Rooij, "The People vs. Pollution."

19. Watts, Jonathan. *When a Billion Chinese Jump: How China Will Save the World—or Destroy It.* London: Faber, 2010, 107.

20. "China Consumes Nearly as Much Coal as the Rest of the World Combined." *U.S. Energy Information Administration*, January 29, 2013. http://www.eia.gov/todayinenergy/detail.cfm?id=9751; Young, Angelo. "China New Auto Sales 2013: Chinese Consumers Bought over 20 Million Vehicles in 2013 as Foreign Automakers Jockey for Market Share." *International Business Times*, January 7, 2014. Accessed July 25, 2014. http://www.ibtimes.com/china-new-auto-sales-2013-chinese-consumers-bought-over-20-million-vehicles-2013-foreign-automakers.

21. Yang, "Smog Pushes Emigration."

22. Shi, Jiangtao. "Factory Axed as Shifang Heeds Protesters' Calls." *South China Morning Post*, July 4, 2012.

23. Wang, Natalie. "Violent Protests Erupt in Maoming, Four Allegedly Killed as Police Seal the City." *Nanfang Insider*, March 31, 2014.

24. Rosenzweig, Joshua. E-mail interview by author, April 2014.

14. THE JOURNALISTS

1. China Digital Times. "Directives from the Ministry of Truth: Wenzhou High-Speed Train Crash." Last modified July 25, 2011. http://

chinadigitaltimes.net/2011/07/directives-from-the-ministry-of-truth-wenzhou-high-speed-train-crash/.

2. Osnos, Evan. "Boss Rail." *The New Yorker*, October 22, 2012. Accessed October 17, 2014. http://www.newyorker.com/magazine/2012/10/22/boss-rail.

3. Branigan, Tania. "Chinese Anger over Alleged Cover-Up of High-Speed Rail Crash." *The Guardian*, July 25, 2011. Accessed May 29, 2014. http://www.theguardian.com/world/2011/jul/25/chinese-rail-crash-cover-up-claims.

4. "Ministry of Railways Faces Sharp Questions at Press Conference." CCTV News, July 26, 2011. Accessed October 23, 2014. http://english.cntv.cn/program/china24/20110726/103573.shtml.

5. "伊伊，等你长大的时候" [Letter to Yiyi—When You've Grown Up]. *Economic Observer*, July 30, 2011. Accessed May 29, 2014. http://www.eeo.com.cn/ens/2011/0801/207710.shtml.

6. Liu, Zhiyi. Interview by author, Beijing, June 2013.

7. Ping, He, and Wei Ling. "Milk Scandal Reporter Quits." Radio Free Asia, September 5, 2012. Accessed May 29, 2014. http://www.rfa.org/english/news/china/melamine-09052012122927.html.

8. Zhang, Zhian, and Fei Shen. "中国调查记者行业生态报告" [Chinese Investigative Reporter Industry Ecosystem Report]. *Modern Communication* no. 183 (2011): 51–73.

9. Zhang, Yueran. "Winter for Chinese Media: Why So Many Respected Journalists Are Leaving the Field." *Tea Leaf Nation*, September 11, 2012. Accessed May 29, 2014. http://www.tealeafnation.com/2012/09/winter-for-chinese-media-why-so-many-respected-journalists-are-leaving-the-field/.

10. Shen, Nianzu. Interview by author, Beijing, August 2013.

11. Branigan, Tania. "Wang Keqin and China's Revolution in Investigative Journalism." *The Guardian*, May 23, 2010. Accessed May 29, 2014. http://www.theguardian.com/world/2010/may/23/wang-keqin-china-investigative-journalism.

12. Bandurski, David. "Veteran Muckraker Forced to Leave Paper." China Media Project, March 1, 2013. Accessed May 29, 2014. http://cmp.hku.hk/2013/03/01/31597/.

13. Baihe and the Committee of Wedding Service Industries China Association of Social Workers. "2012 中国人婚恋状况调查报告" [2012 Chinese Love and Marriage Report]. 2013.

14. Zhu, Xuedong. "China's Corrupt Media." China Media Project. Last modified September 19, 2014. http://cmp.hku.hk/2014/09/19/36099/.

15. Branigan, "Wang Keqin and China's Revolution in Investigative Journalism."

16. Branigan, "Wang Keqin and China's Revolution in Investigative Journalism."

17. Zhang, Hong. Interview by author, Beijing, January 2014.

18. Denyer, Simon. "Chinese Journalists Face Tighter Censorship, Marxist Retraining." *Washington Post*, January 10, 2014. Accessed October 23, 2014. http://www.washingtonpost.com/world/chinese-journalists-face-tighter-censorship-marxist-re-training/2014/01/10/6cd43f62-6893-11e3-8b5b-a77187b716a3_story.html.

19. China Media Project. "The Marxist View of Journalism" 马克思主义新闻观. July 5, 2007. Accessed May 29, 2014. http://cmp.hku.hk/2007/07/05/424/.

20. Denyer, "Chinese Journalists Face Tighter Censorship."

21. Shi, Anbin. Interview by author, Beijing, January 2014.

22. Beech, Hannah. "China: Forced-Abortion Victim Promised $11,200, but Family Fears for Life." *Time*, July 13, 2012. Accessed October 23, 2014. http://world.time.com/2012/07/13/china-forced-abortion-victim-awarded-11200-fears-for-life/.

23. Lu, Rachel. "Online and Off, Social Media Users Go to War for Freedom of Press in China." *Tea Leaf Nation*, January 7, 2013. http://www.tealeafnation.com/2013/01/online-and-off-social-media-users-go-to-war-for-freedom-of-press-in-china/?utm_source=feedburner&utm_medium=feed&utm_campaign=Feed%3A+Tealeafnation+%28Tea+Leaf+Nation%29.

24. Bandurski, David. "Students Speak Out against Censorship." China Media Project, January 6, 2013. Accessed May 29, 2014. http://cmp.hku.hk/2013/01/06/30375/.

25. Gao, Helen. "A Press Renaissance? The Legacy of China's 'Southern Weekend.'" *The Atlantic*, January 11, 2013. Accessed May 29, 2014. http://www.theatlantic.com/international/archive/2013/01/a-press-renaissance-the-legacy-of-chinas-southern-weekend/267081/.

26. Lam, Oiwan. "China's Southern Media Group Turns Back on Anti-Censorship Supporters." *Global Voices*, December 29, 2013. Accessed May 29, 2014. http://globalvoicesonline.org/2013/12/29/chinas-southern-weekend-newspaper-turns-back-on-anti-censorship-supporters/.

27. Li, Amy. "Pharmaceutical Company Loses 1b Yuan after 140-word Weibo Message." *South China Morning Post*, February 1, 2013. Accessed May 29, 2014. http://www.scmp.com/news/china/article/1140943/pharmaceutical-company-loses-1b-yuan-after-140-word-weibo-message.

28. Jacobs, Andrew. "China's Crackdown Prompts Outrage over Boy's Arrest." *New York Times*, September 23, 2013. Accessed October 24, 2014. http://www.nytimes.com/2013/09/24/world/asia/crackdown-on-dissent-in-china-meets-online-backlash-after-boys-arrest.html.

29. Buckley, Chris. "Crackdown on Bloggers Is Mounted by China." *New York Times*, September 10, 2013. Accessed October 24, 2014. http://www.

nytimes.com/2013/09/11/world/asia/china-cracks-down-on-online-opinion-makers.html?pagewanted=all.

30. Reporters Without Borders. "World Press Freedom Index 2014." 2014. http://rsf.org/index2014/en-index2014.php.

31. "这个时代的媒体责任" [Media's Responsibility in This Era]. *Economic Observer*, April 12, 2013. Accessed May 29, 2014. http://www.eeo.com.cn/2013/0412/242483.shtml.

15. GENERATIONS

1. The Face of China. "English Corner: China's Free Speech Zone." Last modified January 9, 2014. http://thefaceofchina.com/2014/01/09/english-corner-china%E2%80%99s-free-speech-zone/.

2. Weiss, Jessica Chen. *Powerful Patriots: Nationalist Protest in China's Foreign Relations*. New York: Oxford University Press, 2014, 108–9; Mann, Jim. "Student Protests Challenge Deng's Policies in China." *Los Angeles Times*, December 5, 1985. Accessed October 24, 2014. http://articles.latimes.com/1985-12-05/news/mn-352_1_student-protest.

3. Mann, "Student Protests Challenge Deng's Policies."

4. Weiss, *Powerful Patriots*, 110.

5. Weiss, *Powerful Patriots*, 111.

6. Mann, "Student Protests Challenge Deng's Policies."

7. Weiss, *Powerful Patriots*, 133.

8. Pepper, Suzanne. *Deng Xiaoping's Political and Economic Reforms and the Chinese Student Protests*. Indianapolis, IN: Universities Field Staff International, 1987.

9. Schell, Orville. *Discos and Democracy: China in the Throes of Reform*. New York: Pantheon Books, 1988, 213; Wasserstrom, Jeffrey. "Student Protests in Fin-de-Siècle China." *New Left Review* 237 (1999): 52–76.

10. Sautman, Barry. "Anti-Black Racism in Post-Mao China." *China Quarterly* 138 (1994): 413–37.

11. Sullivan, Michael J. "The 1988–89 Nanjing Anti-African Protests: Racial Nationalism or National Racism?" *China Quarterly* 138 (1994): 438–57.

12. Sullivan, "The 1988–89 Nanjing Anti-African Protests"; Holley, David. "Chinese Students Bar Traffic, Taunt Police in Anti-African Protest." *Los Angeles Times*, December 29, 1988. Accessed October 24, 2014. http://articles.latimes.com/1988-12-29/news/mn-1285_1_african-student.

13. Holley, David. "Chinese March in 4th Day of Anti-African Protests." *Los Angeles Times*, December 28, 1988. Accessed October 24, 2014. http://articles.latimes.com/1988-12-28/news/mn-912_1_african-students; Chung,

Erin. "Nanjing Anti-African Protests of 1988–89." The Institute for Diasporic Studies, Northwestern University, n.d. Accessed October 24, 2014. http://diaspora.northwestern.edu/mbin/WebObjects/DiasporaX.woa/wa/displayArticle?atomid=711.

14. Chung, "Nanjing Anti-African Protests of 1988–89."

15. Sullivan, "The 1988–89 Nanjing Anti-African Protests."

16. Wasserstrom, Jeffrey N., and Elizabeth J. Perry. "Acting Out Democracy." In *Popular Protest and Political Culture in Modern China*, 2nd ed. Boulder, CO: Westview Press, 1994, 35.

17. Schmetzer, Uli. "Chinese Find Spot to Speak the Language of Democracy." *Chicago Tribune* (Beijing), July 3, 1989. Accessed May 29, 2014. http://articles.chicagotribune.com/1989-07-03/news/8902140570_1_Tiananmen-square-english-corner-democracy-movement.

18. "Chinese Defy Police Orders, Meet to Practice English." Associated Press (Beijing), December 26, 1989. Accessed May 29, 2014. http://news.google.com/newspapers?nid=861&dat=19891226&id=CBtQAAAAIBAJ&sjid=ZlYDAAAAIBAJ&pg=1677,6055183.

19. The Face of China, "English Corner."

20. Chubb, Andrew. "Exploring China's 'Maritime Consciousness': Public Opinion on the South and East China Sea Disputes." Perth USAsia Centre, 2014.

21. Gao, Helen. "Diaoyu in Our Heart: The Revealing Contradictions of Chinese Nationalism." *The Atlantic*, August 22, 2012. Accessed May 29, 2014. http://www.theatlantic.com/international/archive/2012/08/diaoyu-in-our-heart-the-revealing-contradictions-of-chinese-nationalism/261422/.

22. Gao, "Diaoyu in Our Heart."

23. *The Gate of Heavenly Peace* (documentary). Long Bow Group Inc. 1995. Transcript, http://citationmachine.net/index2.php?reqstyleid=0&stylebox=10.

24. Yu, Xie. "中国民生发展报告 2014" [China Minsheng Development Report 2014]. Beijing: Peking University Institute of Social Science Survey, 2014.

25. Poushter, Jacob. "Inflation, Corruption, Inequality Top List of Chinese Public's Concerns." Pew Research Center, November 8, 2013. Accessed May 29, 2014. http://www.pewresearch.org/fact-tank/2013/11/08/inflation-corruption-inequality-top-list-of-chinese-publics-concerns/.

26. Gao, George. "Where People Say Giving Bribes Gets You Ahead in Life." Pew Research Center, October 23, 2014. Accessed October 25, 2014. http://www.pewresearch.org/fact-tank/2014/10/23/where-people-say-giving-bribes-gets-you-ahead-in-life/.

27. Wen, Philip. "China's Post-90s Youth in Daring Online Tiananmen Protest." *Sydney Morning Herald*, May 9, 2014. Accessed May 29, 2014. http://

www.smh.com.au/world/chinas-post90s-youth-in-daring-online-Tiananmen-protest-20140509-zr8bw.html.

28. Liao, Minyue. E-mail interview by author, June 2014.

29. Zhang, Lijia. Interview by author, Beijing, June 2014.

30. Han, Han, and Allan Hepburn Barr. *This Generation: Dispatches from China's Most Popular Literary Star (and Race Car Driver).* New York: Simon & Schuster, 2012, 213.

31. Zhang, Xiaonan. Interview by author, Beijing, September 2011.

32. Li, Hao. Interview by author, Beijing, September 2011; Fish, Eric. "March of the Freshmen." *Foreign Policy*, November 10, 2011. http://www.foreignpolicy.com/articles/2011/11/10/march_of_the_freshmen.

INDEX

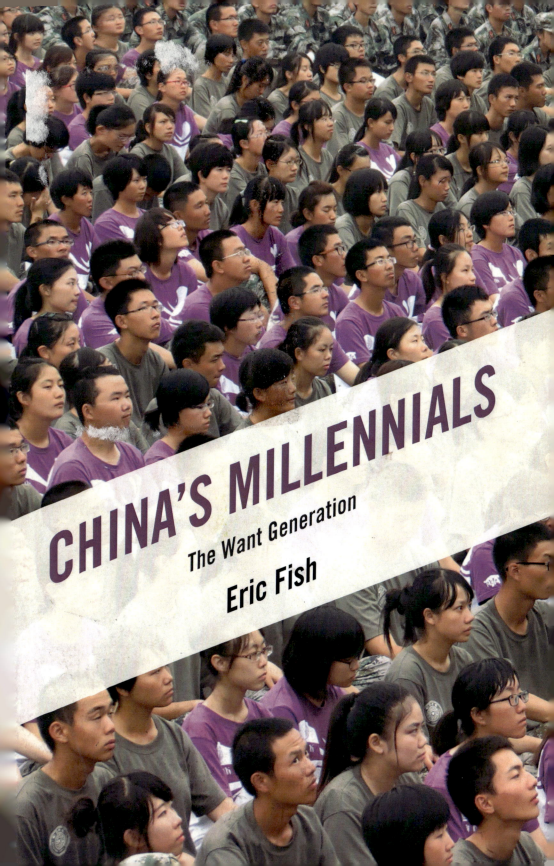

CHINA'S MILLENNIALS

The Want Generation

Eric Fish